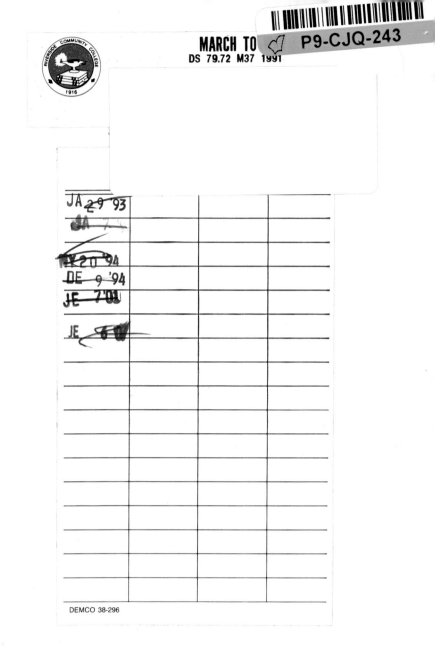

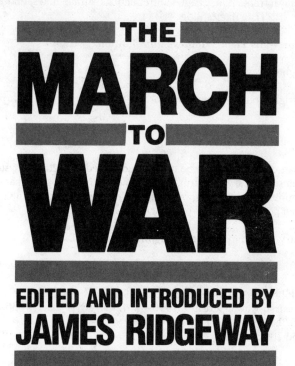

THE MARCH TO WAR

EDITED AND INTRODUCED BY
JAMES RIDGEWAY

Four Walls Eight Windows

New York

General introduction, chapter introductions, article notes, and epilogue ©1991 by James Ridgeway.

A Four Walls Eight Windows First Edition.

Copyright notices to individual articles appear beginning with page 242.

First printing April 1991.

Library of Congress Cataloging-in-Publication Data

The March to war / edited and introduced by James Ridgeway.
    p.   cm.
   ISBN 0-941423-61-1 (pbk.) : $9.95
   1. Iraq-Kuwait Crisis,   1990–   I. Ridgeway, James, 1936–
DS79.72.M37 1991
956.704'3—dc20
                                       91-11607
                                         CIP

Four Walls Eight Windows
P.O. Box 548
Village Station
New York, N.Y. 10014

Illustration preceding Table of Contents shows the size of the Middle East region relative to the continental United States.

Designed by Martin Moskof.

It is true that this assembly was called to deal with the preparation to be made for sailing to Sicily. Yet I think that this is a question that requires further thought. Is it really a good thing for us to send the ships at all? I think that we ought not to give such hasty consideration to so important a matter and on the credit of foreigners get drawn into a war which does not concern us. . . . What I am saying is this: In going to Sicily you are leaving many enemies behind you, and you apparently want to make new ones there and have them also on your hands. . . .

Thucydides

Nicias' statement on the proposed Athenian expedition against Syracuse 413 B.C.

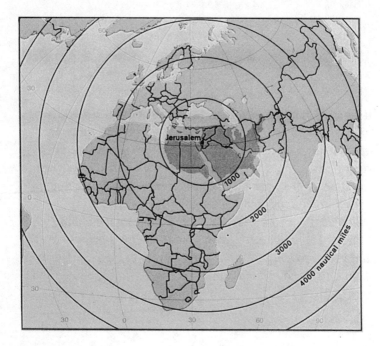

Contents

Chapter Two
August 1990: Iraq's Gamble

Epilogue: The Unquiet Peace

U.N. Security Council Resolutions on the Gulf Crisis

Author's
Acknowledgements

I am especially indebted to Joe Stork and the staff of the
Middle East Research and Information Project in Washington, who have provided me with analysis, information, and guidance throughout the Gulf war. MERIP and
its monthly magazine, *Middle East Report*, are among the
unheralded reservoirs of knowledge on the Middle East
in the United States.

I want to thank the *Village Voice*, in which portions of
this book originally appeared, and especially the editor-
in-chief Jonathan Larsen; my editor Dan Bischoff, and
my colleagues Murray Waas, Curtis Lang, and Robert
Hennelly. Waas's reportage on Iraq's ties to the U.S.
helped to provide a fresh perspective on the background
of the war; Lang's work on the costs of the conflict were
valuable in helping me to understand its context; and
Hennelly's environmental knowledge assisted me in
appreciating that aspect of the crisis. In addition, I am
indebted to Bill Arkin and Peter Dykstra of Greenpeace,
who published a daily report on the war that was faxed

to journalists, and to Peter Montague of Greenpeace, who provided the most sensible environmental assessments of a chaotic situation. Pacific News Service also supplied valuable research on Kuwait.

My thanks go to Dan Simon, co-publisher, who conceived the idea for this book and supported it throughout; and to Jean Casella, whose astute and patient editing was essential to the manuscript. Without them, the book would not have been possible.

I also want to thank Loren Berger, who spent long hours gathering material; Anne Galperin for her research; Don Kennison for proofreading, Martin Moskof for design, and CRC for typesetting, all under unreasonable deadlines; Abigail Scherer and Chris O'Brien of the Four Walls Eight Windows staff; and my assistants at the *Village Voice*, George Spiegler, Nicole Volpe, Rosalie Yee.

—J.R.
Washington, D.C.
March 1991

Introduction

WHY DID WE GO TO WAR WITH IRAQ?

A nation's march to war quickly develops its own momentum, and once war begins, it can appear to have been inevitable. The background and causes of the conflict are rapidly overshadowed by the daily occupation with military strategy.

But the advent of war between the United States and Iraq was neither as sudden nor as simple as it might seem. Rooted in over a century of Western involvement in the oil-producing regions of the Middle East, the causes of the Gulf war go far beyond the question of Kuwaiti sovereignty, to include the debate over domestic environmental and energy policies, the struggle to control the world's resources, and the political and economic shakeups that came with the end of the Cold War. And they involve conflicts and events that long predate the Iraqi invasion of Kuwait on August 2, 1990.

Prelude to War

In the first six months of 1990, Iraq's president Saddam Hussein sent what in hindsight can be seen as a series of signals announcing his growing bellicose intentions in the Persian Gulf. At an anniversary celebration for the Arab Cooperation Council in late February, he angered Egypt's president Hosni Mubarak by attacking the motives of Egypt's ally, the United States, in the Gulf. In a speech on that occasion, Saddam stormed against those rich Arab states that were advancing what he called an "imperialist-Zionist plot"—undercutting OPEC by pumping oil at faster and faster rates, driving down prices—and raised the possibility that Arab nations should consider withdrawing their investments in the West, instead channeling oil capital into Eastern Europe and the Soviet Union. Saddam taunted those Arab states ready to submit to the designs of the United States in the Gulf.

In April Saddam threatened to use chemical weapons against Israel if it did "anything against Iraq." A month later, at an Arab League meeting, he again accused the Gulf states of overproducing oil. In July Saddam labeled both Kuwait and the United Arab Emirates imperialism's agents in the Gulf, and sent a formal protest to the Arab League on Kuwait's overproduction and alleged theft of oil from Iraq.

Neither the United States nor Great Britain showed much concern for any of these signals. Evidently they believed that the war with Iran had transformed the Iraqi dictator into a kinder, gentler leader, ready to take his place on the side of the West. Even towards the end of July, with Iraqi columns formed on the Kuwait border, the Bush administration representatives appearing before Congress continued to advocate maintaining support for Iraq as a countervailing power to Iran.

On August 2 Saddam invaded and annexed Kuwait, renewing a claim first made by Iraq in the 1930s that Kuwait is the "lost" nineteenth province of Iraq. His primary goal was to gain control of the disputed Rumailah oil fields and two tiny islands that would give Iraq direct access to the Persian Gulf.

Early History

Kuwait—the tiny, oil-rich patch of desert that was suddenly the focus of world attention—was founded in the early 1700s, when a group of tribes settled the town of Kuwait. By 1800 the Sabah family had emerged as the ruling clan, creating a dynasty that continued to rule Kuwait until the 1990 Iraqi invasion. In 1899 the Sabahs signed a treaty that made the sheikhdom a protectorate of Britain, agreeing not to sell or lease any land without British approval. The British were anxious to improve their trading positions against the Germans and Russians, and the Sabahs needed British support against the encroaching Ottoman empire and against the Saud family, which was then creating Saudi Arabia. In 1922 the British unilaterally drew borders between Iraq, Kuwait, and Saudi Arabia; in 1961 Kuwait officially gained its independence from Britain.

The modern state of Kuwait revolves around oil production. Before the discovery of oil, Kuwait's economy was based on trade and pearl diving. After oil, the Sabahs maintained power autocratically. Noncitizens, many of them Palestinian and Indian, did the work of the state. They came to comprise two-thirds of the population and 80 percent of the work force. Yet noncitizens could not own property and could not vote. Their wages were a fraction of those paid Kuwaitis for the same work. Even among native born Kuwaitis, the right to vote was restricted to literate males over twenty-one—about 3.5 percent of the population. The last parliament, elected in February 1985, was dissolved the following year.

During the 1970s the Kuwaitis set aside $100 billion in two reserve funds to finance the future needs of the nation. Much of the money was invested abroad in stocks, including shares in British, West German, and American companies. In the 1980s the Kuwaitis found themselves making a greater return from these investments than from the exportation of oil. Yahya Sadowski argues, in the

Winter 1990/91 issue of *The Brookings Review,* that "this discovery suggested a way for Kuwait to deal with the crisis of the Arab state system. Kuwait's rulers dreamed of turning their country into a Middle Eastern analogue of South Korea: economically linked to the West and defended by American power." As the 1980s drew to a close, Kuwait proceeded to expand and consolidate its holdings in the West. In order to do this it decreased its financial aid to poor Arab states—turning away Jordan, which sought emergency relief, and telling Iraq it would have to repay the $10 billion borrowed during the Iran-Iraq war. (Fearing revolutionary Iran, Kuwait sided with Iraq throughout the eight-year conflict). During the same period, the Kuwaitis stepped up the production of oil, exceeding OPEC quotas and driving down oil prices. And, unsure of Iraq, they strengthened ties to the United States, which had been willing to help them by reflagging tankers and by naval intervention in the Gulf. They wanted to secure with the U.S. the sort of special relationship enjoyed by Saudi Arabia. Sadowski writes, "The Kuwaitis and other Gulf regimes began to exit from the Arab state system. They began to rely more on an American security umbrella. In some ways they were returning to the conditions of the 1960s, when Great Britain protected the Gulf states from their hungry neighbors."

Oil

The present geopolitical contours of the oil-producing regions of the Middle East were set in place by the Western powers to facilitate the expropriation of oil. The roots of the United States' current involvement go back to the early 1900s, when a young Winston Churchill, then Lord of the Admiralty, decided to change the fuel used by the British fleet from coal to oil in order to enhance the fighting power of battleships, the strategic weapons of the day. The British backed explorers who had discovered oil in the Mesopotamian desert, and established control over oil production. By the early 1920s the British, having acquired a mandate from the League of Nations to govern most of present-day Iraq, Iran, and Jordan, were threatening to invade American markets, worrying the new oil monopoly of the Rockefeller family. To counter that threat, the American government began to voice dire warnings of an oil shortage, opening the way for forceful American expansion into the Middle Eastern markets. With the sun setting on their empire, the British cut the U.S. companies in on the oil business by including them for the first time in a so-called cooperative venture named the Iraq Petroleum Company. This venture was the predecessor to the Seven Sisters cartel—a consortium of one British, one Anglo-Dutch, and five American companies—that would dominate the oil trade through World War II, the Cold War, and the rise and decline of OPEC. Today the power of the Seven Sisters has shifted from oil production to oil distribution.

While the U.S. has maintained and expanded oil holdings in the Middle East since the 1920s, Arab oil did not become really significant in the world oil game until after the Second World War. As Joe Stork and Ann M. Lesch point out in *Middle East Report* ("Why War," November-December 1990), the appeal of Middle Eastern oil lay in its extremely low production cost: In the mid-1950s, it ran between five and fifteen cents a barrel, while the world market price for oil was around $2.25 a barrel. The Seven Sisters companies, with interlocking concessions, were able to set the world price on the basis of the much higher production costs in the U.S.

The growing importance of Middle Eastern oil coincided with the rise of nationalism in the region and the decline of the British and French colonial powers. Determined not to let this new nationalism cut off their supply of cheap petroleum, for decades the West dealt with Arab countries by playing them off against one another or by undermining individual regimes. Thus when Mohammad

Mossadeq nationalized British oil holdings in Iran in 1951, the U.S. took a major role in the subsequent oil embargo against Iran, and eventually the CIA organized a coup to unseat Mossadeq and install the Shah on his "peacock throne." During the embargo against Iran, the West called on Kuwait to produce sufficient oil to tide over the international market system.

A decade later, in 1961, when a nationalist Iraq sought to gain control over its own oil, it was faced with a Western embargo. Once again the Seven Sisters called on Kuwait, this time together with Iran, to make up the oil shortfall on the international market. Iraq was punished with reduced production, resulting in reduced revenues.

In *Middle East Report*, Stork and Lesch describe the situation this way: "The agenda of economic nationalism set first by Iran and later by Iraq, Libya, Algeria, and other countries has redefined the oil industry. Despite these changes, Iraq's complaints in 1990 about Kuwaiti over-production sound all too plausible in a region where people have an acute memory of the manipulative role of the Western companies and governments, usually with the eager compliance of the local beneficiary regime."

Political Realignments
During the 1950s and 1960s the Arab countries were divided among "radicals" and "moderates." Georges Corm, the Lebanese economic scholar and historian of the contemporary Middle East, outlines the division between these groups in *Revue d' études Palestiniennes* (September 14, 1990). The radicals were military republics that tended to be Arab nationalist in ideology, socialist when it came to economic policy, and close to the Soviet Union in foreign policy. They included Egypt, Syria, Iraq, and Algeria. The moderate governments were pro-Western— Jordan, Lebanon, and the Gulf sheikhdoms of Kuwait, Saudi Arabia, Qatar and Bahrain, as well as Bourguiba's

Tunisia. This division made it difficult for the Arab world to speak with one voice on such issues as Palestine—which, since the creation of Israel and the first Arab-Israeli war of 1948-49, had remained on the agenda of every Arab nation.

In the late 1960s—especially after defeat in the 1967 Six Day War with Israel, which yielded Arab lands to Israeli occupation and brought on a crisis in Arab nationalism—the radical countries began to temper their positions towards the West. And at the Khartoum Arab summit, which ended the 1972 war between Yemen and South Yemen, the moderates and radicals reached an accord: The radicals agreed that they would cease trying to disrupt and destabilize the sheikhdoms along the Gulf, countries that were rich in oil money and relatively unpopulous. The sheikhdoms agreed in return to redistribute oil income to the poorer, more densely populated Arab countries, and work towards their economic development. They also promised to provide arms to Arab countries confronting Israel, and to work towards recognition of the rights of the Palestinians.

The 1973 war with Israel, which ended with a U.N. cease-fire, accelerated the Arab nations' push towards moderation. Egypt, under Anwar Sadat, formally joined the West—reestablishing diplomatic relations with Washington, cutting ties to the Soviets, and falling in with Henry Kissinger's Mideast negotiations. Syria normalized relations with the United States. Algeria became more moderate, and ceased to play a major role in the Arab world. Iraq drew closer to the West and, between 1980 and 1988, waged war with the West's principle enemy in the region, Iran.

Corm provides an overview of the lull which directly preceded the recent hostilities: "What we had on the eve of the present crisis was a regional Arab system that for all practical purposes had entered into the political orbit of the West. This was true notably for Iraq. And the PLO over the past two years had met all the Western conditions, even declaring in May 1989 the Palestinian charter to be obsolete, and had entered the peace and negotiating process; it should be noted that Iraq, on which the PLO increasingly relied, had not disapproved of the peace process. One can thus say that the quasi-totality of the 21 Arab countries had foreign policies more or less in harmony and that they were trying to conform to the Western line. This rather spectacular evolution was facilitated by the well-known problems of the Soviet Union, which began to distance itself from its Arab clients, moved closer to Israel and—a very important fact— opened the door to Soviet Jewish emigration to Israel. The reaction of the Arab countries to this extremely important phenomenon was, in the last analysis . . . extremely moderate. In other times, there would certainly have been a great outcry, threats of retaliation. Instead the measure passed virtually unnoticed, whereas in fact it was an extremely dramatic disruption of the demographic status quo in Palestine."

Our Friend in the Middle East

While Iran under the Shah acted as the main American policeman in the Gulf throughout the 1950s, 1960s, and most of the 1970s, Saudi Arabia came to play an ever more significant role in U.S. foreign policy.

Ever since the early 1930s, when Standard Oil of California and Texaco (joined as partners in ARAMCO) produced their first barrels of Arabian crude, the United States had embraced Saudi Arabia almost as it might a colony. Under Franklin Roosevelt there were discussions of an American participation in oil explorations along the lines of the British government's involvement in BP (British Petroleum), which was partly owned and financed by the English government for decades. Roosevelt's influential secretary of the interior, Harold Ickes, at one point suggested building U.S. government–owned refineries in Saudi Arabia, and during World War II the Roosevelt administration entertained the idea of constructing a Saudi pipeline. Saudi oil was considered to be all-important to the Allied war effort, and after the Allied victory, the Gulf was viewed as one of the earliest testing grounds in the Cold War.

In 1962, partly as the result of pressure from the United States, King Saud was displaced and Faisal took power in Saudi Arabia. Under Faisal, Saudi society was made to appear less primitive: Slavery was abolished, education was expanded, a formal budget was introduced, and a modern army was formed.

But OPEC (the Organization of Petroleum Exporting Countries), formed in 1961 to help the Arab nations maintain greater control over oil production and prices, stood to be a long-term thorn in the side of American foreign policy in the region. Under King Faisal, the oil minister Abdullah Tariki, who had been among the first and boldest proponents of increased OPEC control of oil, was replaced with a man more to American liking: Ahmad Zaki Yamani. It was through Yamani that Saudi Arabia denied the radicals in OPEC fundamental control over oil by refusing to agree to OPEC-determined production levels.

Faisal was assassinated in 1975, and from then on a more diverse family team ran the desert kingdom. In the early 1970s Saudi Arabia provided financial assistance to help pull Egypt away from the Soviet orbit. The Camp David Accords formally put Egypt on the U.S. side, and its military eventually became part of the American regional defense system. In *Middle East Report*, Jonathan Marshall sets forth in great detail just how Saudi Arabia helped out the Reagan administration in its efforts to counter Soviet influence in the Third World ("Saudi Arabia and the Reagan Doctrine," November–December 1988). The Saudis also gave millions of dollars to the pro-Western

Yemen Arab Republic in its 1972 war with the pro-Soviet People's Democratic Republic of Yemen. In the late 1970s Saudi funds paid for the Moroccan troops that rescued the Mobutu regime in Zaire from secessionist Katanganese, and the Saudis provided aid to Somalia to help move it into the U.S. sphere.

When the Shah of Iran was overthrown in 1979, the U.S. pinned its hopes and plans for the region ever more openly on Saudi Arabia. Reagan's secretary of defense, Caspar Weinberger, argued for increased American military aid to the Saudis in the form of AWACS planes, and after heated debate the Senate narrowly approved the plan.

Weinberger's support of the AWACS shipments was part of a wider strategy. Under President Reagan, the U.S. embarked on a foreign policy aimed at "rolling back" Third World Communism by means of so-called low intensity conflict. It has been reported that in exchange for the AWACS deal, the Saudis agreed to partially under-write U.S. covert operations abroad. Even while Carter was in the White House, the Saudis had joined China, Egypt, and Pakistan in supporting the Afghan rebels, financing both the rebels themselves and their base country, Pakistan. As Marshall notes, the Saudis also provided funds to Morocco to help pay for training Jonas Savimbi's UNITA guerrillas, who were trying to overthrow the pro-Soviet government of Angola. Support for UNITA was dear to Reagan's heart, but under the Clark Amendment, in force from 1976 through 1985, Congress had forbidden aid to Savimbi. To the New Right conservatives with their theories of roll back, this was an act of unconscionable liberal treachery. Thanks to the Saudis, both the Clark Amendment and a U.N. embargo on sales of oil to South Africa were circumvented: The Saudis set up a private company that sold oil to South Africa at higher than market rates, using the profits to support Savimbi. Beginning in 1984, the White House stepped up defense spending in Saudi Arabia, and the Saudis began to funnel

$1 million a month to the contras in Nicaragua. Both President Reagan and Vice President Bush had been informed of this fortuitous gift, and Reagan's gratitude was conveyed to the Saudi royal family.

Saudi Arabia also tried to help out Reagan and Bush with their domestic political problems. In the 1980 presidential election, Ronald Reagan won the support of "Little Oil," the influential independent oil and gas producers of the American Southwest, who for years had been faithful supporters of the Democratic party. Reagan promised them he would speed up the process of deregulating oil and gas prices, begun under Jimmy Carter. And upon his election, Reagan set about liberating the energy industry from government rules and regulations —freeing prices and opening public domain territories to greater exploitation. Prices for fuels did rise, but were quickly overturned by the long-term nemesis of the oil industry, a worldwide oil glut.

The glut of inexpensive international oil helped deepen the recession in Texas, Louisiana, and Colorado, centers for the independent oil producers. The situation was worsened by the recessionary tendencies in the overall economy. To curb inflation, the Federal Reserve had raised interest rates, thereby increasing unemployment and sending already marginal small businesses and farming in the Midwest into a steep recession. The recession, especially as it affected the farm belt and the oil men, threatened the conservative Republican hold on Congress, where the Democrats were making a pitched campaign to regain the Senate in 1986. With Republican control of the Senate facing challenge, then–Vice President George Bush made a trip to Saudi Arabia. He sought to persuade the Saudis to reduce production and increase prices to spur the economic recovery of America's independent oil and gas business. The Saudis complied, although too late to help Reagan. Buoyed by a populist surge, the Democratic party regained control of the Senate.

Throughout the 1980s, Saudi Arabia operated as a member of the secret team, the hidden government that advanced American foreign policy outside the scrutiny of Congress according to the political designs of the Reagan and Bush administrations. All in all, the Saudis showed themselves, over thirty years, to be loyal functionaries of Washington. It is hardly surprising, then, that in 1991 we would find U.S. troops massed in the Saudi desert, or that the Washington-Riyadh axis would become the strategic center of the war against Iraq.

Iraq and the United States

Iraq, unlike Saudi Arabia, has not historically shown itself to be a predictable or malleable ally of Western interests. For decades it struggled against British influence: protesting British rule throughout the 1920s, seeking Nazi support for a failed coup attempt against the British-installed monarch during World War II, finally over-throwing its monarchy in 1958, and falling under the control of the nationalistic Baath Party in 1968. Saddam Hussein signed a friendship pact with the Soviet Union in 1972, and nationalized the Iraq Petroleum Company the same year; he maintained a radical stance against Israel, and became a figurehead for Arab nationalism, winning himself few friends in the West.

Attitudes changed for a while, however, when Saddam went to war against fundamentalist Iran, then considered the region's main threat to the West. Throughout the eight-year conflict, Iraq had the support of the moderate Gulf sheikhdoms and Jordan.

Early in the Iran-Iraq war, United States policy towards Iraq also shifted. Faced with what looked to be an expansive Islamic revolutionary movement, the U.S. sought ways to make fresh political openings into what it thought to be the more moderate elements in Iran, which were gathering their resources for a post-Khomeni era. But, as a May 1985 memorandum to then-CIA director William Casey describes, the U.S. had also sought to find ways to curry favor with Iraq as a counterweight to Iran: "The specter of the U.S. and the U.S.S.R. standing on the same side of a major international strategic conflict, like the [Iran-Iraq] war, is extraordinary. It is also an unstable situation and cannot persist for long. We are both on Iraq's side because we lack our preferred access to Iran. Whoever gets there first is in a strong position to work towards the exclusion of the other." The memo concludes, "Our tilt to Iraq was timely when Iraq was against the ropes and the Islamic revolution was on a roll. The time may now have come to tilt back..."

The United States' "tilt" toward Iraq was expressed in several concrete ways. In 1979, during the Carter administration, Iraq had been labeled a terrorist state, which meant that it was prohibited from purchasing many U.S. goods, including civilian aircraft and military equipment of any kind. In 1983 the Reagan administration removed Iraq from the terrorist list, opening the door for U.S. government–guaranteed agricultural exports to Iraq, which began that year. In 1984 the U.S. reestablished diplomatic relations with Iraq, even though that same year Iraq had used chemical weapons in its war with Iran. And despite continuing human rights abuses, the U.S. expanded its credit guarantee programs to Iraq. From 1985 to 1990 the U.S. authorized over $4 billion in U.S.– guaranteed agricultural exports to Iraq, with a peak of $1.1 billion in 1988. In 1987 the Export-Import Bank provided a $200 million line of short-term insurance coverage for U.S. manufacturing exports to Iraq. The Export-Import program began even though Iraq had been in default up to 1987.

Growing reliance on American farm products allowed Saddam to begin the shift of his agriculture away from collective farming to privately owned spreads, which discarded staples such as wheat for more profitable tree crops, chickens, and dairy products. The move away from basic agriculture coincided with the move of the population from rural areas to the cities, a shift quickened by the flow of soldiers returning from the long Iran-Iraq war. Like many other Third World countries, Iraq soon was importing much of its basic food supply. Since then the United States has sold as much as 20 percent of its rice crop to Iraq, mostly long grained varieties from Louisiana. Iraqis buy considerable quantities of hard red winter wheat from Nebraska, Colorado, and Kansas (Kansas Senator Bob Dole would be the leader of the congressional delegation that sought to reassure Saddam of America's benevolent intentions in April 1990). And at the height of the Iran-Iraq war, the U.S. replaced the Soviet Union as a main supplier of timber to Iraq. Washington, Georgia, the Carolinas, and Louisiana provided Saddam with the plywood Iraq needed for urban housing, with telephone poles, and with railway ties as well as with wood pulp for paper. The U.S. also outdid the Soviets in providing chickens, chicken feed (including corn), and chicken-processing equipment to the Iraqis.

Iraq was the United States' third largest trading partner in the Middle East, behind Saudi Arabia and Israel, for the fist quarter of 1990, buying $433.6 million in goods, up from $308.7 million during the corresponding period in 1989. In all, during 1989 the U.S. sent $1.17 billion worth of goods to Iraq and $855 million to Kuwait.

American involvement in Iraq in the 1980s went beyond agricultural trade or loan guarantees. In the *Village Voice*, Murray Waas published a comprehensive report on how the United States had sought to provide Iraq with up-to-date weaponry by selling them arms through friendly third nations ("What We Gave Saddam for Christmas," December 18, 1990). As Waas documents, the U.S. also traded weapons systems with Iraq (ostensibly in exchange for new Soviet weapons that had been procured by the Iraqis) and provided Iraq with such items as helicopters, slated for civilian use but speedily transformed for military purposes. In a short time the U.S., along with the several European countries involved in these arms dealings with Iraq, would face an enemy partially armed with weapons they themselves had built and supplied.

Why Did We Go to War with Iraq?

According to President Bush, the Gulf crisis posed a threat to the American way of life. Others said American troops were there to protect oil interests. But Bush invoked a higher principle: The United States must respond to aggression against the small, helpless state of Kuwait. Bush said that "America's freedom and that of America's friends would suffer if the world's oil reserves fell into the hands of Saddam Hussein." He presented the situation in the Gulf as a grim parallel to that in central Europe during the late 1930s, and likened Saddam Hussein to Hitler.

These arguments were vague. Even among those who supported American troop involvement, many thought the administration's goals were confused. Throughout the last six months of 1990 there were other signs that Bush's policy in the Gulf was muddled. At the outset of the crisis, the administration sent elements of a rapid deployment force to help defend Saudi Arabia, and placed its major emphasis on economic sanctions against Iraq. As late as January 1991, William Webster, the director of Central Intelligence, told Congress sanctions were working— making it ever more difficult for the Iraqi military to operate, and bringing Iraq's economy to a standstill.

Yet by November, Bush's policy had changed course. Operation Desert Shield, the administration's term for the defensive troop deployment, had been transformed into an offensive force. Newspapers portrayed Bush as devastated by news of the Iraqi tortures. The President cited Iraq's purported nuclear capability and its chemical warfare facilities as menaces to world peace.

The administration's arguments for intervention remained general. In response to President Bush's principled outrage at Iraqi aggression and his determined obedience to United Nations principles, his detractors asked why the U.S. did not apply these principles to other conflicts—between the Palestinians and Israel, or Libya and Chad. Principles of national self-determination had not stopped the American attacks on Grenada and Panama, the covert war in Nicaragua, or the ongoing counter-insurgency in El Salvador. And as New York's senator Daniel Patrick Moynihan argued on the Senate floor, the U.N. resolution was definitely a worthy document, but it hardly justified a major war. Iraq had submitted its nuclear facilities to inspection by the international Atomic Energy Commission, and Saddam himself had said he believed chemical weapons should be brought under United Nations scrutiny and control. And why this furor over Iraq when Israel had nuclear capability, as, most likely, did South Africa, Pakistan, and several other small nations? Nor was Iraq the only country to have chemical armaments.

After the Cold War

Why war? Some have argued that the decision to go to war was the natural upshot of the realpolitik that grew out of the colonial past, reinvigorated by the end of the Cold War.

Iraq had spent $241 billion in conducting its war with Iran—more than it had earned from oil exports since they began in the 1930s. Iraq's repayment on foreign debts amounted to $4 billion a year, and it needed billions in additional loans to rebuild. Iraqi citizens clamored for relief after the austerity of the war. Saddam Hussein saw Iraq as replacing Egypt as the Arab protector—already, it had saved weaker Arab nations from being overrun by Khomeni. Saddam expected the gratitude and support of his neighbors. He wanted relief from debt and an Arab version of the Marshall Plan to help rebuild his country. In return for that aid, he talked of using his military machine to take on Israel. He used the Arab Cooperation Council to lobby the rich Arab states for larger contributions, and he curried favor with the poor Arab countries, Palestinians in refugee camps, Mauritanians, and Sudanese. When his neighbors stopped short of giving him what he felt he deserved, he decided to go out and take it.

Had the Russians, long the mentors and suppliers of Iraq, been in a position to serve as a deterrent to the United States, the lesser disputes among nations of the Middle East would have been subsumed within Cold War diplomacy. A stand-off between the two superpowers would have prevented war. But the Cold War was over. The Russians were occupied with the breakup of Eastern Europe and rebellion within their own borders. U.S. interests lay exposed to the parochial machinations of the Arab world, which in turn lay exposed to the machinations of U.S. interests.

Resource Wars

But why war now? For the better part of a century, America had successfully managed to coexist with the intricacies of the Arab world, and had seen the Arab states leave the Soviet orbit for that of the West. The last decade had been a period of relative peace.

It is possible that the causes of the war go far beyond the Middle East. According to this view, the war offers a hint of what is to come in the next century, when nations will concern themselves more with issues of the environment and natural resources—which in turn hinge on economic interests. These issues will supercede ideology as points of debate among nations. The apportionment of natural resources will dominate such forums as the United Nations, as well as international banking institutions and trade agreements.

Man has always set fire to the environment for heat and light, but never before have the actions of governments been tied so closely to energy consumption. Many of the issues of the new world order will involve energy and ecology; the debate over reversing the flow of Soviet rivers for electricity and irrigation; the fight to save the Danube, which helped spark Hungary's overthrow of Communist rule; the Canadian-American arguments over the James Bay; the fight over who is to control the Nile; and the American and Soviet race for oil and gas in the frozen, fragile expanses of the Arctic.

Saddam Hussein foreshadowed such struggles by underlining the inherent insecurity of American dependence on foreign oil. And yet, while it is true that the U.S. relies on foreign oil for nearly half its supply, Iraq produces only about 8 percent of the world total. Its untapped resources are plentiful, but at the time the crisis began, the world was awash in oil. America's petroleum-dependent way of life was in no immediate danger. Still, the crisis in the Gulf—in tandem with an increasingly powerful and broad-based environmental movement —might have promoted a recognition that the world must move towards more varied energy sources, turning to both energy conservation and renewable fuels.

But not everyone wanted this to be the lesson of the Gulf crisis. No sooner had Saddam Hussein moved his troops into Kuwait than the oil industry was on Capitol Hill, demanding tax breaks and stepped-up drilling of domestic reserves in Alaska and along the outer-continental shelf. As time went on the Bush administration set forth the outlines of a new energy policy that emphasized oil, alternative fuels made from coal, and nuclear power. In that sense the crisis and the war, it might be argued, provided the political rationale for reorganizing foreign oil to America's advantage, as we had already done repeatedly earlier in this century. And within the United States the war provided a strong political platform for renewing the energy industry along the lines favored by the traditional proponents of fossil fuels. In this sense the war has served to reassert the fundamentals of the industrial revolution. War has given the Bush administration a clear base of popular support for its energy policies in the face of what had been a growing environmental movement that challenged these policies.

These explanations are part of a larger picture that reaches well beyond the narrow economic imperatives conditioned on oil. Some analysts have suggested that this larger picture includes the fact that the United States now has a permanent war economy, where military production is an enduring and substantial facet of the overall economy. To those with interests in preserving the permanent war economy, the "peace dividend" was never a viable concept, and the end of the Cold War only created a pressing need for new enemies and new conflicts. And the interests of this war economy did not always coincide with those of certain sectors of private industry. Thus, as pumping stations are bombed and oil wellheads burned, we see the war state effectively destroying the oil industry in the Persian Gulf.

Agriculture and Power

While Iraq is best known for its only export—oil—the backbone of life and society there is agriculture. Most of this agricultural activity is centered around the ancient, oblong strip of arable land that lies between the Tigris and Euphrates rivers. Although nearly three quarters of the river basin lies within Iraq, more than 80 percent of the country's measurable supply of water derives from sources outside its borders, primarily in Turkey and northwestern Iran.

Despite the oil boom, which lured people from the countryside into the cities, a quarter of the population of Iraq farms. And it is farming, more than oil, that holds the key to a viable economic future in a region that is desperately short of both water and food.

But from the short-term U.S. point of view, the destruction of Iraq's environment and the ruin of its agriculture would open markets for American foodstuffs. That in turn would foster a growing political dependence on the United States—as has already been the case in Ethiopia and Egypt.

"Famine takes root when farmers lose their means of production," Gayle Smith points out in *Middle East Report* ("Ethiopia and the Politics of Famine Relief," March-April 1987). In Africa grain yields and overall food production have declined over the last decade. Food production is down by 15 percent from 1981. One out of every five Africans now depends on food aid. The famine has depleted Africa of more people than in any period since the slave trade.

Famine opens the door to enormous aid programs aimed at reorganizing local economies and hooking national production into a global system. As the provider of economic and humanitarian assistance to Africa, for example, the U.S. is able to set the terms of economic development across the continent. When our main enemy was Communism, AID (Aid to Independent Development) policies were targeted against socialist ventures —collective farms and cooperatives—in favor of private enterprise.

With food aid comes a change in the way people live. Egypt is a good example. It was once more than self-sufficient in grains, but its grain imports have dramatically increased with American aid, while domestic grain production has fallen off. Most of these grain imports go to feed animals, the remaining domestic grain production has shifted from human to animal consumption as well, in order to produce meat for foreign consumption. Reflecting a growing gap between the rich and poor, there is now more money to be made by redirecting the nation's food output from staples to luxury items. The government uses the aid imports to provide staples, taxes farmers who grow grain heavily, and uses subsidies to encourage the production of meat.

If the war leaves Iraq's environment devastated—an effect that seems guaranteed—it will have created yet another dependent state, a more than docile recipient of Western aid and of American political and economic influence.

The last flash of empire blinds us to the emerging world order. What is slowly coming into focus in the Middle East is the post-Cold War world, where environmental economics, not political ideology, will be the defining principle.

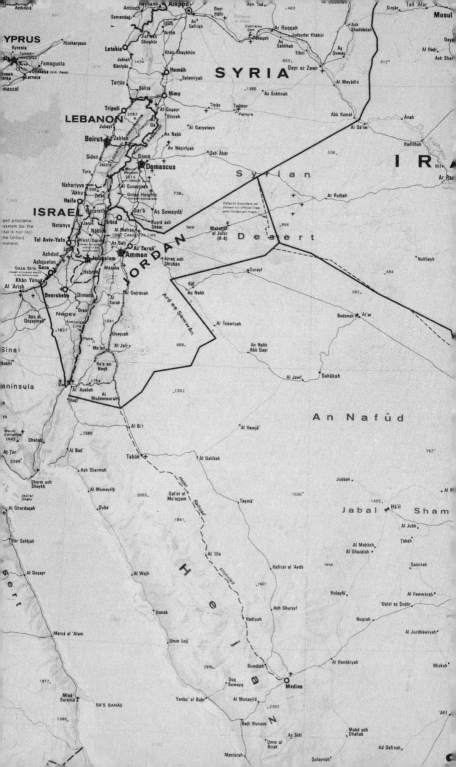

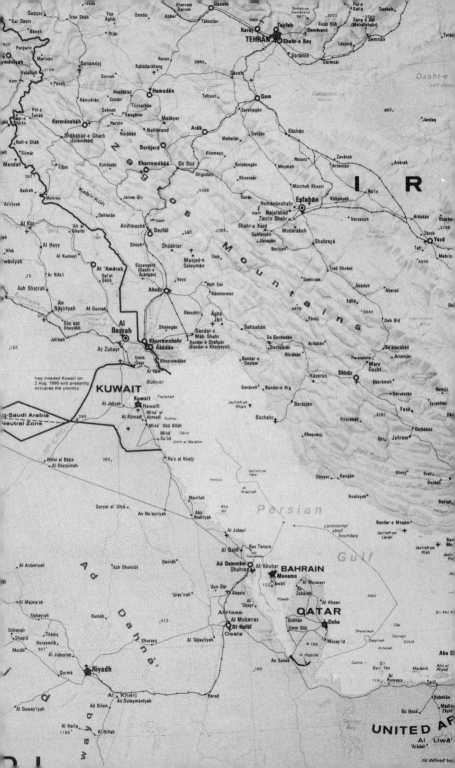

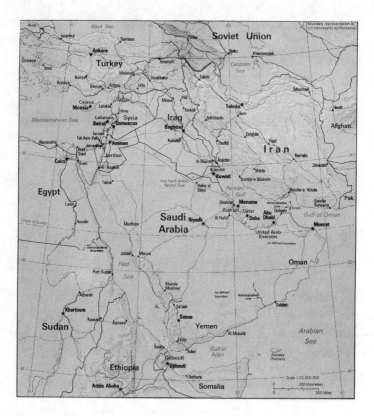

Chapter One

JANUARY–JULY 1990

WARNING SIGNALS

Chronology

The first signal of the coming crisis in the Gulf comes in Amman on February 24, at the first anniversary meeting of the Arab Cooperation Council. The meeting breaks up a day earlier than anticipated because Egypt's president Mubarak resents Saddam's unseemly verbal attack on the United States, made in a speech broadcast on Jordanian television the same day. In its September 29, 1990 issue, *The Economist* traces Saddam's early warning signals, beginning with this February speech. Pointing out the declining influence of the Soviet Union, Saddam predicts that the United States will enjoy unusual freedom of maneuver in the Middle East, and use that freedom to the detriment of the Arabs. The U.S., Saddam says, has been helping Soviet Jews emigrate to Israel and, despite the end of the Iran-Iraq war, has kept its warships in the Persian Gulf. (Actually there are but a handful left.) He says that "the country that will have the greatest influence in the region, through the Arab Gulf and its oil, will maintain its superiority as a superpower without an equal to compete with it. This means that if the Gulf people, along with all Arabs, are not careful, the Arab Gulf region will be governed by the wishes of the United States . . . [Oil] prices would be fixed in line with a special perspective benefiting American interests and ignoring the interests of others." To counter American influence, Saddam proposes using Arab oil money invested in the West as a lever to make changes, perhaps pulling the money out of Western banks and reinvesting it in Eastern Europe or the Soviet Union. He suggests that there is no role among Arabs for the "faint-hearted"—a clear reference to Egypt, Kuwait, and the United Arab Emirates—who would argue that, as a superpower, the United States will be the decisive factor and others have no choice but to submit.

In the United States and Great Britain, the experts discount Saddam's February speech, reading it not as a warning of aggressive intent but as a sign of uneasiness over the future. The prevailing view is that Saddam has been chastened by the long and costly war with Iran, coming to learn the limits of his own power; he is seen as a moderated radical now desiring to lead Iraq onto a larger world stage. Saddam continues to make bellicose statements, but in London and Washington no one seems to take them very seriously.

Then, on April 2, Saddam sends a second signal of the events to come. He announces that Iraqi scientists have developed advanced chemical weapons, and promises to "make the fire eat up half of Israel if it tries to do anything against Iraq." The U.S. State Department admonishes him for being "inflammatory, irresponsible and outrageous," and the Israelis hint that any chemical attack will bring a nuclear response. But to the experts it is just sabre-rattling, an edgy reaction to world opinion. After all, in March, Iraq was sharply attacked in the international press for hanging a foreign journalist, then exposed and condemned for attempting to obtain triggers for nuclear weapons.

On April 12, Saddam meets with a group of U.S. senators led by Robert Dole of Kansas, the Senate minority leader. Saddam takes the group to task for a Voice of America broadcast critical of him and for efforts to impose economic sanctions against Iraq because of human rights abuses. But Dole reassures Saddam that such actions in no way reflected the Bush adminstration's true policy. Dole says Bush opposes economic sanctions. In a transcript subsequently released by the Iraqi government, Dole says, "We believe—and we are as leaders in the U.S. Congress—that the Congress also does not represent Bush or the government. . . . I assume that President Bush will oppose sanctions, and might veto them unless something provocative were to happen."

Alan Simpson, a leading Republican from Wyoming and the minority whip, lays the blame for the dictator's distorted impression of American politics on the press, which he attests, from personal experience, is "haughty and pampered." On their return to Washington, both Dole and Simpson meet with Bush and counsel forbearance. (Kansas, it should be remembered, has sold large quantities of wheat to Iraq.)

On Capitol Hill, the Bush administration reiterated its generally conciliatory line toward Saddam, as Murray Waas would subsequently document in the *Village Voice* ("Who Lost Kuwait?" January 22, 1991). On April 25, Secretary of State James Baker appears before a Senate appropriations subcommittee, where New Jersey's Democratic senator, Frank Lautenberg, confronts him on American "forbearance" towards Iraq: "We hear from President Hussein of Iraq too often, too bellicose . . . On April 2, he threatened to scorch one-half of Israel with a . . . chemical weapon . . . The testimony of numerous arms experts proves that Iraq is developing or already has nuclear capabilities despite their denials."

Baker tells the committee that the Bush administration views "the use of chemical weapons . . . very seriously and it is very disturbing to us," but reports that Saddam told the Dole mission that "chemical weapons [would only be used if Iraq were] attacked with nuclear weapons."

On April 26 Assistant Secretary of State John Kelly, testifying before a House Foreign Affairs subcommittee examining U.S.-Iraq relations, states that "Iraqi actions have raised new questions about Iraqi intentions in the region." He notes Saddam's challenge to American naval power in the region, and criticizes Saddam for the hanging of the foreign journalist and what appears to be an Iraqi-approved murder of an Iraqi dissident in the United States. But Kelly also says that Bush's policy towards Iraq remains unchanged. He reiterates the administration's opposition to economic sanctions, and even seems to praise Saddam for "talking about a new constitution and an expansion of participatory democracy."

Subcommittee member Tom Lantos of California remonstrates with Kelly, likening Saddam's statements to those of Hitler. "I don't think he would have the slightest pangs of conscience for killing half the people living in Israel. He would probably rejoice and have a banquet at the end of the day." Lantos asks, "At what point will the administration recognize that this is not a nice guy, and that conceivably sanctions are appropriate? They were appropriate vis-a-vis Nicaragua in the previous administration ... Did Nicaragua threaten to wipe out its neighbors with poison gas? Did Nicaragua use poison gas on the Contras?"

But Kelly argues that Saddam's threats are mere rhetoric. "I remember hearing Khruhschev saying 'I will bury you,'" he says.

In the following months there are more ominous signs from Saddam Hussein. In May the United States vetoes a PLO proposal at the U.N. to send neutral international observers to the occupied territories, and in Tel Aviv, seven Palestinians are killed by an Israeli. On May 28, at the Arab League summit conference in Baghdad, Saddam takes the lead in the counterattack on Israel. "Not since Nasser," *The Economist* of London notes, "had an Arab leader uttered such chilling, and chillingly plausible, threats against Israel. Arabs everywhere were thrilled." In private Saddam lambastes not the Israelis, but his fellow Arabs. He accuses them of waging what amounts to an economic war against Iraq by pumping too much oil and thereby keeping the price of oil too low. Every dollar off the price of a barrel of oil costs Iraq, badly strapped by its war with Iran, $1 billion a year.

The experts let these statements pass, as they have the others, and the situation is largely ignored by the press. On Capitol Hill, Bush administration representatives continue to argue against the imposition of sanctions against Iraq. It is revealed that U.S. Attorney General Richard Thornburgh apparently slowed an Atlanta investigation into Saddam's laundering of $3 billion through the Atlanta branch of Italy's Lavoro bank for the purchase of U.S. weaponry—including nuclear devices. William Safire, an early and ardent foe of Saddam, writes in the *New York Times* on May 25 that "because the Bush administration does not want to upset the Iraqi dictator . . . no questions are being asked of the National Security Agency about why it failed to spot the huge transfers of dollars."

On July 11, at a special meeting of OPEC, Iraq is unable to persuade other members to raise prices and cut production. On July 16 Saddam's foreign minister, Tariq Aziz, at the Arab summit in Tunisia, declares, "We are sure some Arab states are involved in a conspiracy against us. And we want you to know, our country will not kneel and our women will not become prostitutes and our children will not be barred from food."

On July 17, in his Revolution Day speech, Saddam attacks imperialists, saying they would not dare attack Iraq, the one true defender of the Arabs, because of its great military strength. He implies that Kuwait and the United Arab Emirates are tools of the imperialists, and says the real agents of imperialism are the Gulf rulers who, by keeping oil prices low, are thrusting "a poisoned dagger" into Iraq's back. The day before the speech the Iraqi government had sent a letter to the Arab League stipulating its complaints against Kuwait, which have gone far beyond the overproduction of oil to include stealing oil from Iraq and setting up military outposts inside Iraq.

On July 24 two Iraqi armored divisions move from their bases to positions on Kuwait's border. Later that day Margaret Tutwiler, the State Department spokesperson, is asked at a press conference whether the U.S. has any commitment to militarily defend Kuwait. She replies, "We do not have any defense treaties with Kuwait, and there are no special defense or security commitments to Kuwait."

The next day April Glaspie, the U.S. ambassador to Baghdad, repeats these sentiments to Saddam himself. She has been summoned to appear before Saddam, who dresses her down. In a text subsequently released by Iraq, Ambassador Glaspie is recorded as saying that the U.S. has no position on the Kuwait border question, and that Americans understand Iraq's desire to increase oil revenue. At this meeting, Glaspie reportedly suggests that Saddam should go on American television so Americans could better understand his aspirations. Glaspie does ask "in the spirit of friendship—not . . . confrontation," why Saddam is massing his troops on the Kuwait border.

In response, Saddam promises that there will be diplomatic meetings between the two belligerents, and relates a conversation with Egypt's president Mubarak, who had told Saddam that the Kuwaitis were frightened by the troops. "I said to him that, regardless of what is there . . . assure the Kuwaitis and give them our word that we are not going to do anything until we meet with them. When we meet and when we see that there is hope, then nothing will happen. But if we are unable to find a solution, then it will be natural that Iraq will not accept death, even though wisdom is above everything else. There you have the good news."

On July 27 the Senate and House vote to impose limited economic sanctions against Iraq, prohibiting agricultural credits to the country. (During the Reagan-Bush years, those credits had risen to $4.5 billion.) But for all practical purposes the sanctions are worthless, since they contain a clause allowing President Bush to override them if he judges them a threat to the export competetiveness of American products.

On July 31, Waas notes, with both the CIA and the Defense Intelligence Agency agreeing that some sort of Iraqi military action against Kuwait is imminent, Assistant Secretary of State John Kelly is back before the House Foreign Affairs subcommittee, where, in response to chairman Lee Hamilton's questioning he declares, "We have no defense treaty relationship with any Gulf country. That is clear...We have historically avoided taking a position on border disputes."

Two days later, on the morning of August 2, Iraq invades Kuwait.

March 19, 1990

New York Times columnist William Safire's early salvo against Saddam Hussein is fired at a time when the U.S. government is still acting primarily *on behalf* of the Iraqi president. In mid-March, Safire's position seems marginal and extreme—but it foreshadows the rhetoric that will overtake the nation less than six months later.

A DANGEROUS THING
WILLIAM SAFIRE
The New York Times

Washington

Saddam Hussein, widely feared as "the Butcher of Baghdad," declared a school holiday last Saturday to swell the crowds ordered to demonstrate in front of the British Embassy.

The dictator took offense because Mrs. Thatcher's Government dared to protest—as "an act of barbarism deeply repugnant to all civilized people"—his hanging of a reporter for The London Observer.

"Mrs. Thatcher wanted him alive; we gave her the body," crowed the Iraqi propaganda minister, after the remains were turned over to the British Embassy in Baghdad.

The accredited journalist, Farzad Bazoft, had heard reports of an explosion at a plant to the southwest of Iraq's capital. Reporters were denied permission to investigate; suspecting trouble at one of Iraq's poison-gas or missile plants in that area, the reporter disguised himself and went anyway. He was caught, tried as a spy, and promptly hanged.

Not all the people of the civilized world found the lynching repugnant: "moderate" King Hussein of Jordan, no relation to Saddam, deplored "a concerted attack on Iraq for a long period of time without any reason to justify it."

Arab apologists are busily trying to besmear the victim: Mr. Bazoft had a prison record in his early 20's, was stateless, confessed to spying under the always gentle Iraqi interrogation, etc. The PLO's Salah Khalef broadcast support of Iraq's gleeful leader.

Saddam sent no demonstrators to the U.S. Embassy for good reason: the Bush Administration's reaction was of such studied indifference as to border on condoning the assassination.

President Bush refused to join in the worldwide appeals for clemency. After the hanging, the President's spokesman, Marlin Fitzwater, said only that "we regret those [appeals] went unheeded. But we don't have a lot of details on the case itself."

At the State Department, our rip-'n'-read spokeswoman, Margaret Tutwiler, read "We deplore Iraq's decision . . ." but when asked what our Government intended to do about it, went into her usual flustered state: "I did not think to ask . . ."

A couple of questions we should all ask:

What terrible secret was the journalist trying to uncover? President Bush knows, from the same satellite observation that showed poison-gas production at Libya's Rabta plant, that Saddam is producing poison gas at 10 different locations. Some of that gas was used in the Iranian war, some in killing thousands of Iraqi Kurds. Three months ago, Iraq launched a three-stage, 48-ton rocket, demonstrating its missile capability. Was the damaged plant producing gas, rockets or nuclear weapons?

Why is Mr. Bush so eager to help the dictator of what has become the world's most dangerous nation? When the Congress identified Iraq as a terrorist nation to be denied U.S. favor, Mr. Bush invoked an exception enabling him to ignore this ruling "in the national interest."

That's why Iraq still gets loan guarantees from us on grain purchases. The Atlanta branch of Italy's Bank of Lavoro scandalously slipped $3 billion in financing to Iraq, in a deal being laconically prosecuted by our Justice Department. Even after the scandal broke, and our Agriculture Secretary promised a Senate Committee no new loan guarantees would be issued without notification, Secretary Yeutter supplied an additional $500 million guarantee.

When these fishy dealings were outlined in this space, with wonderment at Mr. Bush's needless exposure of U.S. taxpayers, the Iraqi press counselor in Washington, Abdul Rahman Jamil, wrote to my editor to insist our aid was used for grain, not missiles, explaining: "It is not uncommon to expect delays of payments in financial arrangements." That tipped off future repayment problems.

"Mr. Safire ought to be reminded," Mr. Jamil added, "that a little knowledge is dangerous, and he is using this knowledge dangerously."

A colleague cheerfully passed this along with "Hope you weren't planning a holiday in Baghdad." (I did not take Mr. Jamil's reminder to be intimidation, noting it only as a misquotation of Alexander Pope's "A little learning is a dangerous thing.")

So now they're hanging foreign journalists in Iraq and nobody in the Bush administration gives a damn. Mr. Bush ignores this state murder, allows the U.S. to become dependent on Arab oil while Saddam urges OPEC to raise prices, and keeps guaranteeing loans to a country that spends billions on mustard gas and missiles.

In what national interest? What hold does the Butcher of Baghdad have on the President of the United States.

April 12, 1990

On April 12, with the Congress showing anger over Iraq's human rights record, Bob Dole, the Senate Republican leader from Kansas, leads a delegation of five senators on a visit to Saddam Hussein. The other senators are Idaho Republican James McClure, Ohio Democrat Howard Metzenbaum, Wyoming Republican Alan Simpson, and Alaska Republican Frank Murkowski. Saddam will later release a text of their meeting—which appears to have been almost cordial—under the now-ironic heading "Message of Peace."

TRANSCRIPT OF MEETING BETWEEN U.S. SENATORS AND SADDAM HUSSEIN
Baghdad

President Hussein: It has been claimed that Iraq threatened Israel, although my words clearly state my conviction, that this campaign has been intended to provide a psychological, propaganda and political cover for Israel to attack us, as it did in 1981. It is similar to the campaign that occurred in 1981, although this one is harsher.

Senator Dole: Once again I assure you that the U.S. government is not the cause of this campaign.

President Hussein: In any case, it was waged in the U.S.

Senator Dole: Mr. President, we condemned the Israeli attack in 1981.

President Hussein: Yes, you did condemn it, but many reports have surfaced that the U.S. knew about it in advance.

If the U.S. didn't know, then so much the worse, because the U.S. is the one who gives Israel the means of power. If any great power provides the means of power to a country in the same region or outside of it, and it has no control whatsoever over the way that power is used, this is what threatens peace, and this is what exposes the world to unexpected events whose outcome cannot be controlled.

Again, in my statement I said that if Israel strikes, we will
strike against it. I assure you now that if Israel strikes, we will
strike against it. I believe that this is a fair position, and that
such a known, previously stated position is what helps peace,
and not the opposite... Senator Dole, other members of the
delegation, I know that chemical weapons have been banned
in the Geneva Accords. I have not forgotten our commitment
that we have signed. However, are chemical weapons more
dangerous to mankind than are nuclear bombs?

You are citizens and officials of a superpower, and you know
in theory as well as in practice what the significance of each
weapon is. You know that when chemical weapons were
banned, all these types of weapons were banned. How could
you want Iraq not to use chemical weapons when confronting
the atomic bombs of an authority that continually raves and
threatens the Arab nations and Iraq?... Regardless of how this
discussion is interpreted by the media, it goes as follows: if
Israel strikes, then we will strike against it. What we say is
clear and written in both Arabic and English, and recorded on
paper and on tape. We will not retract what we have
said... We do not apologize for the statements we have made.
Our position is clear, fair and defensive. And it is correct.

* * * * *

Senator Dole: Mr. President, I want to say that we know the
importance of Iraq. You are the second country in terms of oil
reserves: you are the second largest country in the region, and
you have a long, long history. We understand the importance
of Iraq, even in the peace process although you are not at the
forefront of it. When we talk about peace in the region, about
peace for all the countries in the region—and also about arms,
whether biological, chemical or nuclear—we hope that this
will be part of a total disarmament to make this region free of
these types of weapons.

President Hussein: This would do well with the Arabs.

* * * * *

Senator Murkowski: I think that we have come to your
country, Mr. President, well aware of the history of the Middle
East, and we acknowledge the history of conflict in this
region. You are still in the process of this conflict after the
long war with Iran, and you are still reorganizing in your
country. We in the U.S., I believe, view the Middle East as a
powder keg. It has incredible amounts of war and military

potential, and advanced technological weapons, while in Eastern Europe we have an atmosphere of peace.

We look at this part of the world and note that the tension here is very high. We have come to you, Mr. President, with good intentions. We look forward in the future to the opportunities that make it easier for us right now. In Israel they are now in the process of establishing a new government. It appears to me that there is a golden opportunity right now. In our discussions with the leaders of the states in the region, they all strongly assured us of their conviction that this is an opportune time. However, in order to achieve real peace, we must reach a compromise, and a commitment from the concerned parties must be made, as happens in our legislative bodies in the U.S. That is, we agree to a compromise ... I highly appreciate your openness and your views on protecting your country. This is something we understand. We sense that there is similar concern in Israel. They, too, are aware of the opportunity that is now available, and that they must benefit from it.

President Hussein: Until now, this has not been very apparent.

Senator Murkowski: I understand that.

President Hussein: Because Israel has embarked on this widespread immigration to the occupied territories, this does not convince us that Israel wants peace. Where can these numbers of immigrants go? You know that in Gaza the population is already very dense. The same can be said about Jerusalem as well, and the rest of the occupied territories can barely absorb but a few more. We look at this new wave of immigration as the basis for a new phase of Israeli expansion ... If there is a wise person in Israel, he should be attempting the impossible to achieve peace now, not in ten years.

Senator Simpson: We all realize that they must adopt something different in their government. But I say that Presidents Bush and Gorbachev have started to grow closer to each other, and there is a personal relationship between them. However, the last thing you talked about was democracy. Democracy is a very confusing (sic) issue. I believe that your problems lie with the Western media, and not with the U.S. government. As long as you are isolated from the media, the press—and it is a haughty and pampered press—they all -consider themselves political geniuses. That is, the journalists do. They are very cynical. What I advise is that you invite them to come here and see for themselves.

President Hussein: They are welcome. We hope they will
come to see Iraq, and after they do, write whatever they like,
and say that they liked this and they didn't like that. No, we
are not at all too sensitive toward the media. We hope they
will come. I will grant your Ambassador my approval for all
the media in the U.S. We welcome anyone who wants to
come here: there is no veto against anyone...

April 24, 1990

On April 24, before anyone begins to think of war with
Iraq as a real possibility, Robert H. Kupperman of the
Center for Strategic and International Studies argues
convincingly for strong measures to limit Saddam
Hussein's power. He accuses the Bush administration,
which still opposes such measures, of engaging in
"psychological denial" and "wishful thinking" with
regard to the Iraqi threat.

PRESIDENT BUSH'S OPTIONS ON IRAQ
ROBERT H. KUPPERMAN
The Christian Science Monitor

It is unprecedented. A foreign despot with a record of using
chemical weapons to murder thousands of his own people has
uttered public threats to destroy half the population of
America's most reliable ally in the Middle East. Thus far, the
only reaction from the Bush administration to Iraqi President
Saddam Hussein's threat against Israel has been verbal criticism.

Anyone who seriously expects such admonishment to
chasten Saddam Hussein is deluded. It was only in the last
two weeks that Iraqi agents were intercepted on United States
soil before they could execute visiting Iraqi dissidents. At
Heathrow Airport in London, British and American customs
officers defeated an Iraqi effort to smuggle nuclear-warhead
triggering devices from the U.S. to Baghdad. Iraq's leader
has an agenda of domination and is utterly determined to
carry it out.

Like most others, dictator Hussein learns from experience.
He got away with invading Iran, with the chemical-weapons
slaughter of Kurdish people in Iraq, with the execution of a
British journalist who dared to seek out Hussein's nuclear-
weapons research center, and with the missile attack on the
USS Stark. Hussein also got away with creating biological,
chemical, and nuclear weapons programs that will soon
menace not only Israel but the entire Arab world, much of
Europe, and hundreds of thousands of Americans visiting the

region. All will be within easy range of missiles currently under Iraqi development.

Saddam Hussein has long wished to command a global power. The post-Vietnam American mentality, the after-Afghanistan Soviet mindset, the exquisite emotional relief brought on by the end of the Cold War, and the public-relations body blows suffered by Israel during the *intifadah* have all encouraged the Iraqi dictator and may lead him to believe that he can get away with committing new atrocities.

President Bush, national security adviser Brent Scowcroft, and others close to Mr. Bush who have great experience must know that Saddam Hussein poses an unpredictable but increasing threat to American and allied lives and interests. They must also understand that left alone, Iraq is quite capable of unleashing weapons of mass destruction.

The Bush administration has the following options, complete with attendant risks:

•Public and private diplomacy aimed at "putting back in the bottle" the genie of mass destruction weaponry, a noble effort likely to fail and distract attention from the nature of the threat and inadvertently provide cover for an Iraqi surprise attack.

•Coordinating with Moscow the total economic and diplomatic isolation of Iraq, a course of action also likely to fail because of greed and political cowardice among many U.S. allies.

•Covert military action by the U.S. against Iraq's biological, chemical, and nuclear weapons facilities. This option is extremely difficult, with high risk of U.S. commandos being captured, tortured, and killed, with negative domestic political reaction resulting, to say nothing of the fueling of fundamentalist Islam predictably flowing from any U.S. action.

•Open military action, including conventionally armed cruise missile and bomber attacks on Iraqi weapons plants and laboratories. This option would lower physical risks to American operatives, but has high political risk for the U.S., including loss of credibility as Middle East peace-maker.

•Washington can do nothing, hoping that Israel will have no such option and will soon feel that it must act to forestall Hussein's making good on his public pledge to massacre half the Israeli populace. Israeli bombs would fall as commandos destroy small, difficult-to-target weapons facilities.

The great sadness in this case is that the U.S. will probably choose this last option, that is, let Israel do the necessary dirty work and then castigate the Jewish state for saving its own life and that of thousands, perhaps millions of others.

If the Bush administration pursues that path, you can expect strong pressure to cut off U.S. aid as punishment for Israel's action. Any action of any kind is bound to lead to hand-wringing from anti-interventionists who would probably have opposed the assassination of Hitler if that opportunity had presented itself.

Remember, Saddam Hussein launched the invasion of Iran in 1980 to seize control of the Shatt Al-Arab waterway, which he now has. He used American-provided intelligence for strategic planning, German and Japanese technology to build chemical weapons, and his own brutality to perpetuate a war that slew more than 1 million human beings. During the past decade, Hussein's home-grown and foreign hired help have manufactured an array of biological weapons infinitely more dangerous than his chemical arsenal.

Today Saddam Hussein has them, and they do not require the most sophisticated delivery systems. Terrorists in his employ could smuggle them into the U.S. over border crossings or bring them in under cover of diplomatic pouch.

So long as the Iraqi dictator is permitted to possess weapons of mass destruction, we are all in real danger. What will our leaders do about it and when? Other than psychological denial and wishful thinking, there are no easy options, only very hard and costly choices with little time.

April 26, 1990

On April 26, John H. Kelly, Assistant Secretary of State for Near Eastern and South Asian Affairs, appears before a House Foreign Affairs committee to give a formal statement and answer questions on Iraq. Carefully evasive, Kelly shies well clear of recommending sanctions.

TRANSCRIPT OF HOUSE SUB-COMMITTEE HEARING ON U.S.-IRAQI RELATIONS
Washington, D.C.

Mr. Kelly: Early in this Administration, Mr. Chairman, a review of our policy in the Persian Gulf was conducted ... The result was a conclusion that U.S. interests in the Persian Gulf—and in Iraq—were likely to be increasingly important in the decade to come.

One reason, of course, is energy. Gulf producers account for about 70 percent of world excess oil production capacity, and over the next 10 years, they will be called on to cover increasing percentages in world consumption. Worldwide, Iraq's oil reserves are second only to those of Saudi Arabia.

Another reason is the danger of proliferation of nuclear, chemical, or biological weapons, and the missile systems to deliver them. Again, the importance of Iraq is clear.

We also knew, of course, that in the final analysis only a policy based on American values and principles will succeed. This meant that human rights would be a central consideration for us.

These fundamental concerns and interests will continue to guide our diplomacy with Iraq. We had reestablished full diplomatic relations with Iraq in 1984, after Iraq expelled the Abu Nidal terrorist gang and was removed from the list of states that support international terrorism. The establishment of diplomatic relations helped us work with Iraq in efforts to end the Iran-Iraq war. In subsequent years we developed a dialogue with Iraqi leaders on issues from the Middle East peace process to Lebanon.

By October 1989, we could point to some modest developments on issues of concern to us . . . Since then, Iraqi actions
have raised new questions about Iraqi intentions in the
region . . . Mr. Chairman, our policy towards Iraq has been to
attempt to develop gradually a mutually beneficial relationship with Iraq in order to strengthen positive trends in Iraq's
foreign and domestic policies. Recent developments, taken
together, are serious. They raise questions in our minds about
the intentions of Iraq's leaders towards such international
commitments as the Non-Proliferation Treaty and the Geneva
Protocol banning the use of chemical weapons. Behind this
lies the broader issue of what Iraq's political and military aims
are in the region.

To summarize quickly the remainder of my statement, Mr.
Chairman, we have no economic support or military
assistance programs for Iraq. We limit and monitor closely
sales of articles which might be useful in the military domain
or might be dual-use items.

We have an active program of providing insurance for
agricultural credits for Iraq and a modest program of export-
import bank guarantees. We are concerned by the activities of
Iraq and deeply so. We are active in trying to prevent the
spread of missiles in volatile areas such as the Middle
East . . . . Mr. Chairman, this brings me to the question of
sanctions. I am well aware there is strong sentiment on this
committee and in the Congress for trade sanctions against
Iraq. If those of us in the Administration thought legislating
trade sanctions would have the effect of promoting the goals
we share with this committee and the Congress, we would
not hesitate to support their imposition. We simply do not
believe that to be the case. While we do not rule out
appropriate responses to recent actions by the Government of
Iraq, we are not prepared to see economic and trade sanctions
legislatively imposed at this point. Instead, we believe that
Iraq has clearly received the important message of unanimous
U.S. Government concern over its recent actions, and we are
hopeful that the Government of Iraq will move quickly to
bring U.S.-Iraq relations to a more positive level. . . .

Another result of sanctions would be to worsen the existing
imbalance in our trade with Iraq. In the first two months of
1990, we imported Iraqi oil at a level of some 675,000 barrels
per day. If this rate of purchase holds through the year, we will

buy at least $3.7 billion worth of oil from Iraq. Our exports to Iraq last year amounted so some $1.2 billion, or roughly the levels of the CCC and EXIM guarantee programs combined.

For these reasons, the Administration continues to oppose imposition of legislated sanctions. They would hurt U.S. exporters and worsen our trade deficit. I do not see how sanctions would improve our ability to exercise a restraining influence on Iraqi actions.

The Government of Iraq is well aware that its recent actions have caused a deterioration in U.S.-Iraq relations. The visit of Senator Dole and his colleagues to Baghdad helped bring home to Iraqi leaders the damage which has been done. We believe it is important to give the Government of Iraq an opportunity to demonstrate that it does indeed wish to reverse this deterioration in relations, and we are therefore opposed to legislation to impose economic sanctions.

* * * * *

Mr. [Tom] Lantos: Welcome, Mr. Secretary. With all due respect, Mr. Secretary, I detect an Alice in Wonderland quality about your testimony. Let me tell you why. You recite accurately a chamber of horrors. The Department of State calls Saddam Hussein's outrageous and preposterous comments, I quote, "inflammatory, irresponsible, and outrageous." You talk about Iraq using poison gas against its own people, diplomats engaging in murder plots in the United States and the government smuggling nuclear trigger devices from here and from the U.K. and other places.

We now have the big gun episode which is lied about as all other episodes are lied about and a human rights record which according to the State Department's human rights annual report is a nightmare. Then you express the hope, which boggles my mind, that somehow this will change and Iraq under Saddam Hussein will turn in the direction of being a responsible and civilized and peace loving and constructive member of the international community.

I find this, to put it mildly, a non sequitur. I also find it remarkable that while the Administration uses the word "fungible" with great glee on the numbers of other occasions, meaning dollars saved in one place can be used elsewhere, it fails to see the fungibility that our extension of agriculture and Ex-Im Bank credits provide Iraq.

There is another inconsistency that I would like to ask you to clarify for all of us, in the opening sentences of your presentation, you pointed to Iraq's enormous oil wealth. You are absolutely correct. If Iraq has such enormous oil wealth why does it need these commercial and financial subsidies from the United States. Why can't it buy at open market rates?

Let me make one observation before I ask you to respond. You drew a dichotomy between words and deeds. We are not just dealing with words, although the words that Saddam Hussein is spewing forth I have not heard since Adolf Hitler who also had to be believed when he said he would wipe out by gas a very significant portion of the people. I believe Saddam Hussein. I don't think he would have the slightest pangs of conscience for killing half the people living in Israel. He would probably rejoice and have a banquet at the end of the day. There are such people, Mr. Kelly. Saddam Hussein by his statements and by his actions, poison gassing Kurdish children, running the most bloody and murderous dictatorship on the face of this planet, is one of these people. At what point will the Administration recognize that this is not a nice guy, and that conceivably sanctions are appropriate? They were appropriate vis a vis Nicaragua in the previous administration. Did Nicaragua have a worse human rights record? Did Nicaragua threaten to wipe out its neighbors with poison gas? Did Nicaragua use poison gas on the Contras? At what point can we hope that the Administration will wake up to the reality which is shouting into the ears of anybody who is prepared to listen with an open mind?

Mr. Kelly: Thank you, Congressman. You have put your finger on a very difficult decision that successive administrations have to make in dealing with countries or leaders of countries who do atrocious things. I remember the great debate in the early years of the Reagan Administration when President Reagan referred to the Soviets as an evil empire. The Soviets were engaged in shooting down the Korean airliners: their disrespect for human rights, to put it mildly, a whole long catalog of things. There was great argument in the United States as to whether the United States ought to abjure contracts with the Soviet Union or to engage in them.

The same occurred with regard to the government of South Africa, should the United States engage? In other words, is

there the potential of improvement in countries, regimes and
leaders who advocate atrocious and unconscionable acts. This
is not a new argument. It is a legitimate one.

Mr. Lantos: With all due respect, Mr. Kelly, the Soviet regime
since the end of the Second World War did not threaten to
wipe out half the population of Europe with poison gas.

Mr. Kelly: I remember hearing Krushchev saying I will bury
you.

Mr. Lantos: You know the contest. It related to economic
competition. I don't think it is fair for you retroactively to
reinterpret Krushchev's comments. Nobody in the American
government took those words to mean a physical annihilation
of the United States. You are the first one to make this observation.

Mr. Kelly: That may be true. I was not in government at that
time.

Mr. Lantos: But you were an adult and you heard that
statement?

Mr. Kelly: I don't think I had reached voting age.

May 1, 1990

On May 1 Secretary of State Baker appears before a Senate appropriations subcommittee and, as he has done repeatedly in the past, backs away from any hard stands against Iraq. The CCC program Baker refers to is the Commodity Credit Corporation, by which the U.S. government guarantees commercial bank loans used to finance the purchase of various agriculture products. Without the guarantees, Western banks would not make loans to countries like Iraq because they might default.

TRANSCRIPT OF SENATE SUB-COMMITTEE HEARINGS ON IRAQ'S USE OF CHEMICAL WEAPONS
Washington, D.C.

Senator Robert Kasten: Iraq's statements regarding the use of chemical, biological, and nuclear weapons in the Middle East have been termed by the State Department as "inflammatory, irresponsible, and outrageous."

There have been attempts, as we all know, to smuggle nuclear trigger devices into Iraq. We have statements from a number of government officials concerning different kinds of threats being made.

Iraq has proved its willingness to use chemical and biological weapons against Iran and, even more outrageously, against its own population. It has recently deployed missiles within range of Israel, and has threatened to use them.

What kinds of sanctions is the administration prepared to impose against Iraq for these actions?

Secretary Baker: Senator Kasten, we have made it clear to the Iraqis that their recent actions in several areas have damaged the relationship between Iraq and the United States. You have mentioned their continuing efforts to develop and

improve missile and chemical weapons capabilities. These are
particularly disturbing to us.

We have got some measures in place now to try and block
Iraq's proliferation programs. Iraq is barred from buying United States munitions list items. All of the high technology
items that they want to buy from us are carefully screened.
And if I might suggest it, the recent arrests in London were a
part of that effort.

And in addition to that, we are working through the
Australia group and the missile technology control regime to
block international support for their chemical weapons and
missile programs. And finally, we are in the process of
reviewing the future of our CCC program with Iraq.

Senator Kasten: You mentioned the fact that in last year's
appropriations bill Iraq had been removed from the list of
terrorist states. Therefore, Iraq is now eligible for Ex-im Bank
loans and a couple of other trade-related programs.

Do you believe that we should add Iraq back onto that list
of terrorist countries?

Secretary Baker: Well, Senator Kasten, I think we have to
take a look at that, and we will be taking a look at that issue
in connection with the preparation of a report for 1990.

The actions that I have referred to as having damaged our
relationship with Iraq will certainly be considered. It is a little
bit premature for me on May 1 to sit here and make that
determination just as we sit here.

We will obviously be looking at that and we will be looking
at the factors that I mentioned.

Senator Kasten: Well, I believe that they ought to be put
back on that list of terrorist countries based on what they
have said and are doing, and I am going to make an effort to
do that at a minimum.

There is some legislation that Senator Inouye and others
have developed that goes significantly beyond that, involving
agricultural credits and of other programs.

Secretary Baker: That is the CCC program I am talking
about.

Senator Kasten: Exactly, and I would not object to going
further. The PLO, Mr. Secretary—

Secretary Baker: Senator, could I just say there, without in any
way defending, because I certainly do not, what has happened,
and I think you heard what I said about the damage to our

relationship, I think we ought to at least be conscious of the fact that if we take that action with respect to CCC or other economic measures, Senator Kasten, that in all probability our allies will be very quick to move in there and pick up our market share.

There will be some people in the United States that will be less than enthusiastic about that. That is not in any way said as a defense of what has happened or to take a position to try and prejudge what the CCC review will decide.

July 25, 1990

On July 25, a little more than a week before the invasion of Kuwait, Ambassador April Glaspie meets with
Saddam in Baghdad. The transcript later released by the
Iraqis shows a conciliatory and reassuring U.S. attitude
towards Iraq's president.

TRANSCRIPT OF MEETING BETWEEN U.S. AMBASSADOR APRIL GLASPIE AND SADDAM HUSSEIN
Baghdad

Saddam Hussein: I have summoned you today to hold comprehensive political discussions with you. This is a message to
President Bush... Iraq came out of the [Iran-Iraq] war burdened with $40 billion debts, excluding the aid given by Arab
states, some of whom consider that too to be a debt although
they know—and you know too—that without Iraq they
would not have had these sums and the future of the region
would have been entirely different.

We began to face the policy of the drop in the price of oil.
Then we saw the United States, which always talks of democracy but which has no time for the other point of view. Then
the media campaign against Saddam Hussein was started by
the official American media. The United States thought that
the situation in Iraq was like Poland, Romania or Czechoslo-
vakia. We were disturbed by this campaign but we were not
disturbed too much because we had hoped that, in a few
months, those who are decision makers in America would
have a chance to find the facts... But when planned and
deliberate policy forces the price of oil down without good
commercial reasons, then that means another war against
Iraq. Because military war kills people by bleeding them, and
economic war kills their humanity by depriving them of their
chance to have a good standard of living... Kuwait and the
U.A.E. were at the front of this policy aimed at lowering Iraq's

position and depriving its people of higher economic standards. And you know that our relations with the Emirates and Kuwait had been good. On top of all that, while we were busy at war, the state of Kuwait began to expand at the expense of our territory.

You may say this is propaganda, but I would direct you to one document, the Military Patrol Line, which is the borderline endorsed by the Arab League in 1961 for military patrols not to cross the Iraq-Kuwait border.

But go and look for yourselves. You will see the Kuwaiti border patrols, the Kuwaiti farms, the Kuwaiti oil installations—all built as closely as possible to this line to establish that land as Kuwaiti territory...

April Glaspie: ... Mr. President, you mentioned many things during this meeting which I cannot comment on on behalf of my Government. But with your permission, I will comment on two points. You spoke of friendship and I believe it was clear from the letters sent by our President to you on the occasion of your National Day that he emphasizes—

Hussein: He was kind and his expressions met with our regard and respect.

Glaspie: As you know, he directed the United States Administration to reject the suggestion of implementing trade sanctions.

Hussein: There is nothing left for us to buy from America. Only wheat. Because every time we want to buy something, they say it is forbidden. I am afraid that one day you will say, "You are going to make gunpowder out of wheat."

Glaspie: I have a direct instruction from the President to seek better relations with Iraq....

Hussein: Your stance is generous. We are Arabs. It is enough for us that someone says, "I am sorry, I made a mistake." Then we carry on. But the media campaign continued. And it is full of stories. If the stories were true, no one would get upset. But we understand from its continuation that there is a determination.

Glaspie: I saw the Diane Sawyer program on ABC. And what happened in that program was cheap and unjust. And this is a real picture of what happens in the American media—even to American politicians themselves. These are the methods the Western media employs. I am pleased that you add your voice to the diplomats who stand up to the media. Because your appearance in the media, even for five minutes, would help us to make the American people understand Iraq. This would increase mutual understanding. If the American President had control of the media, his job would be much better.

Mr. President, not only do I want to say that President Bush wanted better and deeper relations with Iraq, but he also wants an Iraqi contribution to peace and prosperity in the Middle East . . . Frankly, we can only see that you have deployed massive troops in the south. Normally that would not be any of our business. But when this happens in the context of what you said on your National Day, then when we read the details in the two letters of the Foreign Minister, then when we see the Iraqi point of view that the measure taken by the U.A.E. and Kuwait is, in the final analysis, parallel to military aggression against Iraq, then it would be reasonable for me to be concerned. And for this reason, I received an instruction to ask you, in the spirit of friendship—not in the spirit of confrontation—regarding your intentions.

I simply describe the concern of my Government. And I do not mean that the situation is a simple situation. But our concern is a simple one.

Hussein: We do not ask people not to be concerned when peace is at issue. This is a noble human feeling which we all feel. It is natural for you as a superpower to be concerned. But what we ask is not to express your concern in a way that would make an aggressor believe that he is getting support for his aggression . . . .

Glaspie: Mr. President, it would be helpful if you could give us an assessment of the effort made by your Arab brothers and whether they have achieved anything.

Hussein: On this subject, we agreed with President Mubarak that the Prime Minister of Kuwait would meet with the deputy chairman of the Revolution Command Council in Saudi Arabia, because the Saudis initiated contact with us, aided by President Mubarak's efforts. He just telephoned me a short while ago to say the Kuwaitis have agreed to that suggestion.

Glaspie: Congratulations.

Hussein: A protocol meeting will be held in Saudi Arabia. Then the meeting will be transferred to Baghdad for deeper discussion directly between Kuwait and Iraq. We hope we will reach some result. We hope that the long-term view and the real interests will overcome Kuwaiti greed.

Glaspie: May I ask you when you expect Sheik Saad to come to Baghdad?

Hussein: I suppose it would be on Saturday or Monday at the latest. I told brother Mubarak that the agreement should be in Baghdad Saturday or Sunday. You know that brother Mubarak's visits have always been a good omen.

Glaspie: That is good news. Congratulations.

Hussein: Brother President Mubarak told me they were scared. They said troops were only 20 kilometers north of the Arab League line. I said to him that regardless of what is there, whether they are police, border guards or army, and regardless of how many are there, and what they are doing, assure the Kuwaitis and give them our word that we are not going to do anything until we meet with them. When we meet and when we see that there is hope, then nothing will happen. But if we are unable to find a solution, then it will be natural that Iraq will not accept death, even though wisdom is above everything else. There you have the good news.

Foreign Minister Tariq Aziz: This is a journalistic exclusive.

Glaspie: I am planning to go to the United States next Monday. I hope I will meet with President Bush in Washington next week. I thought to postpone my trip because of the difficulties we are facing. But now I will fly on Monday.

July 29, 1990

Only four days before the invasion, the West still appears to be "misreading the nature of Iraq's president" and "entertaining false hopes"—practices which, Middle East expert Shireen T. Hunter astutely predicts, will put "Western interests in the Gulf . . . in deep jeopardy."

IRAQ IS NOT THE LESSER OF TWO EVILS
SHIREEN T. HUNTER
Los Angeles Times

The West is once more in danger of misreading the nature of Iraq's president, Saddam Hussein, and his ambitions for his country. Unless there is a clear-sighted view of his intentions and an effective response to them, Western interests in the Persian Gulf will be in deep jeopardy.

The record of Western misapprehension about Hussein's regime is extensive, going back to 1980, when Iraq invaded Iran. Ignoring a raft of evidence, Western analysts and policy-makers attributed Iraqi aggression to fear of Iran and its revolution, rather than to Iraq's ambitions to become the dominant power in the Persian Gulf and the Arab world.

These analysts made their next serious mistake by inter-preting Hussein's downshifts in rhetoric, necessitated by war needs, as indicating deep and long-lasting ideological and institutional transformation of Iraqi behavior that could only be characterized as wishful thinking. For example, it was generally expected that Iraq would liberalize its political system and play a positive role in resolving the Arab-Israel conflict. Perhaps it would even join Egypt and Jordan in an Arab coalition willing to make peace with Israel. The pay-off: total Western support for Iraq in the Persian Gulf war.

Because of this sort of analysis, the West—the United States and Europe—helped Iraq economically and militarily far beyond what was necessary to contain Iran. Simultaneously, by weakening Iran more than was necessary to keep it from dominating the Persian Gulf, the West helped to create a dis-equilibrium in the regional balance, which Saddam Hussein has exploited ever since.

After the cease-fire in the Iran-Iraq war, and despite the obvious shift in the regional military balance, the West persisted in viewing Iran as the greater threat and refused to force Iraq to live up to its commitments under U.N. Security Council Resolution 598, the basis for the cease-fire.

The West also continued to turn a blind eye to Iraq's massive human-rights violations and was years late in condemning Iraq's use of chemical weapons, the most extensive since World War I. The Western attitude toward Iraq's drive for nuclear capability has also been muted.

Last week Iraq's threat to Kuwait's security and territorial integrity was seen by many Western analysts as mere posturing in order to boost oil prices at the OPEC meeting in Geneva. As usual, they cautioned against antagonizing Hussein.

This analysis is seriously in error. There can be no doubt that Iraq wants to become the dominant power in the Persian Gulf, which its own 30 miles of coastline does not merit. Thus, it must control the Iranian shoreline or that of Kuwait.

Saddam Hussein is a typical Arab nationalist, in the Nasser mold, who views the Gulf rulers as reactionary Western surrogates and impediments to achievement of Arab nationalists' goals. Now that he is riding high in popularity among the Arab masses and because of Arab frustration over the Palestinian problem, he is testing to see whether he can supplant these Gulf leaders or at least bring them under his control. Nor would Iraq need to launch a full-scale military invasion of Kuwait to achieve its goal. It could force Kuwait to surrender or lease strategic islands or even to unite with Iraq.

If successful, critical Iraqi influence over the West's oil lifeline would lead Hussein to pressure the West on the Palestinian problem.

Under these circumstances, what is the West to do? It has already narrowed its options by having indulged Hussein for too long. For example, given Iraq's current military strength, it would not be easy to mount a U.S. naval operation similar to the re-flagging and protecting of Kuwaiti tankers that was carried out at the height of the war in 1987-88.

Nevertheless, the West must act before it is too late. First, it must finally see Hussein for what he really is and stop entertaining false hopes. It must be more prudent about Iraq's nuclear program, and it must apply economic pressure while Iraq is still financially vulnerable. Let's hope the U.S. Senate's voting of economic sanctions Friday marks the start of a long-term policy re-evaluation. The West, including Europe, must stop new credits and loans to Baghdad, and if that is not sufficient, an economic boycott, including Iraq's oil, may be necessary.

The West also must try to restore some balance in the region by helping Iran's moderates, easing Iran's re-integration in the world community and encouraging Arab-Iranian reconciliation.

Finally, the West must do all it can to break the deadlock on the Arab-Israeli peace process and find a solution to the Palestinian problem—the single most important rallying cry for frustrated Arabs and the best tool of manipulation for their ambitious leaders.

July 31, 1990

On July 31, Iraqi armored divisions are at the Kuwait border, and Assistant Secretary of State John Kelly is back on Capitol Hill to clarify the Bush administration's position for the increasingly puzzled members of the House Foreign Affairs Subcommittee on Europe and the Middle East.

TRANSCRIPT OF HOUSE SUB-COMMITTEE HEARING ON U.S. COMMITMENTS IN THE GULF
Washington, D.C.

Mr. Kelly: . . . I am confident in the Administration's position on the issue. We have no defense treaty relationship with any Gulf country. That is clear. We support the security and independence of friendly states in the region. Ever since the Truman administration, we have maintained Naval forces in the Gulf because of our interest in stability in that region.

We are calling for a peaceful resolution of any differences in that area and we hope and trust and believe that the sovereignty of every state in the Gulf ought to be respected.

Mr. Hamilton: Do we have a commitment to our friends in the Gulf in the event that they are engaged in oil or territorial disputes with their neighbors?

Mr. Kelly: As I said, Mr. Chairman, we have no defense treaty relationships with any of the countries. We have historically avoided taking a position on border disputes or on internal OPEC deliberations, but we have certainly, as have all administrations, resoundingly called for the peaceful settlement of disputes and differences in the area.

Mr. Hamilton: If Iraq, for example, charged across the border into Kuwait, for whatever reason, what would be our position with regard to the use of U.S. forces?

Mr. Kelly: That, Mr. Chairman, is a hypothetical or a contingency, the kind of which I can't get into. Suffice it to say we would be extremely concerned, but I cannot get into the realm of "what if" answers.

Mr. Hamilton: In that circumstance, it is correct to say, however, that we do not have a treaty commitment which would obligate us to engage U.S. forces?

Mr. Kelly: That is correct.

Mr. Hamilton: That is correct, is it not?

Mr. Kelly: That is correct, sir.

Chapter 2

AUGUST 1990

IRAQ'S GAMBLE

Chronology

On August 2 Iraqi troops invade Kuwait, occupying the capital of Kuwait City. The emir of Kuwait, Sheikh Jabir Ahmad al-Sabah, flees to Saudi Arabia, where he sets up a provisional government. The Iraqis announce they are in control.

The same day, President Bush signs an executive order banning trade with Iraq except for humanitarian aid such as medical supplies, and freezes $30 billion in Iraqi and Kuwaiti assets in the U.S. Britain and France follow suit and the Soviet Union, Iraq's long-time arms supplier, suspends arms sales. Bush dispatches a battle group of seven warships, led by the USS Independence, to the Persian Gulf. The United Nations Security Council, in a 14-0 vote (Yemen abstaining), passes Resolution 660, condemning the invasion and calling for Iraq to withdraw.

At a meeting of the Arab League on August 3, fourteen of twenty-one members demand that Iraq withdraw. Japan, West Germany, Belgium, Italy, and the Netherlands freeze Kuwaiti and Iraqi assets. The Soviet Union and the U.S.

issue a joint statement calling on the world to end arms shipments to Iraq. The European Community imposes economic sanctions.

On August 3 President Bush says that "the integrity of Saudi Arabia" is one of the United States' "vital interests," and warns that "further [Iraqi] expansion would be even more unacceptable." When told that Saddam Hussein has announced he will withdraw his troops by August 5, Bush responds, "Let's see him haul them out right now, then." Two days later, Bush warns that the U.S. will not accept the establishment of a puppet government in Kuwait, and when reporters ask him how he might stop that, he replies, "Just wait, watch, and learn."

There follows a rush of events, all moving the world closer to war. Bush sends Defense Secretary Richard Cheney to Saudi Arabia, and on August 5 King Fahd agrees, for the first time, to permit U.S. troops to be based in Saudi Arabia. On August 6 the Security Council passes Resolution 661, imposing a comprehensive economic embargo on Iraq and occupied Kuwait. (Yemen and Cuba abstain.) The same day, British prime minister Margaret Thatcher and NATO secretary general Manfred Woerner are at the White House to discuss the crisis.

By August 7 the rapid deployment forces of Operation Desert Shield begin arriving in Saudi Arabia in what will become the largest U.S. mobilization since the Vietnam War, and the largest airlift since the Second World War. This first contingent of troops and materiel includes fighters, fighter-bombers, paratroopers, and AWACS planes.

The same day, Saddam Hussein promises to "pluck out the eyes of those who attack the Arab nation," and declares, "We would rather die in dignity than live in humiliation." Saddam says it was necessary for him to go into Kuwait to redraw the boundaries that had left wealth in the hands of a "corrupt minority" of Arabs.

On August 8, in a nationally televised address from the Oval Office, President Bush proclaims, "Four simple principles guide our policy. First we seek the immediate, unconditional, and complete withdrawal of all Iraqi forces from Kuwait. Second, Kuwait's legitimate government must be restored to replace the puppet regime. And third, my administration, as has been the case with every president from President Roosevelt to President Reagan, is committed to the security of the Persian Gulf. And fourth, I am determined to protect the lives of American citizens abroad." Likening the situation in the Gulf to that of Europe in the late 1930s, Bush says that "appeasement does not work." But he says that the mission of American troops is "wholly defensive. Hopefully they will not be needed long. They will not initiate hostilities."

Oil is Iraq's only real export product, and an important pipeline runs north to Turkish ports. On August 7 Turkey announces it will enforce sanctions and stop ships from loading Iraqi crude. The pipeline is shut down.

On August 8, three days after the date it originally set for troop withdrawal, Iraq formally annexes Kuwait, apparently in response to U.S. military moves. Saddam says the annexation was undertaken in response to an appeal from a provisional Kuwaiti regime to return their country "to the mother homeland" of Iraq. "Thank God that we are now one people, one state that will be the pride of the Arabs," Saddam declares.

Twelve members of the Arab League vote, on August 10, to send troops to Saudi Arabia. The same day, Saddam delivers a speech in Baghdad urging the "Moslem masses" to launch a "holy war" against the "aggressive invaders" and "disfigured petroleum states" who, with the aid of the colonialists, had "kept the wealth away from the masses." He appeals to "Moslems and believers everywhere" to "rise and defend Mecca, which is captured by the spears of the Americans and Zionists," and to "burn the land under the feet of the aggressive invaders."

In a speech at the Pentagon, Bush speaks of "atrocities" in Kuwait, and declares that the U.S. action in the Gulf is concerned with "fighting aggression—and preserving the sovereignty of nations... And we are also talking about maintaining access to energy resources... Our jobs, our way of life, our own freedom..." The U.S. announces that American, British, and French warships around the Gulf will blockade any oil shipments from Iraq.

On August 13 the crisis worsens, as Iraq announces that foreign citizens will not be allowed to leave Iraq or Kuwait. The U.N. speedily passes a resolution demanding that Iraq let the foreign nationals go, but the speaker of the Iraqi parliament says that his country will continue to "host" the foreigners, placing them at strategic military and industrial sites. Iraq surrounds foreign embassies in Kuwait after they refuse to close, shutting off electricity and water and demanding that they move to Baghdad. Hemmed in, Iraq seeks allies. On August 15 it offers Iran a permanent peace settlement on terms favorable to Iran.

On August 21 Iraqi Foreign Minister Tariq Aziz urges the U.S. to begin peace talks, but says Iraq will not be intimidated into withdrawing from Kuwait. "If the American leader thinks that this is a vacation like they had in Panama or Grenada, they are mistaken..." says Aziz. "It will be a bloody conflict, and America will lose and... be humiliated." By this time nine European Community nations, as well as the dozen Arab League countries, have agreed to send forces to the Gulf to oppose Iraq.

In an open letter to President Bush, Saddam compares his detention of Westerners in Iraq to the United States' internment of Japanese-Americans during World War II. On August 23 Saddam has his first televised visit with Western hostages, but a few days later he announces that he will release all foreign women and children held by Iraq.

On August 26 British prime minister Margaret Thatcher says that any peaceful solution to the Gulf crisis seems "most unlikely," and rules out negotiations with Saddam. "This man is a despot and a tyrant," she says, "and must be stopped." On August 28 Saddam calls for televised debates between himself and both Thatcher and Bush. The American State Department calls the offer "sick," and the British Foreign Office dismisses it as "pure gimmickry."

The U.S. begins to evacuate its embassy in Kuwait and, in the last weeks of August, for the first time since the Tet offensive in Vietnam, the president begins calling up the reserves.

Iraq's Gamble

In the ancient world, the territory that now makes up Iraq was called Mesopotamia, the "cradle of civilization." It was part of the Ottoman Empire from the fifteenth century until World War I, then a British protectorate until 1932, when it gained full independence. A military coup toppled the monarchy in 1958. After another ten years of internal struggle the Baath Party took control. Saddam Hussein quickly rose to power behind the scenes, exercizing his control through the Revolutionary Command Council, and in July 1979 he officially became president of Iraq. Saddam for the first time brought the disparate races of Iraq under autocratic control. Prosperous Sunni Moslems from around the Baghdad area ruled over both the poor, uneducated Shiite Moslems in the lowlands of the South and the non-Arab Kurds in the oil-bearing regions of the North. Although Saddam's Sunni Moslems are fewer in number than the Shiites, they share no power with them, or with the Kurds, whose independence movement Saddam attempted to crush with poison gas attacks.

During twenty years in power, Saddam built an economy on the Soviet model, nationalizing oil and agricultural concerns. Saddam used oil revenues to build highways and hospitals, instituted education programs that achieved a 70 percent literacy rate, and gave women more rights than they enjoyed elsewhere in the Arab world. But he showed himself to be ruthless toward his rivals, both domestic and foreign. The war he launched against Iran, which lasted from 1980 to 1988, saved Iraq from its ancient enemies and protected the other nations of the Persian Gulf from Iranian domination, but at a terrible cost in life and resources.

Saddam has always been inspired by Nasser's Pan-Arabism, and in August 1990, marching into Kuwait, he carries the banner of Arab conquerors of old, giving the Arab masses new pride. Having suffered in humiliation five defeats at the hands of Israel and watched as Arab lands were occupied by the Israelis, many Arabs believe that Saddam's jihad in Kuwait will not only clear the Holy Lands of American infidels and their lackeys in the Gulf, but also open the way for a new society. In August, it surely seems that Saddam will do to Kuwait what he did to Iraq: destroy it in order to rebuild a new autocratic society.

August 10, 1990

At the end of a cataclysmic week that saw the invasion of Kuwait, the imposition of U.N. sanctions against Iraq, and the birth of Operation Desert Shield, Christopher Flavin of the Worldwatch Institute identifies an immediate lesson of the crisis: the folly of American oil dependence and overconsumption.

COLD WAR ENDS, OIL WAR BEGINS

CHRISTOPHER FLAVIN
The Christian Science Monitor

On Aug. 2 Iraqi tanks rumbled into Kuwait and initiated the most profound change in the world oil picture in decades. In the space of a few hours, Saddam Hussein raised his share of world oil reserves from 10 percent to almost 19 percent. The petroleum reserves captured amount to nearly three times U.S. reserves and almost double the Soviet total. In a night's work, Hussein altered not only the balance of power in the Middle East, but the balance of supply and demand in the world oil markets.

In the short run, the world has already lost over 4 million barrels per day, or 15 percent of the oil traded on the world market. Given the military buildup in the Persian Gulf, it is unlikely that Saudi Arabia or any other country can fully make up for this loss. Future price increases are likely as long as this conflict persists.

Iraqi and United States forces now face each other across oil fields that represent about half of world oil reserves. Most of the nations that own those reserves—including Abu Dhabi, Dubai, and Qatar—possess tiny populations and military forces even weaker than Kuwait's. Even the military forces of the largest of the nearby oil states, Saudi Arabia, are no match alone for the large and battle-tested divisions that Iraq can bring to bear. It remains to be seen if the forces that the U.S. and perhaps other countries are sending to Saudi Arabia will deter Hussein.

An open-ended period of extreme military and political instability now pervades the nerve center of the world's energy system. Indeed, the world is already seriously overdependent on Middle Eastern oil, which accounts for 17 percent of world production and 44 percent of world exports.

The Middle East's share of world oil exports is destined to increase steadily during the '90s. Global oil demand has been rising by more than 2 percent a year since 1985, and production by the two leading producers—the United States and the Soviet Union—is falling steeply. U.S. oil imports have increased by 3 million barrels per day in just the last five years. Already Middle Eastern dominance of the world oil market is nearing the dangerously high proportions of the 1970s.

How has such a disastrous situation crept up on political leaders as unexpectedly as Hussein's tanks? The Western world's energy policymakers slept through the 1980s, slashing many of the government programs that could have reduced oil consumption.

In the United States, for example, the federal government allowed auto fuel-economy standards to lapse at the level achieved in 1986. New cars rolling off Detroit's assembly lines in 1989 were actually less efficient than those of the year before. Meanwhile, home weatherization efforts have been gutted, as have energy efficiency R&D programs. Federal spending on improved energy efficiency fell from $700 million in 1981 to a budgeted $150 million in 1990.

President Bush, who finally discovered the words "energy conservation" in the midst of this military crisis, was part of an administration that attempted to eliminate virtually every program designed to reduce U.S. oil dependence.

The folly of such moves has been evident for some time. Oil production in the continental 48 states has been declining for two decades, a trend interrupted only briefly by the massive drilling efforts of the '70s. Oil analysts have long warned that the old, depleted U.S. fields were beginning to run dry. Yet the country's energy-guzzling habits have continued as if it were still in the oil gusher days of the 1920s. Americans' per capita oil consumption is well over twice that of Europeans.

The military confrontation under way in the Persian Gulf will result in a substantial shortfall in world oil supplies for as long as it lasts. Beyond the oil lost from Iraq and Kuwait, oil companies will be reluctant to send tankers into the region to carry oil from Saudi Arabia, Iran, or any other country. The U.S. action, while intended to bring Iraq's economy to its knees, could soon cripple the world economy as well.

The resting period between the cold war and the "oil war" of the '90s has proved shockingly short. This new conflict may well turn out to be equally tense and more difficult to contain. At stake is a sizable share of the world's energy resources. While the local players may be smaller states, the United States and other major powers have gotten involved. Chemical and perhaps nuclear weapons are available to the combatants.

The Middle East is and will remain a dangerous place. It is reckless to rely on such a region for the bulk of the Western world's future energy supplies. Unless efforts begin immediately to reduce oil dependence, we may soon long for the economic and military stability of the former superpower standoff. Not only the industrial countries, but the entire third world is now vulnerable to a serious oil shock.

August 16, 1990

Two weeks after the invasion, U.S. troops are massed on
the Saudi/Kuwait border, and Saddam Hussein has been
declared the "new Hitler." But *Wall Street Journal* and
Nation columnist Alexander Cockburn will not let the
U.S. forget how recently it supported this "monstrous
tyrant," nor how selectively it seems to apply its foreign
policy principles.

THE LAST TEMPTATION OF GEORGE BUSH
ALEXANDER COCKBURN
The Wall Street Journal

In times like these memory is the first casualty. No harm then
in pausing for a moment to look back at history as old as a
day, a week, even three months.

*Did the Gulf States declare economic war on Iraq, thus
provoking Saddam Hussein's subsequent military invasion?*

In the *London Financial Times* for Aug. 8, Lamis Andoni
reported from Amman that at the emergency Arab summit in
Baghdad in May, both Jordanian and Iraqi officials argued
that Kuwait's insistence on boosting oil production above
OPEC guidelines was part of the Gulf States' attempt to
undermine Iraq's emergence as the major regional power.
King Hussein's concerns were further heightened by
indifference to his pleas that Jordan's existence was
endangered unless more political and financial aid was
forthcoming from the Gulf States.

"Some Jordanian politicians also believe that [King]
Hussein has given up the idea of receiving any serious
American backing," Ms. Andoni wrote. "'We would not be
very surprised if some circles in Washington pushed for
sacrificing Jordan if necessary to ensure Israel's stability and
security,' a former Jordanian minister said in reference to
widespread speculation in Amman that the U.S. might
concede to Israeli extremist calls for the transformation of
Jordan into a substitute homeland for the Palestinians."

At the OPEC meeting in Geneva in July, Saddam Hussein said that every dollar off the price of oil cost Iraq $1 billion annually. Iran was being similarly injured by the overproduction by Kuwait and the United Arab Emirates. Even Saudi Arabia added its voice to Iraq's and Iran's protests. Why then did Kuwait push ahead with overproduction despite Iraq's increasingly threatening posture?

Is Saddam a monstrous tyrant, and if so, how did he get that way?

He certainly is a monstrous tyrant, and the parallels with Hitler are not entirely misplaced. Iraq has long had one of the most appalling human rights records in the world. In 1985, Amnesty International reported that 300 children, aged 10 to 14, had been tortured to extract information about the activities of their relatives. Two years later the bodies of 29 youths, arrested in 1985, were returned to their parents bearing the marks of their interrogation. Mass executions of civilians have been frequent. In December 1987, some Kurds were killed with thallium, a rat poison. In 1988, around 6,000 civilians, many of them Kurds, were killed in chemical-weapon attacks.

Yes, the U.S. helped Saddam become the leader he is today, even leaving aside the belief of many in the Middle East that the CIA assisted Saddam's Baath Party in seizing control in 1963, giving it lists of communists who were then murdered.

To help Saddam win his eight-year war against Iran, the U.S. gave him satellite intelligence, helicopters, agricultural credits and naval protection in the Gulf. The reason that a U.S. Navy vessel, the Vincennes, was able to shoot down an Iranian civilian Airbus filled with innocent people, is that it was in the Gulf aiding Iraq.

The U.S. supported Iraq in this fashion, though perfectly aware of Saddam's abominations, as were the French, who lent him fighter-bombers, the Germans, who made him mustard gas, and the British, with whom he was a major trading partner. On March 7, the U.N. Commission on Human Rights, in which the U.S. is very influential, decided not to take action on a draft to bring human-rights violations in Iraq before it, despite a mass of information provided by Amnesty International.

On July 29, the former U.S. assistant secretary of state for Near Eastern affairs, Richard Murphy, was asked by the

International Herald Tribune whether he thought Saddam resembled Hitler. Mr. Murphy thought the comparison "far too glib" and said Saddam was "a rough, direct-talking leader."

Is the U.S.'s sudden discovery of the virtues of the U.N. and of collective sanctions via the Security Council hypocritical?

Very much so. If the U.S. truly adhered to the principle enunciated by George Bush that "the acquisition of territory by force is unacceptable," then its behavior in recent years would have been very different. It would have exerted itself in the U.N. Security Council to condemn Israel, which continues to occupy and settle the Jordanian (Palestinian), Syrian and Lebanese territories it seized in 1967, 1973 and 1982. It would not have been complaisant to Turkey's occupation of northern Cyprus, seized in 1974. It would have condemned Iraq's invasion of Iran in 1980. In that instance, the Security Council did nothing for two weeks and then, when Iraq was 40 miles inside Iranian territory, called for a "cease-fire in place."

If the U.S. was truly principled in opposing aggression against small nations and interference in their affairs it wouldn't have attacked Cuba, Grenada, Nicaragua, Libya and Panama. It wouldn't have sponsored attacks on Angola and Mozambique or encouraged Indonesia's occupation of and genocide in East Timor. It wouldn't have sanctioned Israel's occupation of Lebanon, the West Bank and Gaza.

T. S. Eliot wrote, in "Murder in the Cathedral," that "The last temptation is the greatest treason: / To do the right deed for the wrong reason." It was right to organize a collective response under U.N. auspices against Saddam's takeover of Kuwait, but justice is compromised and degraded if it is not evenhanded, and perceived by everybody to be so.

The average "Arab in the street" is well aware of the lack of evenhandedness and principle. The U.S. wants oil on its terms, not Iraq's. As Robert Fisk of the *Independent*, in London, wrote recently, "Oil decides. If Saudi Arabia were just tens of thousands of miles of sandtrap, its people living in abject poverty, its demands a drain on the world's generosity, not a single American soldier would be deployed in the area, whatever Iraq's ambitions."

To the disgust of most Americans and the immense joy of Israel, many Palestinians openly support Saddam. There's tragedy here, because Palestinians know better than most the nature of Saddam, since their PLO leaders were long the targets of terror and assassinations instigated by him. They were comparing him to Hitler a decade ago, when the U.S. saw him as the bulwark against Iran.

But just as many Palestinians in the occupied territories see their future as a U.S.-sponsored catastrophe and probable eviction into Jordan, they and fellow Arabs see the actions today of the U.S. and its allies as the most coarsened realpolitik. So they turn in support of the opposing coarse real-politicker, Saddam, who had a point when he said that Iraq would withdraw from Kuwait if Israel withdrew from the territories and from Lebanon, and if Syria likewise withdrew from Lebanon.

The U.S. dismissed this negotiating posture as "irrelevant," but Saddam's points are not irrelevant at all, because for the United States to use the U.N. and the Security Council as a club only against Iraq and then revert to the contemptuous indifference of the past 20 years would be to deal the institution an irreparable blow in the eyes of the rest of the world.

August 18, 1990

In the weeks that follow the invasion, conservatives are split on going to war. Ted Galen Carpenter of the Libertarian Cato Institute remonstrates that "no one in the Bush administration even considered alternatives to our barging into the region," and that the U.S. has taken on the role of "planetary policeman" without even giving regional powers time to stop Iraq.

BUSH JUMPED THE GUN IN THE GULF
TED GALEN CARPENTER
The New York Times

Washington

The Bush Administration's decision to dispatch American troops to the Arabian peninsula was a knee-jerk, cold-war reaction that the President and the rest of us may soon regret. We now confront a crisis that may ultimately escalate into full-scale combat costing $1 billion a day and untold numbers of lives. In essence, the Bush Administration has made the U.S. the point man in the Middle East, a dangerous and thankless status that prudent statesmen would seek to avoid.

Throughout the cold war, our leaders insisted that the U.S. is the only power capable of preventing aggression. However, that belief was based on the assumption that the Soviet Union or a Soviet surrogate would be the source of aggression and that only a superpower could thwart the other superpower and its agents.

Unfortunately, that attitude has persisted into the post-cold-war era, in which global political and military conditions are vastly different. Moscow is no longer a likely source of expansionist threats. As the Persian Gulf episode demonstrates, smaller, regional powers with their own agendas are now the probable candidates.

But the more limited nature of such threats also means that other regional powers should be able to contain them. There is no longer even a plausible case for the U.S. being the planetary policeman, taking responsibility for all security burdens.

That point is especially relevant to the Persian Gulf. Washington responded reflexively to Iraq's invasion, adopting a high-profile leadership role with all the attendant costs and risks. No one in the Bush Administration even considered alternatives to our barging into the region.

There was, in fact, little need for the dangerous step of introducing U.S. combat forces. The Administration's equation of Saddam Hussein and Adolf Hitler—with the implication that Mr. Hussein had an ability to achieve virtually unlimited expansionist objectives—was fundamentally flawed. Much has been made of Baghdad's million-man army, but Iraq is still a small third world nation with a population of barely 17 million. While oil rich, it has an economy impoverished by the costly war with Iran. This is hardly the foundation for a sustained expansionist push.

Moreover, Iraq's neighbors were quite capable of limiting its expansionism (although probably not of compelling it to disgorge Kuwait). Iran, Syria, Jordan, Saudi Arabia and Turkey have more than 1.8 million troops, outnumbering Baghdad's forces by nearly two to one. Moreover, Iraq has 5,500 tanks to its neighbors' 9,900. Baghdad has only 513 combat aircraft, compared with the nearly 1,300 of its potential foes.

Those figures do not include the additional forces that other regional powers, such as Egypt, could bring to bear. Nor do they take into account the support—especially naval support—that could be provided by outside powers, most notably Japan and the members of the European Community, who rely far more heavily than the U.S. on Middle East oil.

We assume that President Hussein had designs on Saudi Arabia. But he could not have invaded Saudi Arabia without stretching his forces on the southern front dangerously thin. This would have left Iraq exceedingly vulnerable to Syrian, Iranian and even Turkish counter-attacks. This was a danger that Mr. Hussein could not afford to ignore.

The Bush Administration never allowed time for such interested parties to deal with Iraqi aggression on their own. Nor did it give the Arab League a chance to formulate a political solution. The fear was that either Iraq would take Saudi Arabia without effective resistance or that, in the event of determined opposition, the resulting regional conflagration would cut off oil supplies.

But the U.S. buildup—on a scale that portends offensive operations against Iraq—also puts oil supplies at grave risk. Even worse, the dominant American presence enables Saddam Hussein to portray himself as an Arab hero standing up to Western neocolonialist invaders.

The Administration also feared that, even without an invasion of Saudi Arabia, Iraq would dominate OPEC, threatening the West with high oil prices and disruptions in supply. But that would be strange behavior indeed for a country in economic ruin and $80 billion in debt. More likely, it would seek to maximize its oil revenues, which means providing a steady supply at prices low enough to discourage widespread conservation and alternate fuels.

As Washington rushed into the conflict it seemed almost grateful for the opportunity to demonstrate America's continuing global leadership in a post–cold-war setting. Asserting such "leadership" may gratify the egos of policy-makers obsessed with maintaining a hyperactive American military role despite the demise of the cold war. It may also serve the interests of the national security establishment, which desperately needs a justification for $300 billion military budgets. It may even be an occasion for gratitude on the part of nations that were spared the risks and costs of defending their own vital interests (although one should not count on such gratitude).

But a major military deployment that costs more than $15 million a day and risks a shooting war that would cost $1 billion a day—not to mention producing a steady stream of casualties—does not serve the interests of the American people.

August 19, 1990

In mid-August, former Secretary of State Henry Kissinger declares that "America has crossed its Rubicon" in the Persian Gulf, and must act quickly and decisively, even if that means war: "The United States cannot afford to be diddled, and it simply cannot afford to lose."

THE GAME HAS JUST BEGUN
HENRY KISSINGER
The Washington Post

The president's courageous decision to deploy a major military force in Saudi Arabia has raised not only the prospects of success but also the stakes of defeat. The United States has in fact passed the point of no return.

It therefore becomes crucial to assess how success and failure are to be defined. The U.N. Security Council has unanimously demanded the unconditional withdrawal of Iraqi forces and the restoration of the legitimate government. The United States has justified its interdiction of the sea lanes as a response to a request of the exiled Kuwaiti government.

In these circumstances, should Iraq manage to remain in Kuwait or exercise indirect control through some puppet, the American show of force will turn into a debacle. If in the end Iraq controls Kuwait and U.S. forces stay in Saudi Arabia, the crisis will have ended in a demonstration of the irrelevance of America and of world opinion. In any event, neither Arab nor American politics would long sustain significant troop deployments in Saudi Arabia. The argument that we have saved Saudi Arabia will be overwhelmed by the perception of an American failure that would shake political, economic and financial stability everywhere. Indeed, even attainment of the U.N. objectives might provide only a breathing space if Saddam Hussein remains in office and Iraq continues to build up its nuclear and chemical weapons potential.

Time is not on our side. American staying power in the face of public, regional and allied pressures is usually inversely proportional to the scale of our deployment. Thus, if after a certain interval the conflict appears to settle down to a siege, the United States will be obliged to consider new measures to bring it to a conclusion.

Success for Iraq in Kuwait would usher in a series of upheavals certain to culminate in a general Middle East war. A government as cautious and as dedicated to anonymity as Saudi Arabia's would never have asked for the assistance of foreign troops had it not considered the very survival of the state at stake. Nor would the Arab summit have condemned a brother country. Nor would Egypt, Syria and Morocco have sent troops to assist Saudi Arabia. Likewise, in the developing world, where so many countries have more precarious and even more recent frontiers as well as covetous neighbors, a victory by Iraq could inaugurate a time of troubles.

The vital interests of the industrial states are affected most directly. If Iraq succeeds in making the annexation of Kuwait stick, it could determine the price of oil by blackmailing the states of the Arabian peninsula—which together with Kuwait and Iraq control some 40 percent of the world's oil reserves—into reducing their oil production.

The United States had three choices in dealing with the crisis: it could passively endorse whatever consensus emerged in the United Nations; it could support whatever the industrial democracies—all of which are more dependent on Mideast oil than the United States is—were prepared to do in concert; or it could take the lead in opposing Saddam Hussein and try to organize international support for an effort in which the United States would bear the principal burden.

There were ample excuses for avoiding a decision. The most fashionable is the argument that the defense of the area should be an Arab matter. But in the end, alibis cannot change the consequences of failure to resist. None of the Arab states is strong enough even in combination to defeat the Iraqi army, toughened in a 10-year war, supplied with advanced military technology during that time by the Soviet Union and France and buttressed by economic assistance from the other industrial democracies, including the United States. Such an argument marks the reemergence of American isolationism, especially among the conservatives. Allowed to prevail, it would conclude with America's abdication at the very moment when the old East-West conflict has been won.

Another argument to avoid a U.S. role is that even if Iraq controlled all the oil in the Gulf, it would still have to sell it in a world market governed by the laws of supply and demand. But were Iraq to achieve its strategic design, it would be able to determine the level of supply by taking production away from sparsely populated principalities in the Arabian peninsula without hurting its own population. The ability to cause a worldwide economic crisis is not the sort of power to be left in the hands of a ruler who has attacked two of his six neighbors, is engaged in mortal conflict with two others and has used poison gas against his own dissident population.

The administration must have concluded that anything other than a leadership role for the United States would have ended with making Iraqi domination of Kuwait permanent and led to the collapse of the moderate governments in the region including Egypt. Having committed the United States to a leadership role, President Bush made another crucial decision. The American military role could have been confined to interdiction at sea and a token force on the ground to make clear that an attack on Saudi oil fields would lead to war with the United States. President Bush and his advisers opted for a massive deployment. They seem to have reasoned that the U.N.'s unexpected sanction might change Saddam Hussein's calculation. He may well not have originally intended to seize the Saudi oil fields. Had there been no meaningful resistance, he would not have needed to do so. The rulers of the Arabian peninsula—in Saudi Arabia as well as in the Emirates—would have yielded to Iraqi pressures or been overthrown, more likely both.

But once the sanctions were voted, Saddam Hussein's calculus was bound to change. So long as oil prices remain steady, the sanctions are likely to be sustained for many months. And prices will remain at more or less present levels if Saudi Arabia increases its production by 2.5 million barrels. The remaining 1.6 million barrels of the 4.1 million barrel present shortfall caused by the loss of oil from Iraq and Kuwait, can be pieced together (at least until the winter) from Venezuela, the Emirates, Nigeria and other small producers. But if Saudi production can be destroyed or even severely reduced, the absence of Iraqi and Kuwaiti oil will lead to an explosive rise in oil prices. With Saudi production crippled and a

worldwide depression looming, it would become increasingly
difficult to maintain sanctions; Saddam Hussein would win
the endurance contest.

President Bush and his advisers must have concluded that
once they committed military forces, the best hope of ending
the crisis quickly was to assemble an overwhelming force to
over-awe such a threat and to be able to go further if necessary,
but the administration needs to calculate very carefully the
window of opportunity it has available to achieve its objectives.

The administration must take care not to wallow in the
wide domestic and international support it now enjoys. For
the perfectly legitimate concern about the probability of
success expressed by talk show hosts and newspaper colum-
nists coupled with insistent reassurances by administration
spokesmen will over time weaken the credibility of the American enterprise. The longer it lasts, the more American governmental procedures and Congressional inquiries will take
their toll. At some point the familiar question of the light at
the end of the tunnel is bound to surface.

The situation within the Middle East is also likely to grow
more precarious the longer the crisis festers. The impact on
the Arab world of anti-Western propaganda from Baghdad
and the skillful linking of the issues of Kuwait and of Palestine
must not be underestimated. A coup in one of the emirates or
sabotage in the oil fields would send another shock through
the region and the world economy.

The time required for the sanctions to work must be
balanced against the factors undermining international
cohesion. Such an analysis must keep in mind that the acid
test of the sanctions will be not how much oil is prevented
from leaving the region but how few supplies are allowed to
enter Iraq. Iraqi oil exports are relatively easily blocked. But
Iraq's frontiers are long, and less bulky goods such as food can
seep in. And the likelihood of this happening will grow the
longer the crisis lasts and the more Iraq's neighbors conclude
that they may have to live with the Iraqi dictator, however
dangerous he may be.

A sharp and short crisis is far more in the interest of all
concerned with moderation than a long siege. I am not in a
position to know whether sanctions can work within the time
constraints outlined here. I also realize that the United States
must consider the risk that a more aggressive course might

take away some of the current international support. At the same time, that support would not survive the appearance of an American defeat. The United States stands to lose the most from a long siege—whatever the relative immediate economic impact on Europe and Japan. An ignominious withdrawal following the debacle in Lebanon—and any withdrawal however dressed up without achieving our objectives would be ignominious—would end America's stabilizing role in the Middle East. And no other country could take its place. It would gravely weaken the Bush administration's capacity to overcome the economic crisis that would inevitably follow.

It would be a mistake to focus only on America's difficulties. In the end, Iraq is a heavily indebted developing country with a population of only 16 million that has just ended a debilitating 10-year war with Iran, and which has hostile relations with four of its six neighbors. It is in no position to enter into a protracted conflict with the United States. Saddam Hussein proved during the Iran war that he is prepared to negotiate when necessary. His most recent offer agreed to the principle of withdrawal from Kuwait, albeit under outrageous conditions. It may be the beginning of an attempt at negotiation obscured by bluster once the reality of the stark choices before Iraq sinks in. Then the offer to withdraw may reemerge stripped of its absurd baggage.

But the United States cannot afford to be diddled, and it simply cannot afford to lose. If it should be concluded that sanctions are too uncertain and diplomacy unavailing, the United States will need to consider a surgical and progressive destruction of Iraq's military assets—especially since an outcome that leaves Saddam Hussein in place and his military machine unimpaired might turn out to be only an interlude between aggressions.

It would be irresponsible for an outsider to press for a course of action in a situation so dependent on information not available to the kibitzer. But it is important to understand that America has crossed its Rubicon. All those concerned with global peace and world economic well being should subordinate whatever tactical misgivings they may have to standing behind the only policy that can now succeed.

August 23, 1990

One of the most personal—and most powerful—early statements against the war comes from Alex Molnar, a University of Wisconsin professor and the father of a twenty-one-year-old Marine just dispatched to the Gulf.

"IF MY MARINE SON IS KILLED..."
ALEX MOLNAR
The New York Times

Milwaukee

Dear President Bush:

I kissed my son goodbye today. He is a 21-year-old marine. You have ordered him to Saudi Arabia.

The letter telling us he was going arrived at our vacation cottage in northern Wisconsin by Express Mail on Aug. 13. We left immediately for North Carolina to be with him. Our vacation was over.

Some commentators say you are continuing your own vacation to avoid appearing trapped in the White House, as President Carter was during the Iran hostage crisis. Perhaps that is your reason. However, as I sat in my motel room watching you on television, looking through my son's hastily written last will and testament and listening to military equipment rumble past, you seemed to me to be both callous and ridiculous chasing golf balls and zipping around in your boat in Kennebunkport.

While visiting my son I had a chance to see him pack his chemical weapons suit and try on his body armor. I don't know if you've ever had this experience, Mr. President. I hope you never will.

I also met many of my son's fellow soldiers. They are fine young men. A number told me that they were from poor families. They joined the Marines as a way of earning enough money to go to college.

None of the young men I met are likely to be invited to serve on the board of directors of a savings and loan association, as your son Neil was. And none of them have parents

well enough connected to call or write a general to insure that
their child stays out of harm's way, as Vice President Quayle's
parents did for him during the Vietnam War.

I read in today's Raleigh News and Observer that, like you,
Vice President Quayle and Secretary of State Baker are on
vacation. Meanwhile, Defense Secretary Cheney is in the
Persian Gulf. I think this symbolizes a Government that no
longer has a non-military foreign policy vision, one that uses
the military to conceal the fraud that American diplomacy has
become.

Yes, you have proved a relatively adept tactician in the last
three weeks. But if American diplomacy hadn't been on
vacation for the better part of a decade, we wouldn't be in the
spot we are today.

Where were you, Mr. President, when Iraq was killing its
own people with poison gas? Why, until the recent crisis, was
it business as usual with Saddam Hussein, the man you now
call a Hitler?

You were elected Vice President in 1980 on the strength of
the promise of a better life for Americans, in a world where
the U.S. would once again "stand tall." The Reagan-Bush
Administration rolled into Washington talking about the
magic of a "free market" in oil. You diluted gas mileage
requirements for cars and dismantled Federal energy policy.
And now you have ordered my son to the Middle East. For
what? Cheap gas?

Is the American "way of life" that you say my son is risking
his life for the continued "right" of Americans to consume 25
to 30 percent of the world's oil? The "free market" to which
you are so fervently devoted has a very high price tag, at least
for parents like me and young men and women like my son.

Now that we face the prospect of war I intend to support
my son and his fellow soldiers by doing everything I can to
oppose any offensive American military action in the Persian
Gulf. The troops I met deserve far better than the politicians
and policies that hold them hostage.

As my wife and I sat in a little cafe outside our son's base last
week, trying to eat, fighting back tears, a young marine struck
up a conversation with us. As we parted he wished us well and
said, "May God forgive us for what we are about to do."

President Bush, the policies you have advocated for the last
decade have set the stage for military conflict in the Middle

East. Your response to the Iraqi conquest of Kuwait has set in motion events that increasingly will pressure you to use our troops not to defend Saudi Arabia but to attack Iraq. And I'm afraid that, as that pressure mounts, you will wager my son's life in a gamble to save your political future.

In the past you have demonstrated no enduring commitment to any principle other than the advancement of your political career. This makes me doubt that you have either the courage or the character to meet the challenge of finding a diplomatic solution to this crisis. If, as I expect, you eventually order American soldiers to attack Iraq, then it is God who will have to forgive you. I will not.

Chapter 3

SEPTEMBER 1990

ENERGY WARS

Chronology

In the first week of September, Iraq begins to release Western hostages, mostly women and children. Special flights begin to take foreign citizens out of Kuwait and Iraq. These flights will continue on and off into November. Refugee guest workers from Sri Lanka, India, Vietnam, and the Philippines are stranded in Kuwait; more than a million trek across the desert from Kuwait and Iraq into Jordan.

On September 4 Defense Secretary Cheney announces that American troop strength in the Gulf has reached 100,000. The U.S. expects the Saudis to committ $500 million per month to the U.S. military effort, and an exiled Kuwaiti sheikh pledges $5 billion.

Bush and Gorbachev meet in Helsinki on September 9 and issue a joint statement calling for an Iraqi withdrawal. Though they fail to reach accord on other measures, Secretary of State James Baker calls the Russians "very reliable partners" in the Gulf. The next day, Iraq and Iran restore diplomatic relations, but Iran promises not to violate the trade embargo against Iraq.

In his September 11 address to a joint session of Congress, Bush says that "Saddam Hussein is literally trying to wipe a country off the face of the Earth. We do not exaggerate. Nor do we exaggerate when we say: Saddam Hussein will fail." The president adds that "the lion's share" of the world's oil is in the Gulf, and "we cannot permit a resource so vital to be dominated by one so ruthless. And we won't." Bush states that Iraq will not be permitted to permanently annex Kuwait. "That's not a threat or a boast. That's just the way it's going to be."

By mid-September, U.S. Naval forces are regularly boarding ships to check cargos, mostly in the Red Sea. On September 16 Iraqi television airs an unedited taped speech by President Bush in which he warns the Iraqi people of the dangers of war.

Angered by King Hussein's support for Iraq, Saudi Arabia cuts off oil shipments to Jordan. Soviet Foreign Minister Edward Shevardnadze, in a speech before the U.N. General Assembly on September 25, warns Iraq that the Soviet Union will support a U.N. military operation to free Kuwait. "An act of terrorism," he declares, "has been perpetuated against the emerging new world order." The same day, the U.N. Security Council passes a resolution calling for an air embargo on Iraq.

By the end of September, U.S. troop strength in the Gulf has reached 150,000, and the price of oil has reached $39.54 a barrel (up from $20 before the invasion).

Energy Wars
By the second week of September, the United States' energy policy is reflected not only in the crisis raging in the Gulf, but also in the debate raging on Capitol Hill.

America's addiction to foreign oil increased steadily after the election of Ronald Reagan in 1980. When Jimmy Carter left the White House, the country's oil imports were about 30 percent of total consumption. Today they are 50 percent. This growing dependence on oil from the volatile

Persian Gulf is a direct result of the Reagan-Bush energy policy, which was largely dictated by the energy industry itself.

The idea behind this policy was to overturn a half-century's worth of government regulations aimed at controlling energy use and to subject the energy business to the bracing winds of free market economics. It didn't work. We are now involved in what could easily be the first of many resource wars in the Middle East. And in the meantime, we have lost the opportunity to plan for an energy system that could get us through the next century.

The Reagan administration was not the first to appease the oil giants. It was Carter who, under industry pressure, signed a new law that began the process of gas—and, hence, overall energy—deregulation. But while Carter gave in to the energy industry on gas pricing, he also encouraged the country's first steps down the alternative energy path, away from its massive reliance on fossil fuels. Carter set up the Solar Energy Research Agency, a branch of the Department of Energy, to conduct long-term research on renewable energy technologies, such as photovoltaic cells, wind, hydropower, conservation, and cogeneration. By the last year of the Carter administration, the federal budget for renewables was close to $1 billion a year. The program included loan programs, grants to innovative entrepreneurs, and legislation to establish a solar bank to help fund emerging solar technologies. As a symbol of the change, the White House was equipped with solar panels. The hope was that by the year 2000 renewable energy could provide as much as 20 percent of the nation's energy supply.

There was a growing awareness in the 1970s that shifting away from fossil fuels also made compelling environmental sense. If Carter's energy strategy had been pursued, carbon dioxide emissions would have dropped substantially and global warming would have at least slowed. The amount of lead in our air would have been reduced. The hidden social costs of a petroleum-based economy—measured in pollution control, environmental clean-up, and medical expenditures—would have been slashed.

But with the election of Ronald Reagan, all this went out the window. Nowhere was the New Right's assault on government more savage than in the area of energy regulation. At the Department of the Interior, which oversees the vast public domain that encompasses one-third of the nation and holds most of our future energy resources, Secretary James Watt promised to sell or lease as much of that public territory as he could. In terms of energy, this meant leasing valuable tracts of underwater oil and gas along both coasts to oil companies at bargain basement prices, giving them control of how these resources were to be developed, or not developed, for years to come. Watt even moved to disband the big public power systems. All of this, it was argued then and now, made sense because private business was more efficient and more attuned to the times than big, clumsy government bureaucracies staffed with misguided do-gooders.

At the Department of Energy, Reagan's revolutionaries slashed the solar budget by 90 percent. They eliminated most of the tax credits for renewables, and defunded the solar bank bill.

Vice President Bush also got into the act: As head of a task force on regulatory relief, Bush got the administration to repeal federal requirements for energy efficiency in new buildings, and sought to repeal fuel economy standards in automobiles. When Congress refused to agree, the administration on its own rolled back the standards. At the prodding of the Bush committee, the Reagan adminstration also fought renewal of the Clean Air Act, which would have pushed the auto industry towards greater energy efficiency, while at the same time making at least some progress toward improving the atmosphere in urban centers. Instead, the Bush team proposed easing or eliminating thirty-five regulations on auto emissions and auto safety. These proposals were largely based on a hit list circulated in 1980 by General Motors. In a letter leaked to *Environmental Action* magazine, GM chairman Roger Smith thanked Bush: "The administration is to be congratulated on your plans to help American industry improve its international competitiveness. Unquestionably, the regulatory reform measure you have announced in April 1981 constituted an important step in that direction."

Big Oil continued its reign when George Bush moved into the White House. Bush, of course, got his start in the Texas oil industry, operating a company that was a pioneer in offshore oil drilling. In public life, he has consistently viewed energy matters from an oilman's perspective. In April 1986, Vice President Bush became so concerned that low prices in the Persian Gulf were hurting Texas oil producers that he flew to Saudi Arabia to confer with the petro-sheikhs. Bush threatened the Saudis with oil import duties if they failed to raise their price. The Saudis complied.

As president, Bush would deliver a more ominous threat in the Persian Gulf: that he would go to war with Iraq if it failed to relinquish its hold on the sovereign —and oil-rich—nation of Kuwait. And his point man, whom he would entrust to line up international support to carry out this threat, is Secretary of State James Baker, Bush's chief political advisor and best friend, whose family law firm—Baker, Botts—has long been at the hub of Texas's oil business.

Bush also has strong backing for his energy policy in Congress, where leading Democrats support his goals. By far the most important fossil fuel advocate is the congressman from Dearborn, Michigan, John Dingell, who has faithfully represented the interests of the auto industry. Dingell is joined by Senator Bennett Johnston of Louisiana; Johnston represents both the oil and nuclear industries. Other steadfast supporters hail from Alaska, including both Senators Ted Stevens and Frank Murkowski and the state's only congressman, Don Young.

Dingell was too young to do much about the first clean air bill in 1970, but when it came up for reauthorization in 1976 he introduced amendments to gut auto emission standards. They failed, but he was back the next year with more amendments, this time getting them past the House—only to see them killed by the Senate. Year after year it was the same story, with Dingell, backed by a high-powered industry lobby, working to hold the line against the environmentalists. Under his leadership, the Congress was unable to move forward with clean air legislation for thirteen years, until the spring of 1990.

After Bush himself finally gave a push to the clean air legislation, Dingell relented, cosponsoring Bush's bill on tail-pipe emissions; but then, according to environmental lobbyists, he undercut it behind closed doors in Congress. Dingell insists he has done more for the environment than all "the do-gooders at the Sierra Club." "What I am telling you is that this country has to have a balanced policy," he says, meaning a policy that balances environmental goals with economic costs.

Dingell and his allies in the Louisiana and Alaskan delegations are the brokers of an order that in the very best of circumstances will be hard to change. While Carter persuaded Congress to experiment with renewable energy systems, these modest efforts were overshadowed by the existing energy industry's desire to win federal financing for such harebrained schemes as oil shale, coal-based gas, and petroleum synthetics, and, of course, to keep upping the ante on the worst economic gamble in energy history —the pursuit of nuclear power. Essentially, the Carter experiments channeled federal funds into one or another pocket of the international oil companies, since they owned and controlled oil shale and synthetics technology as well as the leading coal and nuclear firms. Since its beginning, the government has shepherded nuclear development, at first as a publicity gimmick to demonstrate the multitudinous peaceful uses of the atom, and to help spread the rationale for building more bombs. It picked up research and development costs, built and ran a uranium enrichment industry, and provided insurance liability through the Price-Anderson Act that no private company in its right mind would have offered. According to one estimate in a study—suppressed, naturally, by the Department of Energy—the subsidies to nuclear power between 1950 and 1979 amounted to more than $37 billion. (In fiscal 1990 the government spent $455.1 million on nuclear research compared to $86.4 million on solar and other renewable energy forms.)

But, despite all these subsidies, nuclear power by the late 1970s just had not panned out. It was more expensive than coal, and in the wake of the Three Mile Island mishap, there were alarming questions about both safety and waste disposal—questions that remain today.

Still, we hang on to nuclear power, and under the leadership of Louisiana's Bennett Johnston in the Senate, the Congress wants to forge ahead with a new generation of plants. Why? Political contributions. Over the last eight years the industry has pumped more than $25 million into the campaigns of senators and representatives, according to a study by the U.S. Public Interest Research Group.

While the government continues to support nuclear power, renewable sources now supply just as much as nukes—about 10 percent. And subsidies to support wind and solar alternatives and energy conservation have all declined over the last ten years. Not only did renewable sources of energy grow—in the face of great efforts to emasculate them—but under the specious "market driven" rhetoric of the Reagan era, the most important legislative initiative of the Carter years was hacked nearly to death. The Public Utility Regulatory Policies Act, aimed at the electric utility industry's stranglehold on the development of energy resources, required power companies to purchase electricity created from renewable sources by private firms—risky ventures in small hydropower production, biomass, windmills, solar energy, cogeneration, etc.—at premium rates. In a very real way, this program was harnessing the private marketplace to meet the energy needs. But the Reagan-Bush administration moved to eliminate the preference for renewable energy sources. So the utilities could buy any type of energy from independent companies—allowing them to favor technologies that in no way threatened their dinosaur-based systems. The existing energy system is an undeniable drag on the economy—and, in the long run, would seem to require that we control the oil output of the Middle East.

We have never dared to inquire into the exact costs of keeping our energy system going—but the Germans studied theirs, and that study can apply to any market economy. Known as the Hohmeyer study, this inquiry sought to quantify the social and environmental costs of a unit of energy produced from fossil fuels, wind, solar, and nuclear power. It found the social costs were roughly equal to the market costs, suggesting the real total costs of conventional fuels are roughly double their market prices.

For example, the social costs for fossil fuels were figured to be as much as 5.5 cents per kilowatt hour, and for nuclear power as much as 13.1 cents per KWH. Photovoltaics and wind power actually registered a net social benefit, in terms of employment, wages, and tax benefits, costing nine cents less for a KWH of electricity made from fossil fuels and sixteen cents less than one made from nuclear power.

Transportation accounts for 60 percent of all American oil consumption, most of it by cars and light trucks. Last year these cars and trucks gobbled up 3.6 billion barrels of crude oil, somewhat more than one third of the oil we produced. All told, renewable energy sources provide the equivalent of one billion barrels of oil per year, or about 40 percent of the oil the U.S. presently imports. The best known way to cut back on these imports would be to make motor vehicles more efficient, so that instead of an average of 27.5 miles to the gallon, cars and trucks could get 45 or even 50 miles per gallon over the next ten years. There's nothing weird or unrealistic about this goal. We've been steadily making cars more efficient: In 1975, the average fuel efficiency of all passenger cars on the road was 13.5 miles to the gallon. By 1988, the efficiency level had jumped to 19.95 mpg. Those improvements achieved a savings of about 36 billion gallons of gasoline in 1989 over what would have been consumed if the fleet average had remained at 1975 levels. But those savings could have been much greater had not the auto industry gone in for promoting more powerful and less efficient cars. They were encouraged by the Reagan-Bush administration, which put the brakes on fuel efficiency by rolling back the standards. Between 1975 and 1985, the average annual increase in new-car fuel efficiency was 5.88 percent. Then between 1985 and 1988, the average annual increase dropped to 1.31 percent. In 1988 the average new car's fuel efficiency actually slipped from the 1988 high of 28.7 mpg to 28.3 mpg, and dipped again this year to 28.2 mpg.

The Congressional Office of Technology Assessment estimates potential average fuel efficiency for new cars can range from a low of 34 mpg to a high of 65 mpg, with a median of around 40. Some commercially available autos already achieve fuel efficiency in excess of 45 mpg in city driving. Several completed prototypes hit 70.

So why not save this energy, make the economy more efficient, and bring the boys back from the Middle East? Ask John Dingell. In the second week of September 1990, at the same time that Dingell was attempting to gut the fuel economy bill, sponsored by Nevada Senator Richard Bryan, Michigan Senator Don Riegle was working with

Oklahoma's Don Nichols to prevent the Senate from even voting on the legislation by means of a filibuster—and Samuel K. Skinner, Secretary of Transportation, threatened that if the measure passed Congress, President Bush would veto it. "The goal set by the Bryan legislation is completely unrealistic, irresponsible, and more importantly, unattainable from a technology viewpoint," Skinner said by way of explanation. He went on to cite a study that purported to demonstrate that reductions in car size made to accommodate current regulations had cost thousands of lives, because the small cars produced to meet the standards tended to result in more accident fatalities.

But an official of the Department's National Highway Traffic Safety Administration told reporters the department could not support these statements. In fact, greater energy efficiency need not involve smaller, lighter cars, but the introduction of new technologies in engine design.

In the end, the filibuster killed the legislation. And perhaps it is not to much to suggest that it was this kind of governmental refusal to develop viable alternatives to fossil fuel dependency, combined with American overconsumption, that made war with Iraq a part of our national energy policy.

September 1, 1990

By September, many Arab nations have joined the coalition opposing Saddam Hussein's annexation of Kuwait—a move that is at once seized upon by some Western commentators as an opportunity to open a new era for the Arabs, bringing them to a kinder, gentler position within the Western camp.

THE OLD ARAB ORDER PASSES
The Economist (London)

It has not yet been said clearly enough that, of all those who have been put to the test by Mr. Saddam Hussein's theft of Kuwait, the test comes sharpest for his fellow-Arabs. Yes, the Saddam challenge could be the making or breaking of Mr. George Bush's presidency. Yes, it will show whether the United Nations can at last speak out clearly, or will produce just another incoherent mutter. It will also reveal how much reality there is in the European Community's hope of standing as one when the world gets rough.

Yet the Arabs have a fair complaint. All this ignores the people most affected: them. How the Arabs themselves respond to the latest act of Saddamery will chiefly decide whether the anti-Saddam coalition in the U.N. holds together. It may also decide whether the Arabs can escape from the corner into which life seems to have painted them.

Intelligent and self-critical Arabs—there are more of them than Western cynics like to admit—lament that history has passed them by. That is a conveniently evasive way of putting it. It is not the fault of "history" that the marvellous half-dozen centuries of Arab culture and science that followed the death of Muhammad have faded into today's sad mixture: on the one hand, a feeble imitation of the Euro-American style of life; on the other, a scowling attempt to revive a long-ago Muslim past. Nothing inexorably ordained that the Arabs should have had to live so long under Ottoman rule, then be carved up into British, French and Italian empires, then be almost powerless in their nominal independence. No law of politics says that, alone of all the world's great peoples, the Arabs should in 1990 be unable to boast a single specimen of working democracy.

But neither does the explanation lie in some taint of racial inadequacy., The Arabs have the backwardness of a people still largely rural, badly educated, horribly poor (aside from the few Gulf petrostates, that is) and without any responsibility for running their own lives. Yet the performance of Arabs in medicine (Magdi Yacoub is one fine example), the arts (Naguib Mahfouz), popular culture (the new vogue for the Maghreb's *rai* music)—in fact, in almost everything except free politics—shows that the fire still flickers. What the Arabs have failed to do in the twentieth century is to give themselves a system of political organisation that could support a new Arab civilisation. It is here that Mr. Saddam Hussein is putting them to the test.

To many Arabs, Mr. Hussein seems to offer the prospect of two things they have long wanted. One is a rediscovery of Arab unity, free of the "artificial" frontiers drawn by the European conquerors after the break-up of the Ottoman empire in 1918. The other is the power to defy the West, that infuriatingly successful new civilisation in whose shadow the Arabs have spent the past 70 years. Both are false goals, for reasons those shrewder Arabs are starting to understand.

As one disastrous experiment after another has shown, the unity so many Arabs yearn for is not the sort that can be drawn on a map. The Arabs share (more or less) the same religion and the same language. That is no better basis for being organised into a single state than it would be for the Germans, the Austrians and the Swiss. One or two of the statelets created since 1918 may not last much longer. The other Arab countries have roots. Their separate existences are not just a matter of the local rulers' self-interest. They rest, behind the misty talk of "unity," on the real differences between these countries. That is why Egypt never blended with Syria, Jordan with Iraq, Libya with any of its invitees. No United States of Araby is in the offing.

Least of all should unity be sought in rejection of the West. The chief danger that most Arab countries now face—a population growing much faster than the means to feed and house it—cannot be beaten by the economics of autarky. Survival requires these countries to be as open as possible to the means of rescue available from outside: new technologies, more investment, better ways of persuading people to have fewer babies. Over the past hundred years one outbreak of

Muslim populism after another has offered salvation through isolation, only to discover that it doesn't work. President Rafsanjani of Iran, nervously trying to pull his country back into the modern world, is the latest example of the recognition that turning the clock back is always a mistake.

Mr. Saddam Hussein holds out false gods: Arab cohesion enforced by dictatorship, Arab hostility to America and its European allies. The Arabs need the opposite. They need reconciliation with the West, so that the means of revival can flow into their economies. At home, they need a change that will release the energising powers of pluralism.

They could do with more pluralism in their economies; too many Arab governments still distortingly try to shape them too much from the center. And pluralism is essential for their politics. Almost all of these countries are getting poorer by the year, as population growth exceeds economic growth. To try to keep the lid of authoritarian, often semi-feudal, government on this turmoil is to guarantee an expansion. A move towards democracy will be dangerous in the short run; but in the longer run it is the only thing that is likely to keep the Arabs at peace with themselves.

If Mr. Saddam Hussein is beaten, the move towards pluralism will pick up speed. Americans will find it hard to accept that they took so great a risk merely to give the antique politics of the Arabian peninsula another generation or two of existence. The handful of families that now run the peninsula, freed from the ruder threat of Saddamisation, may be readier to experiment with democracy. The first seeds of a freer sort of politics have already been planted in Jordan, Algeria, even Egypt. And a slowly democratising Arab world would find reconciliation with the West much easier—not least because a more democratic Palestinian movement might offer the prospect of a peace with Israel that most Israelis could at last trust themselves to accept.

None of this is going to happen painlessly. The period of nascent Arab democracy will be turbulent: its early form could well be a heightened passion for Islam and Arab nationalism. This period will require vigilance from the West: But for it to happen at all requires that the international move against Saddam Hussein and what he stands for should now succeed. In a week of United Nations approval of a naval blockade, and of diplomatic manoeuvering aimed at loosening

Mr. Hussein's grip on Kuwait, it remains just possible that this can be done short of war. It will not be done at all unless other Arabs see that this is a fight for their future as much as anyone's.

September 5, 1990

As debate over the invasion of one Arab country by
another Arab country grows heated, the Arab perspective often seems subsumed by arguments about American interests in the region. But as the Iraqi occupation
enters its second month, Palestinian writer and scholar
Edward Said assesses the "shattering effect" of the crisis
on the Arab countries and the Arab people.

SHATTERING EFFECTS OF
SADDAM'S INVASION
EDWARD SAID
Arab News

It is still far too early to say what the results are of the
immense disruption in Middle Eastern life and politics begun
by Iraq's reckless invasion of Kuwait in early August. We
know only that things will not be as they were and, more
important, a tremendous amount of human misery and waste
will have been caused. Beyond that, the shattering effect of
one Arab state invading and in effect attempting to obliterate
another produces in those of us who are Arab expatriates (in
the United States) a sadness and anger that is equal to and in
some aspects worse than what we felt in 1967 and 1982.

Kuwait was a small and relatively democratic state: its
society was complex and like every other Arab country had
its own problems, but its economy and institutions were
beneficial to the Arab world generally, and to its citizens in
particular; a large number of non-Kuwaitis—Palestinians,
Lebanese, Iranians, Egyptians, Indians, etc.—lived and for the
most part prospered there, and thanks to hard work their
remittances helped their own societies. We must not forget
that the substantial Palestinian community in Kuwait was of
great significance to Palestinians in the Occupied Territories;
and now their work and prosperity is at an end. As for the
many native Kuwaitis who are now either imprisoned in their
own country or in exile, they join the long column of refugees that our region has been producing since World War II,

many but not all of them an ironic consequence of the refugees who came from Europe to Palestine and displaced so many Arabs in the process.

To the greatly shocked and outraged Kuwaitis who look at what has happened to their country every rational Arab extends a hand of deep sympathy and friendship. Whatever the ideals of Arab unity they cannot be implemented by violence or brute force, and whatever the disputes between Arab states they must be settled by discussion, negotiation and adjudication, and never by unilateral force of arms.

We are all now paying the price of forgetting these principles. To non-Arabs the crisis in the Gulf is principally a matter of oil, whereas for those of us who foresee the dire consequences of what is likely now to ensure—I write these lines on August 27, 1990—it is a matter of the Arab future, a matter of societies, of culture, even a civilization now unsettled as never before, precisely at the same moment when the rest of the world seemed poised at the threshold of a new age of peaceful development and international cooperation.

When the present crisis is somehow resolved the deeper issues remain, and it is to only two of these that I would like to address myself here.

Because I am neither a politician nor a military expert I cannot properly assess the realignments that the present crisis has brought on, although it is clear that in all sorts of ways Arabs will be living in a new and perhaps less pleasant world. The divisions in the Arab world are very deep indeed. But neither am I an economist, although here too the massive changes that will occur in the economic order of the Arab world seem perceptible enough. But as someone who has spent a great deal of time examining the interrelationships between the Arabs and Islam on the one hand, and the West on the other, there are a number of things that I can say with some assurance.

In the first place, whereas it is true that there are common economic and strategic interests between the West and the Arab-Islamic world as a whole, there are also some important differences between them. These, I think, remain in evidence during the crisis and will not be resolved by it. One of the major ones (which I discussed in my book on Orientalism) has to do with the misperception and misrepresentation of the Arab-Islamic world by the West. The overall ignorance and fear that the average Westerner (and especially the American) feels about the Arabs and Islam are very much in evidence today. Western interests in opposing Iraq for its illegal annexation of Kuwait are mainly based on the need for Arab oil, which is of course a real interest. But as one watches television and reads the newspapers and journals, one is struck by how little awareness there is that the Arab world is more than a large and empty desert sitting on top of a wide pool of oil. Israel's view of the Arabs is the dominant one. Arabs are not perceived as having hopes, fears and aspirations.

Here are some examples. For the past several years a series of Arabic novels, poems and essays have been translated and published in England and America. During that time of course Naguib Mahfouz won the Nobel Prize for Literature. Yet except for a few articles about Mahfouz the man, literally nothing of this quite impressive output of Arabic literature has been reviewed or even noted in the major British or American press. It is as if an iron curtain exists between Arab culture and that of the West, a barrier unlike that in any other relationship between the West and the rest of the Third World. A great deal is written in the West about African, Indian, Japanese, Chinese, and Latin American literature. Yet Arabic literature is simply ignored. It is as if there is a general preference here for conceiving the Arab and Islamic world as basically empty, or filled with terrorists and oil-suppliers.

Another example is that the attacks on the Arab and Islamic world by experts such as Bernard Lewis, Fouad Ajami, and others like them have increased. Most of them stress the way in which Arabs and Muslims are basically sick and that their problems have nothing to do with the policies either of the West as a whole or of Israel in particular. People like Lewis and Ajami seem to be sought after for their views not because they say anything new or revelatory (they do not) but exactly because as experts—one a British, the other an Arab Orientalist—they confirm what has long been suspected and what is now getting new respectability and authority. I hasten to add that Ajami and Lewis, Daniel Pipes, David Pryce-Jones, Barry Rubin, and others like them are not delivering only the standard anti-Palestinian attacks that are to be expected of pro-Israeli propagandists. Their current work often focuses on the whole, its culture, civilization and soul. Moreover, if as critics they wrote of the Arabs with the concern and

intellectual rigor than many Arabs have themselves exhibited
in critiques of their own society, these people would be doing
something useful. But in fact they do not write that way.
When Lewis writes about the "rage" of Islam or Ajami on television mocks and derides his own people, their attitude is full
of hostility and a deep hatred, mobilized against a civilization
they feel must be despised and above all defeated. There is no
concern or compassion, or commitment in such expressions
of criticism; there is only antagonism and scorn. There is no
sorrow for the present, only delight.

So no matter what happens, the basic cultural maladjust-
ment between us and the West will remain, and will continue
to require our attention and effort to improve. This is not a
matter of cliches like "mutual respect" or "common interests."
It is, however, a matter of the Arab presence in the world
acquiring a human and cultural reality that it now lacks.

To a great extent, this problem is related to the second
issue, the question of Palestine, which has historically been
the cause of a basic contention between the Arabs and the
West, a symbol of incompletely realized Arab sovereignty and
independence. Palestine is a people and a cause. One of my
many fundamental objections to what Saddam Hussein has
done is that single-handedly he has inflicted a tremendous
blow on the intifada. By invading Kuwait he has diverted the
world's attention from Palestine: he has justified the Israeli
right-wing; he has hurt the entire Arab world by dividing it
and above all by fostering illusions and false hopes. The
enormous amount of money now being spent on armies and
airforces could have been spent alleviating poverty, building
Palestinian hospitals and schools, improving the miserable
conditions of refugees in Lebanon, the occupied territories
and elsewhere. Palestinians have paid an unacceptably high
price for his folly, as too have many other Arabs.

Yet whatever the immediate danger, it is important to
remember that the spirit of the intifada continues, not the
temporary rhetoric of the streets but in the true resistance and
soul of the people. Israeli occupation of Palestine, South
Lebanon and the Golan Heights also continues. It is easy for
those of us who live away from the insecurities and
turbulence of exile, dispossession, and statelessness to
counsel wisdom, to regret hasty decisions, to suggest
alternatives retrospectively. As Palestinians our true role

today is to remind the world and especially our Arab brothers and sisters that when the Gulf crisis is settled the immigration of Soviet Jews will continue, the Shamir-Sharon government will still be there, and the brutalities of the occupation will increase. To suggest otherwise would be to forego our responsibility.

One hopes that the end of aggression and illegal annexation in Kuwait will also presage the end of other occupations and annexations—Jerusalem, Gaza, the West Bank, Golan, South Lebanon. If Saddam can be successfully resisted, why not also Israel? The force of the Arab and the whole world can, I believe, be reunited around the cause of Palestine, in which a just peace and reconciliation between Palestinian Arabs and Israeli Jews can be achieved. This is what the intifada has fought for and what every Arab has been proud of. We must not forget the world consensus on this point, and we must press on.

The cause of Palestine is the concrete example that brings the first issue I raised into focus, the rift between the Arab-Islamic world and the West. Not to lose sight of either one or the other, not to forget both matters as together forming the large context of which the current crisis is an aspect: this, I think, furnishes all Arabs with some hope for the future and a more stable understanding between us all and the rest of the world. We are all in the world together, and better dialogue and mutual understanding than violence and conflict.

Why I have also felt so much anger and sorrow about the crisis provoked by Saddam Hussein is that he did not build on what the Arabs have already achieved, insufficient though that may have been. Kuwait after all was a thriving society, its people a vital part of the Arab nation, its institutions prosperous and liberal. What good has it done to attack all this? How can violence against Kuwait have ever been justified? The failure of creativity, morality and principle are so profound as to trouble us all, particularly when there still seems to be some confusion about the kind of "victory" proclaimed by Saddam. There is loss to be mourned and regretted. All Arabs share in the general diminishment.

September 16, 1990

By mid-September there are signs that America's allies,
united on sanctions, may split apart over the question
of going to war. Author and M.I.T. Professor Noam
Chomsky warns against policies that will leave the U.S.
isolated in the Gulf.

AMERICA'S ISOLATION IN THE GULF
NOAM CHOMSKY
The Boston Globe

There are essentially three ways in which Iraq could be forced
out of Kuwait: (1) embargo; (2) war; (3) negotiations. It is
generally hoped that the first method will suffice. Divisions
appear when we consider the prospect—unfortunately, not
unlikely—that it will not.

At the Helsinki summit, the presidents reached a consensus
on the embargo, but divided over the option of force vs.
diplomacy. On this issue, international opinion largely tends
toward Gorbachev's side, a matter of some import, if this
interpretation is correct.

In the Saudi deserts, the near isolation of the United States
is clear. It is illustrated further by the spectacle of cabinet
officials traveling around the world pleading for funds, or at
least symbolic gestures of support, to little avail.

Germany refused to finance U.S. military operations, which
officials termed a bilateral arrangement between the United
States and Saudi Arabia, not authorized by the U.N. Security
Council. The European Community agreed only to under-
write costs connected with the embargo. An E.C. spokesman
stated that the U.S. military action was "taken autonomously,"
reminding Americans of "the principle of no taxation without
representation."

Japan also politely agreed to do little, except in support
of the embargo and countries suffering from it, while South
Korea pleaded poverty. The Third World reaction was muted.
India and China took an equivocal stance. Malaysia, a
member of the Security Council, stressed the "very strict and

well-delineated parameters" of the U.N. resolutions, and their failure to authorize force. The Arab world largely kept its distance, Kuwaiti nationals aside. Saudi Arabia's willingness to pay "in-country costs" for the U.S. military (water, fuel, etc.) was not overly impressive in the light of the sharp increase in oil exports at much higher prices, yielding new profits that more than cover these costs. In pro-Western Tunisia, a poll showed 90 percent support for Iraq, with many noting the U.S. "double standard" all too evident. Egypt sent a few thousand lightly armed men, with further promises, and others added only token contributions. The pretense of a "multinational force" rests on the meager results of pleading and threats, a pitiful and embarrassing spectacle, and such allies as Syria's Assad, whose record matches that of his sworn enemy, Saddam Hussein.

One reaction has been to denounce the wealthy powers as "fair-weather allies" (*New York Times*). There has been little effort, however, to explore the odd refusal to "get on board" on the part of those who, in theory, are the main beneficiaries of the U.S. actions. It is convenient to believe that when the world is in trouble it calls for the sheriff, and we are the only ones honorable and tough enough to shoulder the burden. Convenient, but much too facile. Europe and Japan seem reluctant to risk or spend much to ensure that oil production and price be administered under the guiding hand of the United States and its clients rather than a coalition influenced by Saddam Hussein.

It is also convenient to proclaim that high principles are at stake. But that pose is hard to take seriously in the context of U.S. behavior, past and present. The actual principle at stake is that Might does not make Right—unless we want it to. The cynicism is not relieved by the fact that this lofty ideal is shared with other powers.

No more convincing is the praise for the United Nations for finally escaping the shackles of Russian recalcitrance and Third World psychic disorders. The United States is far in the lead in the past 20 years in vetoing Security Council resolutions, and has regularly been isolated, or almost so, in General Assembly votes on the Middle East, observance of international law, disarmament and other critical issues. The United Nations can function in this case because it is (more or less) conforming to U.S. demands.

Particularly galling in the Arab world is the U.S. record of support (including repeated Security Council vetoes) for Israeli aggression, annexation and harsh military occupation, and the U.S. role for many years in blocking a broad international consensus on a diplomatic resolution of the Arab-Israeli conflict. We may choose not to be aware of these facts, but others are exempt from our self-serving reconstructions of history.

It is easy to imagine an unpleasant scenario a few months hence: a huge U.S. Army suffering in the desert; the embargo leaking; turmoil in the Arab world, perhaps threatening rule elites; our economy heading into decline; the rivals/allies offering symbolic gestures but going about business as usual. Under such conditions, the temptation to resort to force will be strong.

Are there realistic diplomatic options? The answer will remain unclear if the U.S. continues to dismiss all possibilities out of hand, expressing concern that others might be tempted by the diplomatic track. A few offers have been floated. Consider just two.

On Aug. 12, Saddam Hussein offered to withdraw from Kuwait if Syria and Israel withdraw from occupied Arab lands, a proposal with considerable appeal to people not constrained by our doctrinal system. The London *Financial Times* urged that the offer, though unacceptable as it stands, "may yet serve some useful purpose," offering "a path away from disaster...through negotiation."

On Aug. 23, Iraq offered to withdraw in return for guaranteed access to the Gulf and full control of the Rumailah oil field that dips slightly into Kuwaiti territory, in a disputed area. There was no demand that U.S. forces withdraw from Saudi Arabia, or other pre-conditions. An administration specialist on Mideast affairs described the proposal as "serious" and "negotiable."

In these and several other cases, the proposals were instantly dismissed. We therefore do not know how serious they are and where they might lead, if pursued. The same is true for earlier Iraqi proposals, among them, an April 1990 offer to destroy their chemical and other nonconventional weapons if Israel would do the same, rejected here without consideration.

There is no doubt that Saddam Hussein is a dangerous monster. Exactly the same was true on Aug. 1, before he changed from favored friend to new incarnation of Hitler by demonstrating contempt for U.S. interests. The question is whether the proposals, however cynical, offer "a path away from disaster."

Of the many relevant background issues, two might be at least briefly noted. First, it has been a prime U.S. policy concern since the 1940s that the huge energy resources of the Gulf region must be under dominant influence of the United States and its clients. No independent indigenous forces can be tolerated. Second, there is a striking instability in the world system, economically tri-polar but with one military super-power, now more free than before to exercise force, with the withdrawal of the Soviet deterrent. The temptation to "lead with one's strength" is strong. We, of course, regard ourselves as benign. We might bear in mind that great powers typically have had the same self-image, and the costs of such delusions have been large.

The intricacies of the Middle East crises defy brief comment. We would do well to try to face the facts without comforting illusions. The stakes are very high.

September 23, 1990

King Hussein of Jordan, caught between Iraq and the
United States, had sought unsuccessfully to play the
role of mediator in the Gulf crisis. By September 23, he
is expressing his fear that "the current course of events
in the Middle East could, indeed, be a replay of August
1914."

IT'S NOT TOO LATE TO PREVENT A WAR

HUSSEIN IBN TALAL, KING OF JORDAN
The Washington Post

Amman

Is it too late to prevent another major war in the Middle East?
Is the pace of events accelerating at such an uncontrollable rate
that war is inevitable? Are the opposing parties so locked into
their positions that a peaceful solution is no longer possible?

It is the sad conclusion of many of those who live in the
area, and who would be the innocent victims of such a
conflagration, that the answer is probably yes. And it is part of
their despair that they are helpless to do anything about it.

One might ask how such a tragic turn of events could have
occurred in the space of less than two months. Would there
be any victors, and what would be the spoils? Are we
embarked on a noble mission to establish a new world order
of peace and justice and the abolition of aggression? Or are we
witnessing a replay of the quixotic events of August 1914,
when the world stumbled into a war it did not want but could
not stop?

I am stubborn enough to believe there is still a chance to
prevent another war. I refuse to concede that the pace of
events cannot be brought under control. And I cannot
conceive that disputants would commit themselves to a war
that is so obviously contrary to their own vital interests.

As for victors and spoils, Middle East wars have produced
neither, only graveyards for illusions and the seeds for future
wars.

Let us hope that a new world order can be established, but its foundation must be based on conciliation, not conflagration, and on distributive, not selective justice and morality.

I fear the current course of events in the Middle East could, indeed, be a replay of August 1914. To repeat the scenario would be an inexcusable tragedy. If the same effort by the world community in the present marshaling of military forces, the imposition of sanctions and the commitment of colossal sums of money were to be applied to a political solution, I am convinced it could be achieved.

It is very disturbing that some believe military action is the only solution to the current crisis. This is dangerously short-sighted. The effects of a war against Iraq would not be limited to the confines of that country. They would reverberate in every capital throughout the Middle East. They would create the very instability such action was designed to prevent. For these reasons a political solution to the present crisis is imperative.

Since the Iraqi invasion of Kuwait did not occur in a vacuum, it cannot be solved in a vacuum. Any solution must address, if not simultaneously at least sequentially, the major underlying causes—namely, the dispute between Iraq and Kuwait, the imbalance of wealth in the area, the unresolved confrontation between Israel, Palestine and the Arab States, and the perilous escalation and proliferation of weapons of mass destruction.

All of these problems are driven by political differences. To attempt to solve them militarily treats only the symptoms, not the causes, and can only exacerbate the problems, not resolve them.

Because these problems are inter-related, piecemeal solutions are not the answer, as efforts over several years have demonstrated.

This is not as tall an order as it sounds, since proposed solutions to some of these problems already exist in the files of those governments involved. The area is exhausted from the conflicts and tensions it has endured for decades. Most are appalled by the wasteful diversion of so much wealth and energy to the misfortunes of war. They are eager to join the rest of the world in its new march toward freedom, justice and prosperity. Despite the threat of war, the conditions for peace do exist in the Middle East. It is a moment of opportunity, which we should all grasp.

Whatever political solution to the immediate crisis might be devised, I believe it imperative that it include a substantial Arab input. Irrespective of the justice of any solution, there must not be room to misrepresent it as a resolution imposed from outside the area. This would only discredit its legitimacy.

Finally, there is one thing of which I am certain. The Middle East cannot afford another war. The world should not impose one on it. I am also certain that it is not beyond the ingenuity of the leaders of this world to devise a peaceful solution to this crisis. May God help us all if they cannot.

September 23, 1990

With U.S. troop strength in the Gulf exceeding 150,000, James Webb, former Assistant Secretary of Defense and Secretary of the Navy under Reagan, observes that the U.S. lacks "specific military goals," and warns that "momentum is not a policy" that should be followed when so many lives are at stake.

"...AND THE HORRORS OF A DESERT WAR"
JAMES WEBB
The New York Times

Arlington, Va.

President Bush has not only embarked on his own voyage into the Persian Gulf, that Bermuda Triangle of Presidencies. Unlike his two immediate predecessors, he has dragged more than a hundred thousand of our troops with him. And as the President struggles at home, our troops have been learning to cope with a sun that can melt electrical wiring, sand so fine that few filters can keep it out of gear boxes and a growing ennui that seeps through even the most careful monitoring of our press corps.

The debate over our role in the Persian Gulf crisis has focused on national, rather than specific military goals. The fundamental questions, upon which all others inevitably rest, have not been addressed. Why did we send such a huge contingent of ground troops in the first place? And under what conditions are we going to use them or bring them home?

Answers are not forthcoming. Military officials intimate that the question would expose tactical options. Administration officials talk in vague terms: Defense Secretary Cheney is telling us to prepare for a commitment that may take years. Others have been quoted as saying we may be there for a decade. At the same time we are being reassured, amidst many loud calls to initiate a war with Iraq, that the U.S. military commitment is wholly defensive.

As one who opposed the Reagan Administration's overt tilt toward Iraq which caused the Persian Gulf problems in 1987 and 1988, I have no desire to give consolation to Saddam Hussein now that he is getting the attention he deserves. But if our experience since World War II tells us anything, it is that justifiable national goals are too frequently lost through unfocused and ineffective military policy. And the strongest likelihood is that our ground buildup in Saudi Arabia is the product not of conscious strategy, but of an initial overreaction that compounds itself with the arrival of every C-5 transport.

The Kuwaiti dilemma is not new. This is the third time since 1981 that Iraq has asserted, militarily, its claim to Kuwaiti territory. As such, positioning U.S. aviation units into Saudi Arabia with ground forces to defend them was appropriate as a short-term guarantee of Saudi sovereignty. But the huge buildup of forces began after it became clear that Iraq had no military designs on Saudi Arabia. And coupled with escalating rhetoric, it has created an intractable siege, with the survival of President Bush, as well as Saddam Hussein, hanging in the balance.

The U.S., whose interests in the region are far less than Kuwait's, Saudi Arabia's, Israel's, Europe's and Japan's, is carrying the overwhelming burden. True, others are involved in small scale—the Egyptians, who stand to benefit to the tune of at least $7 billion in forgiven debts, the Syrians, traditional enemies of Iraq, who are sending a few thousand soldiers, other Arab nations whose royal families are also threatened, European and other allies who are throwing in a ship or two here, and a military unit there. We appear to have traded the promise of greater economic help to the Soviets for Mikhail Gorbachev's rather noncommittal statement of support.

And now we are out on the international hustings, asking for financial contributions for our effort. Mr. Bush hastens to assure us that this does not make our soldiers mercenaries, but anyone with a relative or loved one in Saudi Arabia will quickly argue that this is not a fair trade.

And what is the impact, strategically, of the introduction of all these ground forces? In grand sum, it can only be judged as negative.

Those who have called for massive, pre-emptive air strikes against Iraq must now contemplate the detriment of tens of thousands of American soldiers within range of Iraqi chemical weapons, as well as possible terrorist attacks from Iraq and now Iran.

Those who worry about the possibility of crisis in other parts of the world must recognize that a large percentage of American maneuver forces—including as much as half of the Marine Corps—are tied down in a waiting game in the desert.

Those who believe we should use these forces offensively should realize that this would galvanize the Arab world, invite chemical retaliation and an expansion of the hostilities, produce great numbers of casualties and encourage worldwide terrorism—in short, open up a Pandora's box.

This is not to say that our soldiers and marines would not fight well. The Iraqi army is not a very good army; it is also war-weary. But it demonstrated against Iran the time-honored maxim that the armies of totalitarian nations are capable of absorbing huge losses—recall the 3.7 million German soldiers who died in World War II, and the million Communist soldiers who died in the Vietnam war.

The President should be aware that, while most Americans are laboring very hard to support him, a mood of cynicism is just beneath their veneer of respect. Many are claiming that the buildup is little more than a "Pentagon budget drill," designed to preclude cutbacks of an Army searching for a mission as bases in NATO begin to disappear.

Others wonder about the predominance of Texans in the Administration, and the dual benefit that higher oil prices will bring to the Southwest: a more robust economy and the concomitant salvation of many S & L's. Others, myself included, worry greatly about a military commitment that has taken on a momentum of its own—or perhaps a hidden strategy.

General Colin Powell is said to have advised the President that the U.S. should take this sort of military action or it would no longer be a superpower. This calls to mind the Suez Crisis of 1956, after Egyptian leader Nasser nationalized the Suez Canal. The British were reeling from a budget affected by the military costs of maintaining the Empire. The Suez Canal was vital for transporting oil. And Anthony Eden, the British Prime Minister who had great antipathy toward Nasser for his anti-British rhetoric, wanted him "destroyed."

Britain went forward, largely to preserve its place at the table of the great powers, drawing in the French and the Israelis. Their attack sputtered in the desert. The U.S., their banker, threatened to withhold support for the British pound if they did not cease their invasion. The Soviets moved into

Hungary. And sure enough, when the dust settled, Britain was no longer a great power.

Too much is at risk, and too many questions remain for this buildup to continue without the Administration clarifying its direction. And if offensive action is in the cards, it should be taken only after the President receives a declaration of war from the Congress.

Chapter 4

OCTOBER 1990

THIRD WORLD IMPACT

Chronology

On the first of October President Bush addresses the U.N. on the crisis, stating that he hopes an Iraqi pullout from Kuwait will provide the opportunity to "settle the conflicts that divide the Arabs from Israel." On October 3 Yevgeny Primakov, Gorbachev's envoy, visits Jordan and Iraq. On his return he is quoted in *Literaturnaya Gazeta* as saying, "I think we should proceed from the fact that [the Gulf crisis] offers a kind of laboratory, testing our efforts to create a new world order after the Cold War....Very much depends on Soviet-American solidarity, on parallel activity or joint political action, on mutual support."

On October 8 Israeli police open fire on Palestinian protesters near Jerusalem's Al-Aqsa Mosque, killing twenty-one and wounding more than one hundred. As a result of this "Temple Mount massacre," tensions between Arabs and Jews, already whipped up by Saddam Hussein, grow even more volatile. The U.N. Security Council begins to debate a response to the massacre, and passes a resolution condemning the violence and calling on the secretary general to send a fact-finding mission to Israel; the Israeli cabinet votes not to cooperate with the investigation. Later in the month, a Palestinian worker will stab three Jews in Jerusalem in retribution, and Israel will temporarily seal the borders leading to the occupied territories.

Iran wants to lessen its isolation from the rest of the world, and its pledge to abide by trade embargos seems to be working. On October 12 the World Bank announces it will soon make a $300 million loan to Iran.

In what will become the most significant step towards an offensive ground war with Iraq, the U.S., on October 19, begins to move heavy armored divisions from Europe —from what once were frontline positions against the Soviet Union—into Saudi Arabia. These tank divisions will become the spearhead of the Allied ground offensive.

The first antiwar protests take place in the United States and Europe. On October 25 the Secretary of Defense Dick Cheney says there never was any "upper limit" on the number of troops to be sent to the Gulf, and announces plans to dispatch 100,000 more to join the 210,00 already there. Allied nations have an additional 200,000 troops in Saudi Arabia. The active-duty service period for American combat reservists is doubled, from 180 to 360 days.

Third World Impact

Even without a shooting war, the Gulf crisis quickly begins to have a damaging ripple effect across the poorer countries of the world's southern hemisphere. These countries, in their struggle to industrialize over the last decade, have come to rely on oil more than ever before. The developing world now accounts for 28 percent of the world's daily oil consumption (as compared with 18 percent in 1973), and in the two months since the invasion of Kuwait, the price of oil has doubled, to nearly forty dollars a barrel.

Many of these nations are struggling under increasing debt burdens and lower commodity prices. Slumps in such major commodities as coffee and cocoa have hit hard at Africa and Latin America: Coffee prices are down by one third from 1979, and cocoa prices are off by two-thirds. According to the Canadian Council for International Cooperation's report, *The Gulf Crisis and Developing Countries*, "For these oil importing countries as a whole, each increase of $1 in the price of a barrel of oil means $2 billion is added to their import bill.... An average cost of $30 a barrel would mean an additional $25 billion added to the import bill over the course of a single year, or about 10 percent of export earnings after payments of debt service obligations. If at the same time, interest rates rise and if recessionary pressures gather in the industrialised countries, reducing demands for developing countries' goods, then damage will be that much more severe."

To save money, Third World nations had maintained a low oil reserve. For example, in August, the month the crisis began, India, a nation with 800 million people and a precarious balance of payments account, was maintaining a reserve of only three days. As India and Pakistan desperately scoured the world markets for oil, they discovered the Japanese had all but cornered the market. India had to go to the International Monetary Fund for more loans, going deeper into debt.

The Gulf crisis produces other crises in the developing nations that had depended upon the "trickle down" of wealth from the Gulf states. While there had been sporadic efforts over recent years aimed at persuading these richer, more sparsely populated countries to spread their wealth through the poorer, densely populated Arab states, the oil-rich shiekhdoms had been laggard in doing so —and it was their refusal, at least nominally, that had led to the Gulf conflict. Still, their wealth had become an important factor to many Third World countries. Hundreds of thousands of "guest workers" from North Africa, the subcontinent, and Asia had been employed in the Gulf states. The guest workers in Kuwait, for one, existed as modern serfs, without rights or citizenship. But these workers sent their earnings home, and those revenues had come to play a significant role in the economies of nations as far away as Pakistan and the Philippines. With the invasion and annexation of Kuwait, thousands upon thousands of these guest workers become refugees, uprooted and seeking escape by trekking across the desert.

As many as 1.2 million Egyptians, for example, had taken jobs in Kuwait and Iraq. There are great costs in resettling these people. Many have returned to Egypt with no visible means of support, even though they earned relatively good salaries in the Gulf states. In addition, the war has raised insurance prices and severely cut back shipping in the region, and Egypt faces declining revenues from its Suez Canal levies.

Other countries—Sri Lanka, India, Bangladesh, Pakistan, Morocco, Korea, and the Philippines—also face heavy losses of income from worker salaries and construction contracts. Their combined loss is estimated at $3 billion yearly, with about two million of their people being dislocated in the Gulf because of the crisis. In India alone, which had about 200,000 workers in Kuwait and Iraq, the loss of salaries will amount to $400 million a year. There are early estimates that money sent home from the approximately 100,000 Indian-held jobs in the Gulf area supported at least 500,000 people on the subcontinent. Most of those displaced workers were migrant workers from the state of Kerala. The Philippines had about 500,000 workers in the Gulf. They sent home billions of dollars a year either through banks, families, or friends. From Kuwait alone, Filipinos were remitting some $100 million annually. Many other countries face similar withdrawal symptoms. Pakistan had 135,000 migrant workers in the Gulf, and Bangladesh had 110,000. Sri Lanka, which had to resettle 110,000 workers, has also been hit by a 20 percent drop in its export earnings from tea due to loss of its Iraqi markets.

Perhaps worst off of all are the Palestinians, who are dispersed across the Arab world, without a home. Two hundred thousand live in Kuwait, where, like the other guest workers, they are denied citizenship and other rights. After the invasion of Iraq, the Palestinians have become collaborators in the eyes of many Kuwaitis, to be hunted down and punished upon liberation.

Looking ahead, there are early signs that future American aid to developing countries may be linked to their positions on the Gulf crisis. And in the coming months, as oil prices fluctuate, refugees stream across borders, and the threat of widespread environmental damage looms large, these Third World countries will continue to experience shock waves from a crisis over which—as usual—they have little control.

October 4, 1990

At the risk of sounding "wimpish and vaguely unpatriotic," *Rolling Stone* political correspondent William
Greider wonders, in early October, whether Americans
should be willing to die to save the Kuwaiti royal family
or to keep oil at twenty dollars a barrel.

LEARNING WRONG LESSONS FROM THE MIDEAST CRISIS
WILLIAM GREIDER
Rolling Stone

Washington, D.C.

The question that now hangs over the Arabian desert is this:
Would restoring the emir of Kuwait to his throne be worth
the life of a single American? The Kuwaiti royals are a greedy
bunch; even other Arab potentates find them obnoxious.
Democracy—a sovereign people endowed with inalienable
rights—is a concept utterly alien to Kuwait, as it is to Iraq or,
for that matter, Saudi Arabia.

Well, if America is not going to war to save democracy, then
try this question: Would you want your son (or husband or
father, daughter or wife or mother) to die to keep oil at twenty
dollars a barrel? Americans do love automobiles and cheap
gasoline, but surely not that much.

Or put it this way: Is America prepared to spill its blood
and treasure to maintain secure supplies of oil for its friends
in Europe and Japan? If Americans are their mercenaries, they
should be paying for the service.

Or are we just going to this fight because we are used to
fighting? When it comes to global relations, that is what
America knows best: a muscular nation with so much of its
energy focused on maintaining its military might, it can't seem
to imagine other approaches to the world's complexities.

So which is it? I am aware that among all the war whoops
in the news media, these questions sound wimpish and
vaguely unpatriotic. But other Americans may soon be asking
them if things go badly in the desert. As this is written, no
shots have been fired at U.S. troops. By the time you read

this, it may already be clear whether we are in a real war or (as is my hunch) a frustrating drama of siege and negotiation. Either way, the question has to be faced eventually: What exactly is our purpose?

George Bush tried to make it easy for us: He invoked Adolph Hitler. Everyone knows Hitler and everyone hates him, even if only from watching television documentaries. In fact, the forty-five-year cold war with the Soviet Union was, in reality, always a love affair with Hitler's ghost. American leaders who—like George Bush—had fought in World War II were determined to act on its lessons as they understood them: no appeasement of aggressors. "Never again" became the organizing rationale for the permanent military mobilization of America.

Iraq's Saddam Hussein is brutal and dangerous, no question, but it's a real stretch to imagine him annexing Austria and marching into Poland, then on to Paris and the English Channel. If Saddam is a Hitler intent on global conquest, we are entitled to a better explanation of why the Bush administration was cozying up to him just a few months ago; why Ronald Reagan supported Saddam in his war of aggression against Iran; and why Reagan's State Department had earlier absolved Iraq of its "terrorist" label.

In other words, questions of territorial integrity in the Middle East are a lot trickier than the repeatedly invoked image of Hitler suggests. This is a region where Syria holds by force a large chunk of Lebanon, where Israel occupies real estate that belongs to Jordan and Syria, where Kuwait itself is a nation only because British colonial map makers invented it early in the twentieth century.

The president, to be sure, was caught short by Saddam's aggression and had little choice but to respond purposefully. And the world would be safer, no doubt, without Saddam in power. But the trouble is, if George Bush gets out of this predicament whole (and I earnestly hope he does), his success is likely to produce its own terrible legacy: the illusion of a powerful and victorious American foreign policy that has proudly reclaimed for the nation its role as the world's riot policeman. The simple-minded specter of Hitler will live on in the minds of policy makers, continuing as the rallying cry for American muscle. And, once again, the United States will try to evade the deeper, harder questions about its role in the world.

Iraq's invasion of Kuwait is, as the secretary of state and countless others have observed, the first crisis of the post-cold-war world. But it threatens to become the pretext for continuing the Cold War under another name.

The United States is genuinely threatened by oil policies, but not in the way George Bush would have us believe. Here is the unpleasant truth: Low oil prices are no longer good for the United States. That assertion would probably start a fistfight at any gas pump. And very few politicians will address that reality because they don't wish to become ex-politicians.

I am not shilling for Texas or the oil companies, but there are two fundamental reasons why this nation's long-term well-being is undermined by cheap gasoline. First the United States is steadily depleting its own oil reserves—a stockpile that has shrunk by nearly a third in the last two decades. This trend will continue, regardless of new discoveries or whether oil companies are allowed to drill in wildlife refuges or coastal waters. Experts all know this: The world isn't running out of oil, but we are. Low oil prices simply encourage overconsumption of this dwindling asset. Ultimately, that deepens our dependence on foreign suppliers and the world market.

Second, cheap gasoline makes it very difficult, if not impossible, to begin a much needed transition in the marketplace to other sources of energy, particularly the so-called soft energy sources like solar power that are both renewable and not environmentally destructive. The phenomenon of global warming, for instance, is driven primarily by burning hydrocarbons such as petroleum, of which cars are the single largest users. As long as gasoline remains cheap, manufacturers have no interest in making the genuinely fuel-efficient cars that are needed, and let's face it, most consumers have no interest in buying them.

The transition to a post-petroleum economy will be fitful and difficult and stretch over many decades, but there is no physical reason why the result has to be economic deprivation or even inconvenience. Since the United States has its own economic and political incentives to make this great transformation first, it ought to be leading the way for other nations. Instead, the U.S. government is pulling in the opposite direction —pretending that somehow we can avoid the fundamental dilemma by controlling foreign geography through military power. Or by drilling more wells in pristine wilderness. George Bush is an oil man himself, and he will soon be hearing from his old friends, urging him to relax environmental laws to ensure plentiful gasoline at low prices.

The belief in our ability to control our own destiny as users of energy is a grand illusion, and someday it will smack us in the face. Certainly, we do not wish to have Saddam setting the price of oil. But here is another unpleasant truth: Somebody has to manage global oil prices, and somebody always has. The law of supply and demand ultimately controls prices, of course, but Western economies learned long ago that without some mechanism for managing total production, prices will soar and collapse, leading to economic chaos for both consumers and producers.

From the early decades of this century, the management of the world's oil supply—and therefore the price—was discreetly supervised by the major oil companies, the Seven Sisters, with formal and informal cooperation from Western governments, including especially that of the United States. Starting in the late Sixties, the Arab nations of OPEC claimed the lead role and engineered two drastic run-ups in oil prices—the so-called oil shocks of the Seventies, which fed American inflation.

In the Eighties, however, oil prices collapsed, in part because consumers everywhere learned to conserve and in part because global recession and slow economic growth weakened overall demand. When oil prices were rising, American families and industry made remarkable improvements in energy efficiency, and alternative fuels were given consideration and study. When oil prices fell, these positive trends were reversed.

Even at thirty dollars a barrel, oil is still much cheaper than it was a decade ago. Pushing the price back to twenty dollars will relieve some short-term economic distress, but it would restimulate bad habits. Higher oil prices would have other benefits, including reviving the economy of the American Southwest and reducing the costs of bailing out the region's failed banks and S&Ls.

Bumping off Saddam may improve our short-term political leverage over oil-producing nations, but it does not alter the fundamental fact of our growing dependency. The Saudi royal family is enormously stronger and more sophisticated than the emir of Kuwait, but it's not the Rock of Gibraltar, either. In fact, the Saudis are threatened by the same forces—Arab fundamentalism and self-determination—that roil so many other Mideast countries. It does seem strange, doesn't it, that as we celebrate the worldwide triumph of democracy, America sends forth its military to defend a feudal monarchy?

If the U.S. government decides that military force is the new, preferred method for managing oil prices, then our soldiers are going to be in the desert for a long, long time. To what end? Eventually, people will begin to ask how much blood we are willing to spill to produce an outcome that is fundamentally not good for us.

Dismantling the cold-war military machine, like facing up to higher oil prices, is painful in the short run but absolutely necessary to our future well-being. In New York, Grumman has eliminated 7400 jobs. Lockheed dropped 5500 workers in Georgia and California. McDonnell Douglas announced cutbacks of 17,000 jobs in Missouri, California and twenty-six other states. This is only the beginning of what promises to be a most painful build-down for the military-industrial complex—that is, if the cold war is truly over.

Right now, George Bush is adroitly positioned on the smart side of the short-term politics: He's basically against ending the cold war, at least in terms of defense spending. So when Bush campaigns for reelection in 1992, he will be able to tour the defense plants and assure nervous workers that he's fighting to save their jobs.

Meanwhile, the Pentagon planners and cold-war theologians are salivating over the Mideast crisis, retooling their arguments for building every weapons system from Star Wars to cargo planes. The defense budget will inevitably shrink whether Bush likes it or not, especially when Western Europe tells us to bring home most of our NATO troops, but no one will ever accuse the Bush administration of leading the nation into a new era.

Once again, this is a tragic moment of evasion. The hard questions are well known to defense experts and economists, but they're not so easy for politicians to articulate. First, a dramatic cutback in defense procurement will eliminate a lot of wasteful spending, but it will also leave a big hole in the economy. The overall defense budget, it's true, is less than ten percent of the gross national product, but that measure is misleading.

The Pentagon's spending on hardware and supplies represents more than twenty percent of American manufactured goods. Since American manufacturing is already being squeezed hard by foreign competitors, shrinkage in the defense market—where American companies have the home-field advantage—will be another heavy blow. No one has figured out how to fill that hole . . .

If defense spending shrinks, private companies will have to learn how to be grown-ups—to make competitive products unsheltered by Pentagon subsidies and protection. The government, meanwhile, has to figure out how to pump R&D capital into the economy without using the cover of national defense. An informed but parochial debate among defense-production experts and manufacturing leaders has already begun along these lines. In time the politicians may even discover there are other, more productive means for priming the pump—such as spending money on non-military goods like roads and schools and health clinics and technical innovation—in the name of "national security." . . .

For the moment, however, the free-market conservatives in the Bush administration have not surrendered their prejudices against government intervention in the economy. Nor are they ready to accept that a demilitarized American economy will ultimately be a stronger competitor in the world. Saddam Hussein has probably extended the life of these illusions.

We are now beginning to feel the aftershocks of last year's political earthquake in the Soviet Union and Eastern Europe. If the Soviets have withdrawn from the field, whom exactly are we struggling against? So far the only healthy debate on that question has surfaced among conservatives, the stalwarts of cold-war anticommunism, who at least recognize that they must rethink the premises for everything in American foreign policy.

Conservatives are splitting, sometimes nastily, into opposing camps, arguing either for a neo-imperialism (under the banner of promoting democracy abroad) or an old-fashioned isolationism. Scattered voices on the left are offering their own fuzzy alternatives—a kind of good-hearted globalism that sets out to heal the environment and tend to the needy and reap the benefits of worldwide disarmament.

If we are lucky, this nascent debate will be allowed to develop and flourish—uninterrupted by nostalgic excursions into war making. America needs to have a good, long argument about itself. Perhaps the worst thing that Saddam Hussein has done is allow many Americans to think that nothing has changed.

October 15, 1990

The nation's accelerating march towards war raises sociological as well as political issues, and for writer Barbara Ehrenreich, the actions in the Persian Gulf offer yet more evidence that America is a "warrior culture."

THE WARRIOR CULTURE
BARBARA EHRENREICH
Time

In what we like to think of as "primitive" warrior cultures, the passage to manhood requires the blooding of a spear, the taking of a scalp or head. Among the Masai of eastern Africa, the North American Plains Indians and dozens of other pretechnological peoples, a man could not marry until he had demonstrated his capacity to kill in battle. Leadership too in a warrior culture is typically contingent on military prowess and wrapped in the mystique of death. In the Solomon Islands a chief's importance could be reckoned by the number of skulls posted around his door, and it was the duty of the Aztec kings to nourish the gods with the hearts of human captives.

All warrior peoples have fought for the same high-sounding reasons: honor, glory or revenge. The nature of their real and perhaps not conscious motivations is a subject of much debate. Some anthropologists postulate a murderous instinct, almost unique among living species, in human males. Others discern a materialistic motive behind every fray: a need for slaves, grazing land or even human flesh to eat. Still others point to the similarities between war and other male pastimes —the hunt and outdoor sports—and suggest that it is boredom, ultimately, that stirs men to fight.

But in a warrior culture it hardly matters which motive is most basic. Aggressive behavior is rewarded whether or not it is innate to the human psyche. Shortages of resources are habitually taken as occasions for armed offensives, rather than for hard thought and innovation. And war, to a warrior people, is of course the highest adventure, the surest antidote to malaise, the endlessly repeated theme of legend, song, religious myth and personal quest for meaning. It is how men die and what they find to live for.

"You must understand that Americans are a warrior nation," Senator Daniel Patrick Moynihan told a group of Arab leaders in early September, one month into the Middle East crisis. He said this proudly, and he may, without thinking through the ugly implications, have told the truth. In many ways, in outlook and behavior the U.S. has begun to act like a primitive warrior culture.

We seem to believe that leadership is expressed, in no small part, by a willingness to cause the deaths of others. After the U.S. invasion of Panama, President Bush exulted that no one could call him "timid"; he was at last a "macho man." The press, in even more primal language, hailed him for succeeding in an "initiation rite" by demonstrating his "willingness to shed blood."

For lesser offices too we apply the standards of a warrior culture. Female candidates are routinely advised to overcome the handicap of their gender by talking "tough." Thus, for example, Dianne Feinstein has embraced capital punishment, while Colorado senatorial candidate Josie Heath has found it necessary to announce that although she is the mother of an 18-year-old son, she is prepared to vote for war. Male candidates in some of the fall contests are finding their military records under scrutiny. No one expects them, as elected officials in a civilian government, to pick up a spear or a sling and fight. But they must state, at least, their willingness to have another human killed.

More tellingly, we are unnerved by peace and seem to find it boring. When the cold war ended, we found no reason to celebrate. Instead we heated up the "war on drugs." What should have been a public-health campaign, focused on the persistent shame of poverty, became a new occasion for martial rhetoric and muscle flexing. Months later, when the Berlin Wall fell and communism collapsed throughout Europe, we Americans did not dance in the streets. What we did, according to the networks, was change the channel to avoid the news. Nonviolent revolutions do not uplift us, and the loss of mortal enemies only seems to leave us empty and bereft.

Our collective fantasies center on mayhem, cruelty and violent death. Loving images of the human body—especially of bodies seeking pleasure or expressing love—inspire us with the urge to censor. Our preference is for warrior themes: the lone fighting man, bandoliers across his naked chest, mowing

down lesser men in gusts of automatic-weapon fire. Only a
real war seems to revive our interest in real events. With the
Iraqi crisis, the networks report, ratings for news shows rose
again—even higher than they were for Panama.

And as in any primitive warrior culture, our warrior elite
takes pride of place. Social crises multiply numbingly—
homelessness, illiteracy, epidemic disease—and our leaders
tell us solemnly that nothing can be done. There is no money.
We are poor, not rich, a debtor nation. Meanwhile, nearly a
third of the federal budget flows, even in moments of peace,
to the warriors and their weaponmakers. When those priorities are questioned, some new "crisis" dutifully arises to serve
as another occasion for armed and often unilateral intervention.

Now, with Operation Desert Shield, our leaders are reduced
to begging foreign powers for the means to support our warrior class. It does not seem to occur to us that the other great
northern powers—Japan, Germany, the Soviet Union—might
not have found the stakes so high or the crisis quite so threatening. It has not penetrated our imagination that in a world
where the powerful, industrialized nation-states are at last at
peace, there might be other ways to face down a pint-size
Third World warrior state than with massive force of arms.
Nor have we begun to see what an anachronism we are in
danger of becoming: a warrior nation in a world that pines for
peace, a high-tech state with the values of a warrior band.

A leftist might blame "imperialism"; a right-winger would
call our problem "internationalism." But an anthropologist,
taking the long view, might say this is just what warriors do.
Intoxicated by their own drumbeats and war songs, fascinated
by the glint of steel and the prospect of blood, they will go
forth, time and again, to war.

October 24, 1990

President Bush's goals in the Gulf remain unclear, and even conservative commentators begin to question the logic of U.S. policy. Recalling other foreign invasions that brought little American response, columnist Patrick J. Buchanan asks, "What makes Saddam a greater enemy, or greater evil, than Mao, Ho Chi Minh or Leonid Brezhnev?"

DECLARE WAR, OR COME HOME
PATRICK J. BUCHANAN
San Jose Mercury News

No one has played his hand better in the Gulf crisis than Hafez al-Assad. Distrusted by Americans for his supected role in the Marine massacre in Beirut, he ostentatiously voted the U.S. position in the Arab League, then sent Syrian troops off to the Saudi desert.

That won Damascus a green light from Secretary of State James Baker to crush Gen. Michael Aoun's Lebanese Catholics. Daniel Pipes describes Assad's victory: "The Syrians are alleged to have asserted their control by committing atrocities aginst the Maronites similar to those attributed to the Iraqis in Kuwait: summary executions, pillage, rape. Thus does a Middle East lion lick his chops."

Now, murdering captured troops is a war crime. Germans were executed for doing that to Americans at Malmedy. Yet, neither the United Nations, which is considering war crime charges against Saddam Hussein, nor the United States, which is pressing Israel to let the United Nations investigate the blood bath on Temple Mount, has protested.

Why not? If the Israelis are enraged at the "double standard" of morality and justice at the United Nations, do they not have a point?

Assad's barbarity toward the Maronite Christians should raise questions in George Bush's mind about the likely beneficiaries of the war being pressed upon him. Already, we have two: Syria now has Lebanon; and Iran has been ceded back all the territory lost in the eight-year war. Both are ready to make land grabs at the expense of a defeated Iraq. Would this advance the ideals for which our Marines would be dying?

Yet, our military buildup, with modern tanks, and perhaps 50,000 more troops coming down from Germany, is leading us inexorably toward war.

Where is the Congress of the United States?

The Consitution, after all, gives Congress, not the president, power to declare war; but, Congress is about to adjourn, leaving Bush two free months to attack, with only some vague admonition that he not do so without congressional approval.

This abdication is appalling; but, no less so than the conduct of conservatives who are supposed to be men of the Constitution.

Last August, the war hawks were shrieking for a U.S. attack, before Congress returned, and before a whipped-up populace could entertain any second thoughts. Is this conservatism?

Having fought two undeclared wars in 40 years, both of which divided America terribly, why not fight this one the consitutional way? As North Carolina's Terry Sanford notes, debating war would not surrender the element of surprise. Saddam Hussein has a fairly good idea of what we have in the desert and why we came.

One reason for debating a declaration of war is the present confusion about our aims. Irritated by a heckler, who said America was fighting for oil, Bush last week retorted that this conflict is not about oil, but naked aggression. A day later, Bush's Senate leader, Bob Dole, said we were there for only one reason "o-i-l."

But, neither is sufficient reason to send thousands of Americans to their deaths. After all, Saddam Hussein stole Kuwait's oil to sell it to the West, to get cash to pay off his debts to the West, and to buy what he needs to modernize, from the West. If the war clouds lift, oil will quickly fall $10 a barrel. But, if war breaks out, Iraqi wells will be destroyed, Kuwaiti wells will be destroyed, Saudi wells will be destroyed; and the price of oil could hit $60 a barrel.

Are we there to fight agression? But, in 1959, China raped Tibet; and we did nothing . In 1975, Hanoi wiped South Vietnam off the map; and, we did nothing. In 1979, the Soviet Union invaded Afghanistan. Rather than go to war, we boycotted Moscow's Olympics and stopped selling grain.

What makes Saddam a greater enemy, or greater evil, than Mao, Ho Chi Minh or Leonid Brezhnev?

Why does this act of aggression call for war by the United States, when Kuwait was never a U.S. ally and no Americans died?

Moreover, what are our war aims? Under what conditions will we agree to stand down? Does Iraq have to give up all of Kuwait? Does it have to destroy its chemical and biological weapons, and nuclear factories? Must Saddam be overthrown? Are unconditional surrender and a Nuremberg-style trial necessary, in which case are we talking about tens of thousands of war dead, as Saddam Hussein will surely prefer, like Hitler to whom he is compared, to die in the last ditch, rather than ascend an American-built gallows?

How many American dead and wounded do we anticipate? How many should we accept? Let's get the politicians and generals on the record. As we will surely debate this after the kids start coming home in caskets, why not debate it now, when they're still alive?

Eighty percent of Europeans, pollsters say, favor war, which is understandable, since 98 percent of the dead will be Arab and American, two people Europeans have always been willing to sacrifice for nobel ideals.

A formal declaration of war would give Bush the authority and support he needs to fight and win. A Congress that authorized war could not cut and run, as Congress did in Vietnam. We would all be on the line, from generals who predict victory in six days, to critics who thought war a mistake.

If Congress refused Bush his ultimatum, and declaration, the president would be off the hook. Surely, this is the way a democratic republic should go to war, the right way, the consitutional way.

If the War Party can't make its case to Congress, maybe it hasn't got a case.

October 24, 1990

As the number of American forces in the Gulf continue to grow, commentators continue to debate the roots of the current crisis. In late October, *New York Times* columnist Anthony Lewis asserts that Ronald Reagan's foreign policies had helped to set the stage for the Iraqi invasion.

PAYING FOR REAGAN'S CONTEMPTUOUS FOLLY
ANTHONY LEWIS
The New York Times

Boston

There has been much soul-searching since Aug. 2 about failures of American policy that helped to encourage Saddam Hussein's aggression. But not enough attention has been paid to the man whose folly led the way: Ronald Reagan.

In three significant ways, President Reagan gave the Iraqi leader reason to believe that he did not have to worry about American opposition. Reagan played down human rights concerns, winking at horrendous cruelties by Saddam Hussein. He destroyed U.S. energy policy, making us more vulnerable to oil threats. And he treated international law with contempt.

Few recent inhumanities in the world have been as shocking as Iraq's use of poison gas to kill thousands of its own Kurdish citizens in 1988. And it was unconcealed. Reporters went to the devastated villages. The world saw the bodies on television.

And what did the United States do? Secretary of State George Shultz, to his credit, condemned Iraq for the use of chemical weapons. But the larger message sent by the Reagan administration to Saddam Hussein was that it did not care.

The administration lobbied against, and blocked, congressional efforts to impose sanctions on Iraq in 1988 because of the use of poison gas. It continued to extend $500 million a year in credit guarantees to Iraq to buy U.S. food products.

At a special international conference on chemical weapons,

held in Paris in January 1989, the United States strongly
opposed efforts to name Iraq as a violator. Because the
administration gave a low priority to human rights, and
because it wanted to sell goods to Iraq, it groveled.

Before the gassing of the Kurds, Saddam Hussein had used
chemical weapons in the war with Iran. The Reagan
administration made no forceful objection to that either.

"In retrospect, it would have been much better at the time
of their use of poison gas . . . if we'd put our foot down."
Richard L. Armitage, an assistant secretary of defense in the
Reagan administration, said that after the invasion of Kuwait.

"The mistake we made," he added, "was not pushing very
hard and loud for international action." The Reagan administration, in short, missed a chance to deter Saddam Hussein.

Shortly after Reagan was elected president, he said energy
conservation meant being too hot in the summer and too cold
in the winter. His policy was in keeping with that ignorant
sneer.

Funds for research on energy conservation were cut toward
the vanishing point. Energy efficiency standards for cars and
appliances were cut back, opposed, delayed. And the Reagan
administration just about ended the search for solar and other
renewable energy sources.

By the conservation measures started in the Carter administration, the United States had reduced its dependence on
imported oil to 28 percent of its total supply. Now about half
the oil we use is imported.

Ronald Reagan's contemptuous attitude toward international
law hardly needs to be described. He reversed the historic
American position, going back to Theodore Roosevelt's time,
of respect for international law and international legal
institutions.

In disregard of treaties and other obligations, the Reagan
Administration made war on Nicaragua. When Nicaragua
sued in the World Court, the Reagan administration rejected
the Court's judgment and withdrew from its jurisdiction.

Again, Saddam Hussein heard the message he wanted; the
United States does not care about international law; it will
look the other way if I break the rules.

President Bush carried on the failed Reagan policies. When
Congress imposed sanctions on Iraq but allowed a presidential waiver, he waived them—and his people were on Capitol

Hill opposing effective sanctions just a few days before the invasion of Kuwait. He did nothing for energy conservation. His invasion of Panama was another expression of contemptuous disregard for international law.

We can hope that Mr. Bush has learned from the experience of these last two months; learned at least that it does not serve American interests to disregard a tryant's cruelties or to trample on international law.

But Mr. Reagan never learned. I thought of him when the superb public television series on the Civil War last week described how President Buchanan's vacuity helped to bring on the war. Americans paid for that war for 100 years. We shall be paying as long for Ronald Reagan's folly.

Chapter 5

NOVEMBER 1990

WHAT'S IN IT FOR US?

Chronology

November begins three days after the United Nations Security Council passes its tenth resolution on the Persian Gulf situation, making Iraq liable for damages, injuries, and financial losses resulting from the invasion and occupation of Kuwait. On visits to Spain and France, Soviet President Mikhail Gorbachev indicates Soviet diplomacy has found signs that Iraq might be willing to compromise and defuse the Persian Gulf crisis. Soviet envoy Yevgeny Primakov, on his return to Moscow from a meeting with Saddam Hussein, notes "a very limited optimism."

But in the United States, President Bush sharpens his attacks on Iraq. In Honolulu, near Pearl Harbor, he says the world is faced with a struggle between "good and evil, right and wrong." In San Francisco he says he is prepared to order the use of military force in the Gulf without Congressional approval. "History is replete with examples where the president has had to take action," he declares, "and I've done this in the past and would have no hesitancy at all." Secretary of State Baker echoes Bush. In Los

Angeles he says, "Let no one doubt: We will not rule out the possible use of force if Iraq continues to occupy Kuwait." In a meeting with a bipartisan group of legislators, a number of Congressmen express the opinion that Bush is creating a pretext for invasion.

On October 31 Bush declares, "The American flag is flying over the Kuwait embassy and our people inside are being starved by a brutal dictator... I've had it with that kind of treatment of Americans, and I know others feel the same way."

On November 3 Baker begins a trip to the Middle East, the Soviet Union, and Europe. In Great Britain, the woman credited with steeling George Bush to the task of war, Prime Minister Margaret Thatcher, minces no words: "Time is running out for Saddam Hussein," she says in the House of Commons on November 7. "Either he gets out of Kuwait soon or we and our allies will remove him by force and he will go down in defeat with all its consequences. He has... been warned."

On November 8 Bush orders a major new deployment of troops to the Persian Gulf, doubling the level of U.S. forces, bringing the total to 400,000. He explains the new troops are being sent to make sure the allied coalition has an adequate military option. "I have not ruled out the use of force at all, and I think that's evident by what we're doing today," Bush now says. He states that he hopes economic sanctions will work within a two-month period, and he believes the U.S. has the authority to launch military action without further U.N. approval.

The new forces deployed to the Gulf will come mostly from what were once Cold War frontline armored divisions stationed in West Germany. It is one of the biggest deployments since the Second World War, and by the time it is completed, one-third of the American Army and two-thirds of the Marine forces will be in the Gulf. The Defense Department announces it won't rotate troops in the Persian Gulf; those that are there will remain for the duration of the crisis.

The Congress, which has remained more or less silent on the president's Gulf policy, now shows signs of potentially serious opposition to the president's Gulf policy. "It's as if that great armed force which was created to fight the Cold War is at the president's own disposal for any diversion he may wish, no matter what the costs," says New York's Democratic Senator Daniel Patrick Moynihan on November 12. "He will wreck our military. He will wreck his administration, and he'll spoil a chance to get a collective security system working. It breaks your heart."

"Not a shot's been fired," White House spokesman Marlin Fitzwater is quick to reply. "What are these guys talking about?" He says Bush hoped to consult with Congress at every stage in the conflict, but then adds that "there are always those unforeseen kinds of provocations that might result in having to move first."

Secretary of State Baker, in Bermuda on November 13 for a meeting with Canadian foreign minister Joe Clark, explains why American forces are in Saudi Arabia: "To bring it down to the level of the average American citizen, let me say that means jobs. If you want to sum it up in one word, its jobs. Because an economic recession worldwide, caused by the control of one nation—one dictator, if you will—of the West's economic lifeline [oil], will result in the loss of jobs for American citizens." Early in the crisis, Bush had said that "our jobs, our way of life" would be placed at risk "if control of the world's great oil reserves fell into the hands of one man, Saddam Hussein." But the administration soon dropped that argument and sought to elevate debate to one of high principle.

On November 18 Saddam Hussein says he is willing to release all the remaining hostages over a three-month period, so long as the U.S. does not start a war. The next day he says he, too, will send more troops to the Gulf —some 250,000, to strengthen his 430,000-strong army already deployed in Kuwait and southern Iraq. The U.S. dismisses his hostage plan as "further cynical manipulation."

On November 21 President Bush arrives in the Middle East, where he will meet with the leaders of Saudi Arabia, Egypt, and Syria, as well as Kuwait's exiled Shiekh Jabir. Bush spends Thanksgiving with the troops in Saudi Arabia, where he describes Saddam Hussein as "a classic bully who thinks he can get away with kicking sand in the face of the world." Bush also offers yet another explanation for America's role in the Gulf. "Those who would measure the timetable for Saddam's atomic program in years may be seriously underestimating the reality of that situation and the gravity of the threat," he tells the troops. "Every day that passes brings Saddam one step closer to realizing his goal of a nuclear weapons arsenal. And that's why, more and more, your mission is marked by a real sense of urgency... He has never possessed a weapon he didn't use." In the end it will turn out that Iraq's nuclear capabilities were grossly overrated.

On November 29 the United Nations approves a resolution authorizing the use of "all necessary means"—including force—against Iraq if it does not withdraw from Kuwait by January 15, 1991. The vote is 12-2 (Cuba and Yemen vote no; China abstains), and is a big victory for the United States. But on Capitol Hill, where the Senate Armed Services Committee has opened hearings on the crisis, several respected former military commanders urge the administration to stop threatening war and let economic sanctions run their course.

On November 30 Bush says that in his determination "to go the extra mile for peace," he is ready to send Secretary of State Baker to Baghdad, and invites the Iraqi foreign minister, Tariq Aziz, to the White House.

At a press conference Bush explains his reasons for sending U.S. troops to the Gulf: They include concern for the hostages and the U.S. embassy staff in Kuwait, the atrocities taking place in Kuwait, and the threat of Iraq's nuclear arsenal. But how much, if any, of this public rhetoric reflects his real reasons?

What's in It for Us?

By November, President Bush seems to have made up his mind to go to war. The president's rhetoric grows increasingly belligerent: He paints Saddam Hussein as an aggressive dictator who can threaten world peace with nuclear and chemical weapons; Saddam's defeat is presented as a matter of great import to America's national security.

It is against the month's gyrating rhetoric that politicians and journalists begin to speculate on underlying reasons for war, beyond those stated by the Bush administration. Some theorists feel that Bush's apparent desire for war is based on the idea that war will make it possible, for the first time, to solve all the problems of the Middle East—opening the way for a solution to the Palestinian problem, and redrawing the map of the region, which had been arbitrarily outlined at the end of World War I after the dissolution of the Ottoman empire, in a way more favorable to the West.

Such ideas give the crisis in Iraq wider significance, and help to explain why the United States should be showing so great an interest in a Third World country with a population of eighteen million, whose only product is oil and whose economy has been badly damaged by its eight-year war with Iran.

As Saddam Hussein and George Bush conduct a war of words in the press, the real war is taking place quietly below the surface. Secretary of State James Baker meets with Syria's president Hafez al-Assad, and some speculate that Baker may have given Syria the green light for crushing Christian general Michel Aoun and his forces, in Northern Lebanon near the Syrian border, in exchange for Assad's participation in the Saudi Arabian expeditionary force—the Arab fig leaf for U.S. military intervention.

Theorists suspect that the American deal with Syria goes much further, perhaps extending to the establishment of new borders, extending into Lebanon, for both

Syria and Israel, and leading to a treaty between the two, similar to Jerusalem's successful deal with Egypt. (Israel's Prime Minister Yitzhak Shamir has said he would be willing to enter into negotiations with Syria alone.) In any such scenario the Palestinians, caught between the expanding Israelis and Syrians, will be crushed.

As part of a deal organized by Baker, the theory continues, Israel will reward Syria for its participation on the American side in the war with the Golan Heights—occupied by the Israelis since 1967—and even, perhaps, complete control of Lebanon down to the Litani River. Israel will be left in control of southern Lebanon, the Gaza strip, the West Bank, and the Old City of Jerusalem.

But U.S. deals with Syria and Israel, whose details remain top-secret, form just part of the possible shape of coming war. It is possible that in return for its participation in the war, Turkey has been promised the disputed northern provinces of Mossul and Kirkuk. Both these provinces were stripped from the Ottoman empire after the First World War. Along with the southern port city of Basra—Iran's longed-for prize in its eight-year war with Iraq—these provinces have only belonged to Iraq since the British stopped controlling them less than three generations ago. Turkey wants to get these provinces back, and since the oil fields in this area are probably near exhaustion, the U.S. would be agreeable to their annexation.

Theoretically, then, the victors in the war might carve up defeated Iraq. Kuwait will be returned to its former rulers, and the U.S. will establish control over the crippled leadership in Baghdad to rule over an amputee Iraq.

By this scenario, or some version of it, the U.S. will be in direct military control of all the oil fields and facilities in Iraq, Kuwait, Saudi Arabia, and the Gulf sheikhdoms —over 50 percent of all the world's oil reserves. We will have a stranglehold on all oil supplies to Japan, Germany, and the rest of Europe. Such control of the world's oil will allay American fears of being left behind Germany and Japan after 1992. They may make our cars, the logic goes, but we will have the oil they need to grease them—not to mention their winter fuel reserves.

In addition to these ideas, there are suspicions that President Bush and Prime Minister Thatcher had gotten together prior to the invasion of Kuwait and agreed to get rid of Saddam Hussein, come what may. This theory suggests that Bush and Thatcher may have purposefully misled Saddam into thinking that they would not react with military force to his invasion, all the while making plans to do just that. By this reasoning, the decision to go to war with Iraq, including a major ground war, was made well in advance, and all the democratic gestures that evolved between August 2 and January 16, 1991 —including the U.N. Security Council resolutions, congressional authorization, and diplomatic entreaties to Saddam—were nothing more than a sophisticated public relations game.

These "wild conspiracy theories" will stay alive throughout the war, evidence of the widespread and persistent suspicions over the Bush administration's true goals in the Gulf. They may prove to be only partly correct. What is clear is that they answer the question "what's in it for us?" more plausibly than many of the official explanations offered by the U.S. government.

November 1, 1990

By November, the embargo on Iraqi oil means Americans are paying higher prices at the gas pumps, and the oil consumers in the already strapped countries of the Third World and Eastern Europe face potentially devastating price increases. But as *The New Republic*'s Michael Kinsley observes, to the oil producers in Texas (in a slump since the mid-1980s) and Saudi Arabia, the Gulf Crisis is a boon that stands to make them $100 billion a year.

WINNERS IN THE OIL CRISIS
MICHAEL KINSLEY
The Washington Post

Texans are trying hard not to appear smug this time. They are not flaunting their renewed oil wealth or sneering at people from less fortunate regions. It's partly superstition—they can't believe their luck—and partly hard-learned tact. After their obnoxious behavior the last go-around, they don't want to offend those who regard the Gulf crisis as no cause for celebration.

Nevertheless, the figures are impressive. Texas pumped 716 million barrels of oil last year. The price bumps around a lot these days, but even without actual fighting it is roughly $15 a barrel higher than a year ago. That works out to a nice $10 billion infusion into the state economy. Texas's proved oil reserves as of 1988 were more than 7 billion barrels. By definition, that was oil that could be profitable at the then-current price of about $13 a barrel. At $33 a barrel, that oil is worth $140 billion more.

The numbers derive from one of my favorite well-thumbed volumes, the Basic Petroleum Data Book, published three times a year by the American Petroleum Institute. When it comes to dreams of avarice, "Dallas" and "Dynasty" have nothing on it. The latest oil crisis, like earlier ones, is redistributing wealth on a scale that trivializes all surrounding "policy" debates, such as our recent tiff over taxes and last spring's discussion about financial aid for the Soviet Union and Eastern Europe.

The world is extracting oil from the ground at a rate of about 21 billion barrels a year. (The petroleum people call it "production," but I prefer "extraction": they didn't make the stuff.) A $15 price increase means a transfer of more than $300 billion a year from unlucky people to lucky ones. Total world reserves as of Jan. 1 were slightly over a trillion barrels (and growing, by the way). The recent price increase, if it holds, raises the value of those assets by almost three times the entire U.S. gross national product. The United States consumes more than 6 billion barrels of oil a year. Our "Gulf crisis surcharge," at $15 a barrel, approaches $100 billion a year, about half of which goes to domestic extractors and half to foreigners.

I do not mean to suggest that anyone actually relishes this crisis. But owners of oil would have to be superhuman not to have mixed feelings with that kind of money at stake.

As in earlier episodes, domestic oil extractors have managed to compound their gain in Washington. The budget bill includes a variety of new tax breaks for oil and gas. Although they are supposedly intended to encourage increased exploration and drilling, these tax favors generally do not distinguish between truly new production and oil that is being pumped anyway. They are piously directed at "small" producers, as if the typical small oil producer really needed to worry where his next Mercedes was coming from.

Who else wins big from the new oil crisis? There have been the usual accusations of rip-off directed at the big oil companies. The charges are somewhat unfair. The companies have not been overcharging at the pump. It's true that pump prices took off quickly after Aug. 2 and have not come down as crude oil prices moderated. But the pump price never reflected the full increase in crude prices. The big windfall is in extracting oil from the ground, not in refining it into gasoline. For Arco, which extracts almost exactly as much oil as it refines, profits are way up. For Mobil, which refines more than twice as much oil as it extracts, profits are down.

Saudi Arabia wins twice: first in higher prices for the oil it is already selling and second by selling an extra 2 million barrels a day as a service to the war effort. Last year's Saudi production was about 1.8 billion barrels. An extra $15 profit per barrel equals $27 billion a year. Two million new barrels a day at $33 a barrel is another $24 billion in revenue (less $1.95 or whatever pittance it costs to get the oil out of the ground out there). Total: more than $50 billion. This should temper our gratitude for the $12 billion the Saudis have offered to pay in support of American forces defending their relative freedom.

The world's biggest oil extractor is the Soviet Union. The Soviets extract more than 4 billion barrels a year and export about a fifth of that. Until recently, most Soviet exports have been to members of the Eastern bloc at essentially fictional prices. But that ends Jan. 1, when the Soviet Union starts charging its former satellites world prices and demanding payment in hard currency. At $33 a barrel, a fifth of Soviet production would bring in something approaching $30 billion. The Soviet Union also exports huge quantities of natural gas, whose price will go up in tandem with oil.

And the losers in the great oil wealth transfer? Eastern Europe, which was just steeling itself for the shock of paying $18 of hard currency for a barrel of oil when it learned it would have to pay more than $30. The cost is in the billions per nation, making our aid offer of the odd $100 million here and there look even more irrelevant. The non-oil Third World loses big again, as usual. And of course American consumers, who, though they lose the least from the highest base, can be counted upon to complain the loudest.

November 12, 1990

Just after President Bush's post-Election Day decision to send 200,000 additional troops to the Gulf, Pulitzer Prize–winning historian Arthur Schlesinger, Jr. urges the administration to observe the wisdom of the Constitution and pursue congressional approval for any use of force against Iraq.

IRAQ, WAR AND THE CONSTITUTION
ARTHUR SCHLESINGER, JR.
The Wall Street Journal

"The use of armed forces outside the country without sanction from . . . the Congress," the president said last March, "is ruled out categorically, once and for all. The only exception will be in the case of a surprise armed attack from outside."

Alas, this was not the president of the U.S. speaking. It was the president of the Soviet Union. The Soviet foreign minister repeated the point the other day. "Any use of Soviet troops outside the country," Eduard Shevardnadze said, "demands a decision of the Soviet Parliament."

The Soviet leadership has thus adopted the theory of the American Constitution. Paradoxically, the American leadership appears to have adopted the old Soviet theory: that the decision to go to war is the prerogative of the executive. "I have an obligation as president," Mr. Bush says, "to conduct the foreign policy of this country the way I see fit." He has thus rejected congressional requests that he agree not to initiate military action in the Gulf without congressional approval during the long adjournment till mid-January.

At a recent hearing of the Foreign Relations Committee, Sen. Claiborne Pell held up a newspaper with the headline "Shevardnadze Promises to Consult Parliament on Gulf Involvement." Secretary of State James Baker rejoined: "We should not have a constitutional argument . . . about whether or not the president, as commander in chief, has the constitutional authority to commit forces. It's been done going all the way back, I think, to World War II."

Does President Bush really have the constitutional power, as commander in chief or otherwise, to take the country into offensive war in the Gulf without congressional authorization?

Senators, Republicans as well as Democrats, told the secretary that they accepted the protection of American citizens as ground for the president to order limited military action on his own but insisted that sustained and massive intervention required congressional approval. In rejecting this argument, Secretary Baker was prudent to confine his case for presidential initiative to the past half century.

The belief that the president has the authority to commit forces to combat on his own is a latter-day novelty. The Constitution of 1789 quite clearly gave Congress the exclusive power to authorize war. Presidents who breached the Constitution before the Second World War, like Lincoln in the spring of 1861 and Franklin Roosevelt in the autumn of 1941, did so knowingly and under the excuse of overwhelming national emergency. They did not claim the right to go to war as an inherent and routine presidential power.

Secretary Baker suggests that the president's role as commander in chief has become a sufficient source of authority to go to war. The Framers would hardly have accepted this argument. In the 69th Federalist, Alexander Hamilton observed that the commander-in-chief clause granted the president no more than the command of the armed forces —in contrast to the British king, whose power "extends to the *declaring* of war and to the *raising* and *regulating* of fleets and armies,—all which, by the Constitution under consideration, would appertain to the legislature.". . .

It is true enough, as President Bush said the other day, that "history is replete with examples" where presidents have ordered military action without congressional authorization. There is indeed a well-known litany of 19th-century military interventions on unilateral presidential initiative. But these actions were not directed against sovereign states. Nearly all were designed to protect the lives and property of American citizens against stateless and lawless bands—revolutionaries, angry mobs, savage tribes, brigands, pirates.

Such interventions differ fundamentally from war against organized governments both in the juridical status of the combatants and in the limited nature of the conflicts. Presidents decided that police actions, not directed against sovereign states and not requiring special congressional appropriations, did not rise to the dignity of formal legislative concern.

Early presidents also engaged in activities directed against sovereign states. But these were furtive, secret and deniable —as if the presidents wanted their agents in the field to do things they knew lay beyond the constitutional right to command. . . .

The fatal moment came in 1950 when President Truman committed American forces to the defense of South Korea. Then Sen. Robert A. Taft said that there was "no legal authority" for President Truman's decision and offered to support a joint resolution authorizing American intervention. But the president was persuaded by Dean Acheson, his secretary of state, an eminent lawyer, former law clerk of the revered Justice Louis Brandeis, to rely instead on presumed constitutional powers as president and commander in chief. (I backed Truman against Taft then. I was wrong.)

Ironically, many who claim the decision to go to war as an inherent presidential right are also advocates of what Attorney General Edwin Meese called "the Jurisprudence of Original Intention." History creates a dilemma for these "originalists." For no one can doubt that the original intent of the Framers was to deny the executive branch the power to authorize war and to reject the monarchical notion that foreign policy was the private property of the president. It is logically impossible to be a champion both of original intent and of unilateral executive war-making power.

As one who regards the Constitution as a document drawn for the ages, I am not troubled by departure from original intent. It may well be that the exact allocation of power as formulated for a minor 18th-century state does not meet the needs of a 20th-century superpower. In a dangerous world, situations may arise where national emergencies require presidents to act as Lincoln and FDR did.

Yet the Founding Fathers were pretty sagacious fellows. When they drafted a Constitution that commanded a partnership between the legislative and executive branches in foreign as well as domestic affairs, we should not lightly discard their broad conception.

November 13, 1990

As the nation gears up for war with Iraq, American policymakers seem quickly to forget that for years the U.S.
supported Saddam Hussein as a stablizing force in the
Middle East and a buffer against a more dangerous
enemy—fundamentalist Iran. Milton Viorst, who covers
the Middle East for *The New Yorker*, warns that a military defeat of Saddam might leave the U.S. facing worse
threats than Iraq: chaotic instability in the region, and
the unchecked fervor of the Iranians.

WAR AND CONSEQUENCES
MILTON VIORST
The Washington Post

It would be ironic if, by the law of unintended consequences,
the Gulf crisis ends where it began—with revolutionary Iran,
the most powerful state in the Middle East, threatening Arabs
and Israelis alike with its militant pietism.

Indeed, once the genies of war are let loose, it is possible to
imagine a range of unintended consequences: the overthrow
of moderate regimes in Egypt and Jordan by Islamic radicals,
multiplying the vulnerability of Israel; the collapse of the fragile sheikhdoms of the Gulf, sending the price of oil soaring for
the next decade; a quixotic uprising of Kurds, shaking the
regimes not just in Iraq but in Syria, Turkey and Iran.

Out of the mix of possible consequences, however, the
greatest likelihood is an abrupt end to the equilibrium on the
Iraq-Iran border, which was Saddam Hussein's gift—Gen. H.
Norman Schwarzkopf, U.S. commander in the Gulf, said as
much in a recent interview in The *New York Times*—to international stability.

A decade ago, the Middle East was in serious jeopardy from
the legions of Ayatollah Khomeini, bent on spreading their
Shiite fundamentalist faith into the Arab world, Iraq's Shiites,
a majority of the population, were tipping to their side. So
were strong Shiite minorities in Saudi Arabia and Kuwait.

Historians may debate whether Saddam committed gratu-
itous aggression or was provoked into initiating war, but the

fact is that he took on Khomeini, fused his own deeply het-
erogeneous people into a nation with a single purpose and
fought the fundamentalist revolution to a dead halt.

The Iraqis did not wage a pretty war. Outnumbered three
to one in population, they enjoyed greater firepower and used
poison gas to win battles when they had to, though military
experts generally agree that gas was not the key to their ultimate victory. Mostly, they won by digging in and inflicting
heavier losses than they took, going on the offensive only
when the Iranians were badly weakened by the attrition of
their manpower.

It seemed obvious as the war approached an end that Iraq's
battle-hardened army of a million men was likely to be a loose
cannon in the region once it had no enemy. Rather wisely, the
United States made serious efforts at that juncture to overcome the animosity that had long marked its relations and to
reach a rapprochement that might contain a restless Iraq.

But dealing with a brutal, dictatorial regime that is
insensitive to international public opinion was not easy. Critics
glibly assert that the State Department did too much to
accommodate Saddam Hussein. The real question, I believe,
was whether we did enough to bring him into a system of
international order.

We know Saddam is an unsophisticated, insular man who
yearns for respect from other world leaders. He believed he
had earned it by his triumph over Iran, and perhaps he had.
Would it have made a difference if he had been invited to
Washington or Paris to take a few bows? I suspect it would, but
after he gassed his own Kurds—insurgents, but Iraqi citizens
—no Western head of state could have received him on an official visit. And so the scenario of the loose cannon came to pass.

It alighted on Kuwait, for reasons that also came out of the
war. Throughout eight years of bloody fighting, the Kuwaitis,
like the Saudis, looked on—as they are looking on now while
others prepare to fight for them. They supported Iraq with
money, which seemed only reasonable; but unlike the Saudis,
they demanded full repayment, with interest. Expecting the
debt to be forgiven, the Iraqis were stunned, and the dispute
became increasingly acerbic until it exploded on Aug. 2 with
the invasion.

It is no defense of that invasion to say that President Bush
must now decide whether it is in America's interest to settle

up with Iraq or make war—and that is where the law of unintended consequences comes in. Do the president's advisers
really believe, even if we win quickly and with minimal losses,
that our Army would be able to pack up and come home?

It would take a monumental effort to put the Humpty-
Dumpty of the Middle East back together, and the United
States—with its money and its men—would be stuck with
doing it.

Iran would be at the top of the agenda. It is naive to think
that the revolution, though currently demoralized, has out-
grown expansionism. Khomeini, before he died, made clear
his belief that the cease-fire was temporary. If we now destroy
Iraq, we would still have to re-create it as a military
power—unless we are prepared ourselves to remain for years
on the Euphrates.

What makes far greater sense is for us to figure out what
kind of order we can live with in the Middle East—taking into
account not just Kuwait but arms and oil prices, and maybe
even the Israeli-Palestinian dispute. Then we ought to get on
with negotiations, because even a victorious war would bring
no end of surprises, unpredictable in nature but surely
unpleasant.

Chapter 6

DECEMBER 1990

THE HOME FRONT

Chronology

On December 1 Saddam Hussein accepts President Bush's offer for talks, although he seeks to link resolution of the Gulf crisis to the Israeli occupation of Palestinian territory. Vice President Dan Quayle, in an interview, says, "Palestine is not an issue on the table. There is no linkage." The next day Secretary of State Baker says the crisis could be resolved if Saddam Hussein left Kuwait and released the hostages.

On December 5 Israeli foreign minister David Levy warns that Israel may attack Iraq if the U.S. fails to force a withdrawal from Kuwait and a dismantling of the Iraqi military machine.

On December 6 Saddam Hussein says he will soon release all the foreign hostages held in Kuwait and Iraq. There are no conditions. (On November 18 Saddam had offered to release hostages in small groups over a three-month period; before that he tied their release to a Western guarantee not to attack.) By the end of the second week in December most of the the hostages have

149

left Kuwait and Iraq, and the U.S. shuts its beleaguered embassy in Kuwait.

The agreed-upon American-Iraqi talks to resolve the crisis founder. Neither side can fix an acceptable date. High-level administration officials travel to Capitol Hill to rebut the string of antiwar witnesses appearing before Congress. Secretary of Defense Cheney says sanctions aren't likely to force Iraq out of Kuwait even if they are "given five years." CIA Director William Webster seems to contradict Cheney when he tells Congress that the sanctions have dealt a "serious blow" but adds, "We do not believe [Saddam] is troubled by the hardships Iraqis will be forced to endure."

As the month ends, there is a gathering realization that war may be inevitable.

The Home Front

On the home front, President Bush begins to encounter resistance to his war policies in Iraq. The Catholic bishops and the National Council of Churches both take a stand against any war in the Persian Gulf. Members of Congress are asking more pointed questions. Chief among them is Sam Nunn, the chairman of the Senate Armed Services Committee. Nunn wants to give sanctions more time to work before rushing into war. A parade of respected military commanders testifies before the House and Senate, urging caution. Some question whether a war would not unavoidably force the country to reinstitute a draft. A growing number of military reservists file as conscientious objectors, claiming they only joined the military to pay for their educations. "I'm a conscientious objector because I don't believe in killing another human being," says one young woman. "I joined the army to pay my way through college. I was more naive than I am now."

The nascent antiwar movement is getting its real push from another source—the environmental movement, which is beginning to see the war fever as a smokescreen for the president's energy policies at home.

Environmentalists, most of whom had long ago abandoned their confrontational approach to corporations and government in search of a middle ground, had hoped to work with Bush, who had promised to address the needs of the environment. They watched and waited as the oil spill legislation dragged on, and as both Democrats and Republicans blocked an auto efficiency bill in the fall of 1990. Now they can scarcely believe the outlines of the real Bush energy policy.

Despite the recent signing of the first Clean Air Act in thirteen years and passage of legislation aimed at controlling oil spills, the Bush administration's National Energy Strategy (NES), made public in December, is unswerving in its pursuit of an economy based on increased use of fossil fuels, especially oil and gas.

The new Bush energy strategy was to have been derived from a series of option papers prepared by the Department of Energy over the past year and a half. Virtually everyone who participated in the process emphasized energy efficiency. But when Energy Secretary James Watkins sent the White House proposals incorporating these different concepts, he got back a redlined version from Bush's chief of staff, former New Hampshire governor and nuke fan John Sununu. What Sununu wanted was an energy policy that opened the Arctic, including the fragile wildlife reserves in northern Alaska, to oil and gas drilling. As an incentive to companies exploring this territory, various tax breaks would be offered, including restitution of the notorious oil depletion allowance, which allowed oilmen to deduct the hypothetical decline in their worth as they pumped the petroleum out of their lands.

Before Congress adjourned for the fall 1990 elections, there had been heated debate over the so-called CAFE standards, which set the levels for automobile efficiency. The new, revised White House option papers don't even mention CAFE standards, nor consider mass transit. The government wants to push ahead with synthetic fuels from coal buried beneath the western prairies. Strangest of all, the plans talk of burning toxic wastes in urban centers, which will spew dioxin and other noxious gases into the air and create tons of hazardous ash.

The NES doesn't cause a ripple in the mainstream press, which is mesmerized by the non-news coming in from the Gulf, but word of Sununu's action spreads quickly through the environmental community—and it becomes one of the major reasons that Greenpeace and other environmental groups decide to join the small and tentative movement against war in the Gulf.

By the 1970s the environmental movement had emerged as the largest white, middle-class political movement, the clear successor to the civil rights movement. Its politics, however, were mainstream, and its tactics were generally cautious and low-key. As time went on, the movement changed, with groups like Greenpeace springing up to challenge the more staid conservation-oriented organizations like the Audubon Society and the Sierra Club. What began as a moderate effort to control pollution and establish parks and wilderness areas by conservatives often aligned with the Republican Party had, by the late 1970s, begun to challenge the fundamentals of the industrial revolution. Under President Jimmy Carter environmentalists achieved a first, tenuous initiative away from fossil fuels to conservation and renewable fuel sources. Reagan, with George Bush as his vice-president, reversed those initiatives. But with the end of the Cold War, and talk of a peace dividend, the enviromental movement once more asserted itself. It challenged the accepted policies of the oil and gas industry by winning legislation after Exxon Valdez towards curbing oil spills, and passage of a clean air act. It challenged the petrochemical industry over the manufacture of ozone-depleting chemicals, and launched a worldwide campaign against global warming.

The war seemed to be the most naked throwback to the policies of an earlier age. And as the war began a peace movement took shape. Just as it did during the Vietnam war, it included students, churches and unions. But this time there were thousands of Vietnam veterans in the marches, and, significantly, organized environmentalists. During Vietnam environmentalists, who were just emerging as a force, had remained on the sidelines. Now Greenpeace, with 2.5 million members in the United States and five million worldwide, takes a position against any war in the Gulf, and by January it will have plunged into the peace movement, helping to organize a mass march on Washington, and even setting up its own reporting system during the war.

By the end of January 1991, the budding antiwar movement will be largely eclipsed by a surge of prowar sentiment. But the war itself brings lasting destruction to the environment of the Middle East, and there are signs that the environmental movement may take the lead in any long-term critical resistance to American policies abroad and at home. In this context, the war is not only a war for resources, which will become increasingly scarce over the next century, but a war to override political opposition at home. It is a war for the future.

December 5, 1990

On December 5, while the military buildup in the Gulf continues, William Webster, the director of Central Intelligence, testifies before the House Armed Services Committee on the effectiveness of sanctions against Iraq.

CIA DIRECTOR WILLIAM WEBSTER'S STATEMENT TO THE HOUSE ARMED SERVICES COMMITTEE ON SANCTIONS AGAINST IRAQ
Washington, D.C.

The blockade and embargo have worked more effectively than Saddam probably expected. More than 90 percent of imports and 97 percent of exports have been shut off. Although there is smuggling across Iraq's borders, it is extremely small relative to Iraq's pre-crisis trade. Iraqi efforts to break sanctions have thus far been largely unsuccessful. What little leakage that has occurred is due largely to a relatively small number of private firms acting independently. We believe most countries are actively enforcing the sanctions and plan to continue doing so.

Industry appears to be the hardest hit sector so far. Many firms are finding it difficult to cope with the departure of foreign workers and with the cutoff of imported industrial inputs—which comprised nearly 60 percent of Iraq's total imports prior to the invasion. These shortages have either shut down or severely curtailed production by a variety of industries, including many light industrial and assembly plants as well as the country's only tire-manufacturing plant. Despite these shutdowns, the most vital industries—including electric power generation and refining—do not yet appear threatened. We believe they will be able to function for some time because domestic consumption has been reduced, because Iraqi and Kuwaiti facilities have been cannibalized and because some stockpiles and surpluses already existed.

The cutoff of Iraq's oil exports and the success of sanctions also have choked off Baghdad's financial resources. This too has been more effective and more complete than Saddam expected. In fact, we believe that a lack of foreign exchange will, in time, be Iraq's greatest economic difficulty. The embargo has deprived Baghdad of roughly $1.5 billion of foreign exchange earnings monthly. We have no evidence that Iraq has significantly augmented the limited foreign exchange reserves to which it still has access. As a result, Baghdad is working to conserve foreign exchange and to devise alternative methods to finance imports.

We believe Baghdad's actions to forestall shortages of food stocks—including rationing, encouraging smuggling, and promoting agricultural production—are adequate for the next several months. The fall harvest of fruits and vegetables is injecting new supplies into the market and will provide a psychological as well as tangible respite from mounting pressures. The Iraqi population, in general, has access to sufficient staple foods. Other foodstuffs—still not rationed—also remain available. However, the variety is diminishing and prices are sharply inflated. For example, sugar purchased on the open market at the official exchange rate went from $32 per 50 kilogram bag in August to $580 per bag last month. Baghdad remains concerned about its food stocks and continues to try to extend stocks and, increasingly, to divert supplies to the military. In late November, Baghdad cut civilian rations for the second time since the rationing program began while announcing increases in rations for military personnel and their families.

On balance, the embargo has increased the economic hardships facing the average Iraqi. In order to supplement their rations, Iraqis must turn to the black market, where most goods can be purchased but at highly inflated prices. They are forced to spend considerable amounts of time searching for reasonably priced food or waiting in lines for bread and other rationed items. In addition, services ranging from medical care to sanitation have been curtailed. But these hardships are easier for Iraqis to endure than the combination of economic distress, high casualty rates, and repeated missile and air attacks that Iraqis lived with during the eight-year Iran-Iraq war. During this war, incidentally, there was not a single significant public disturbance even though casualties hit 2.3 percent of the total Iraqi population—about the same as the percentage of U.S. casualties during the Civil War.

Looking ahead, the economic picture changes somewhat. We expect Baghdad's foreign exchange reserves to become extremely tight, leaving it little cash left with which to entice potential sanctions-busters. At current rates of depletion, we estimate Iraq will have nearly depleted its available foreign exchange reserves by next spring. Able to obtain even fewer key imports, Iraq's economic problems will begin to multiply as Baghdad is forced to gradually shut down growing numbers of facilities in order to keep critical activities functioning as long as possible. Economic conditions will be noticeably worse, and Baghdad will find allocating scarce resources a significantly more difficult task.

Probably only energy-related and some military industries will still be fully functioning by next spring. This will almost certainly be the case by next summer. Baghdad will try to keep basic services such as electric power from deteriorating. The regime also will try to insulate critical military industries to prevent an erosion of military preparedness. Nonetheless, reduced rations, coupled with rapid inflation and little additional support from the government will compound the economic pressures facing most Iraqis . . .

Although sanctions are hurting Iraq's civilian economy, they are affecting the Iraqi military only at the margins. Iraq's fairly static, defensive posture will reduce wear and tear on military equipment and, as a result, extend the life of its inventory of spare parts and maintenance items. Under non-combat conditions, Iraqi ground and air forces can probably maintain near-current levels of readiness for as long as nine months.

We expect the Iraqi air force to feel the effects of the sanctions more quickly and to a greater degree than the Iraqi ground forces because of its greater reliance on high technology and foreign equipment and technicians. Major repairs to sophisticated aircraft like the F-1 will be achieved with significant difficulty, if at all, because of the exodus of foreign technicians. Iraqi technicians, however, should be able to maintain current levels of aircraft sorties for three to six months.

The Iraqi ground forces are more immune to sanctions. Before the invasion, Baghdad maintained large inventories of basic military supplies, such as ammunition, and supplies probably remain adequate. The embargo will eventually hurt Iraqi armor by preventing the replacement of old fire-control systems and creating shortages of additives for various critical lubricants. Shortages will also affect Iraqi cargo trucks over time.

Mr. Chairman, while we can look ahead several months and predict the gradual deterioration of the Iraqi economy, it is more difficult to assess how or when these conditions will cause Saddam to modify his behavior. At present, Saddam almost certainly assumes that he is coping effectively with the sanctions. He appears confident in the ability of his security services to contain potential discontent, and we do not believe he is troubled by the hardships Iraqis will be forced to endure. Saddam's willingness to sit tight and try to outlast the sanctions or, in the alternative, to avoid war by withdrawing from Kuwait will be determined by his total assessment of the political, economic, and military pressures arrayed against him.

December 6, 1990

While Saddam's opponents speculate about Iraq's
nuclear capability, William Arkin, the director of
Greenpeace's Nuclear Unit, points out that it is the
U.S. that has maintained an arsenal in the region—a
fact that raises the stakes in the Gulf conflict to
terrifying levels.

U.S. HANGS NUKES OVER IRAQ
WILLIAM ARKIN
The Cleveland Plain Dealer

Washington

There's been a lot of loose talk recently about Iraq's nuclear
capability, but nary a word has been uttered about the only
real nuclear arsenal in the Persian Gulf—America's. There are
more than 100 B-61 nuclear bombs, deliverable by F-111 jets,
stockpiled just 70 minutes flight time from Baghdad at the
U.S. Incirlik air base in southern Turkey.

In addition, the U.S. Navy has 25 nuclear-armed ships and
submarines in the region. Four aircraft carriers store nuclear
bombs for attack aircraft. And 11 surface warships and a half-
dozen nuclear-powered attack submarines are armed with
Tomahawk sea-launched cruise missiles.

In all, close to 500 naval nuclear weapons are aboard the
mobilized U.S. armada.

What are U.S. nuclear weapons doing in the Middle East?
U.S. military planners have gone on record to assert that the
United States would not and, from a purely pragmatic point
of view, need not use nuclear weapons in a war over Kuwait.
The conventional forces mobilized to the region, they
maintain, will provide a credible offensive force to destroy all
the necessary targets in a war against Iraq.

But this widespread military assessment that nuclear
weapons are unnecessary has not been translated into a
definitive policy statement, and nowhere has there been a flat-
out rejection by President George Bush or Defense Secretary
Dick Cheney of any use of nuclear weapons. Thus, there
remains the possibility that if the conventional force proves
inadequate in a showdown, nuclear weapons could come
under consideration.

Indeed, in October, then-British Prime Minister Margaret Thatcher responded to a report in the Observer newspaper that British troops in the Gulf had been given the go-ahead to use nuclear weapons to respond to an Iraqi chemical attack. Thatcher said she "knew of no authority" for the report, but neither did she deny the option. "You'd have to consider at the time, if chemical weapons were used against us, precisely what our reply should be," she stated.

Various top administration officials have used similar language to describe American options. "If we have to fight a war, we're going to fight it with all we have," declared Defense Undersecretary Paul Wolfowitz. And Secretary Cheney has spoken of our "wide range of military capabilities that will let us respond with overwhelming force."

While no one in Washington interprets such statements as nuclear threats, that doesn't mean Iraq dismisses the option so cavalierly. And that is the point of the U.S. nuclear ambiguity: to keep Saddam guessing.

But what if Saddam guesses wrong? What if, in the midst of an all-out conventional war, he concludes that the U.S. nuclear option will be exercised, even if only as a last resort, and he therefore unleashes a massive chemical assault against American troops—as Foreign Minister Tariq Aziz has promised will happen if nuclear weapons are used?

The consequences of such an action—an action made more possible by the mere presence of our nuclear weapons in the Gulf—are too horrible to contemplate. The fact is, nuclear weapons are "passing through" during this crisis for the simple reason that it is "standard operating procedure." The nuclear bombs in Turkey didn't arrive yesterday; they have been there for 30 years as part of NATO's nuclear strategy against the Soviet Union. The aircraft carriers have been nuclear-armed for Soviet conflict since the 1950s, and surface warships have carried nuclear missiles since 1962.

When conflict with the Soviet Union lurked as an uncertainty behind every crisis, such nuclear deployments were justified as an insurance policy to deter, or respond to, an attack by another nuclear superpower. Yet here they are in the post-Cold War era, positioned not against a Soviet threat but against a non-nuclear (albeit threshold-nuclear) power in the Middle East.

To be fair, the military is struggling to redefine its role in this new era. But if the Pentagon is so accustomed to having nuclear weapons at its disposal that 500 warheads can just pass through the storm in the Middle East like a Mr. Magoo character, then the danger exists that such antiquated habits will be rationalized into new policies. Shipping nuclear weapons around the world, and introducing them into every regional crisis, could create new standard operating procedures and be a temptation for a new nuclear dogma for the Third World.

If, on the other hand, our nuclear weapons are actually intended as a deterrent to Iraq, then this implies that we could use them. This would be a disaster of unimaginable proportions. Any short-term military gains of such an action—or even the threat of such—would be far outweighed by the political fallout, including the probable rupturing of the coalition of Western and Arab nations arrayed against Iraq. It would also cripple our nuclear non-proliferation efforts by serving as a powerful signal to the Third World that development of nuclear arsenals is in their own interest.

If our nuclear weapons are not intended as a deterrent to Iraq, but are merely a meaningless vestige of Cold War policy, then we are foolish to put them in harm's way in a region dominated by a leader whom President Bush equates with Hitler. They would be safer back home, and so would the world.

December 24, 1990

By the end of December, opponents of President Bush's Gulf policy have begun to question the wisdom—and the necessity—of going to war to restore the sovereignty of a tiny, despotic, oil-rich shiekhdom. Noting that as much as $250 billion in Kuwaiti petrodollars is invested in the U.S. and Britain, journalist Peter Dale Scott suggests other reasons behind the rhetoric.

U.S. HUNGRY FOR KUWAITI PETRODOLLARS—NOT JUST OIL

PETER DALE SCOTT
Pacific News Service

Along with Iraq's withdrawal from Kuwait, President Bush has insisted on restoring Kuwait's ruling al-Sabah family as a key condition for resolving the Gulf crisis. The reason isn't just to retain U.S. control over Kuwaiti oil. Equally important, Washington wants to ensure control of a continued flow of Kuwaiti petrodollars into the capital-hungry investment markets of the U.S. and other industrial nations.

The overseas investments of the Kuwaiti government in exile in Saudi Arabia—a government controlled by the al-Sabah family—have long been estimated at more than $100 billion. But educated Middle Easterners believe the figure is much higher—perhaps $250 billion has been invested in the economies of Britain and the U.S. alone. Years of prudent investment of those petrodollars have bought the al-Sabahs extensive political influence in Washington and elsewhere.

The *Manchester Guardian* has reported that Kuwait owns stock in almost all of the top 70 firms on the New York Stock Exchange. In addition to owning the U.S. oil and gas exploration firm Santa Fe International, the Kuwait Petroleum Company by 1981 had invested some $250 million in other U.S. oil companies, including almost 3.89 percent of Atlantic Richfield and 2.39 percent of Phillips Petroleum.

Meanwhile another arm of the al-Sabah government, the Kuwait Investment Office (KIO), has become the largest

foreign investor in Spain, and reputedly the largest foreign
investor in Japan. In Great Britain, the KIO now holds 9.9
percent (down from a high of 22 percent) of British Petroleum,
Britain's largest corporation, and 10 percent of the Midland
Bank.

Such investments do not purchase control, but they do buy
financial and political allies. Kuwait no longer behaves as it
did in the early 1970s, when a former Kuwaiti investment
entity used its clout to exclude Jewish firms from international
lending syndicates. Since then the KIO has generally acted as
a model silent partner, offering capital when it is needed
without interfering with management.

Overall KIO investment strategy has aimed at securing
political allies as well as investment income. In nation after
nation KIO has become a minority partner of those with the
greatest political influence. In the United States, for example,
Kuwait purchased a 45 percent stake in the Hotel Phoenician
of the S&L figure Charles Keating, an investment that has
rendered no profits but gave Kuwait a connection to a man
with demonstrated influence at that time in the U.S. Senate.
Kuwait also invested in the politically influential Houston oil
community which backed Bush's bid to the presidency.

The same investment style has been used in other countries. In Italy the KIO purchased 6.7 percent of Ifil, the holding company of the Agnellis, Italy's most influential family. In
West Germany the KIO bought large passive holdings in the
corporate giants Hoechst (20 percent), Metallgesellschaft (20
percent), and Daimler Benz (14 percent).

In this way, the al-Sabahs guaranteed themselves powerful
allies in the West, from Norway to Canada to Australia. But
the Kuwaiti investment network is truly global, not just
western. In Malaysia, for example, Kuwait bought shares in
the New Straits Times Press, owned by the investment arm of
the dominant party in the ruling government coalition.

In Singapore the KIO became (at 10.6 percent) the fourth
largest shareholder in the Singapore Petroleum Company. It
purchased 49 percent of the securities firm J. M. Sassoon. And
it became an investment partner in a number of firms (including Hong Kong's ninth largest bank) with the powerful Hong
Leong group of the Malaysian Quck family.

The one major area of the non-communist world that does
not seem to have benefited prominently from Kuwaiti foreign

investment is the rest of the Middle East. This is a major source of the resentment felt against the al-Sabah family in the Arab-speaking world, and helps explain the popular Arab indifference to such acts as the Iraqi looting of affluent Kuwaiti institutions.

Kuwait's pro-western, influence-oriented investment strategy has served the al-Sabah family well in Kuwait's current crisis. It would be clearly difficult, if not impossible, for the receiving countries to allow control of these overseas assets to pass to Iraq, or to some subordinate Kuwaiti entity controlled by Saddam Hussein.

The petrodollars of Kuwait, reinforced by those of Saudi Arabia and the other Gulf oil sheikhdoms, are now a significant factor in the deficit-prone economies of the U.S. and Great Britain, and also in those major banks and corporations which (like Chase Manhattan and Chevron) count Arab investors among their largest minority shareholders. Total investment by OPEC members in the U.S. was estimated to be $200 billion in 1980, only seven years after the 1973 oil price increases. It is much larger today.

The al-Sabahs (along with the Saudis) will presumably continue to maintain their economic investment in the United States as long as President Bush continues to support the al-Sabahs politically. Even if the al-Sabahs lose permanent access to Kuwaiti oil fields, moreover, they will retain much of their wealth and influence. The vertically integrated Kuwait Petroleum Company, for example, no longer depends on Kuwaiti oil supplies. As the world's tenth largest oil corporation, it buys and sells oil around the world. And the family now controls roughly as much money from investment income, according to the *Financial Times*, as it does from oil revenues.

December 24, 1990

As the U.N. deadline draws close, the U.S. begins to gear up psychologically for war. And with the enemy located in Baghdad, one inevitable element of war fever is American misunderstanding of and hostility toward anything Arab or Islamic—a mood which, one Muslim teen observes, filters down even to the nation's classrooms.

A "CAMEL JOCKEY" IN AN AMERICAN CLASSROOM
FARIBA NAWA
Pacific News Service

With my blond hair and American accent no one would guess I'm an Afghan-born, Muslim-raised teenager. In school, I blend in with the crowd. At home, however, my mother still wears a scarf and reads the Koran.

Since the Gulf crisis began, I've felt an increased tension between Muslim students and the rest of the kids in my suburban California high school—a kind of Muslim bashing. "Why do Muslims want to be terrorists?" people ask in classes

My classmates don't apply the stereotypes they have of Muslims and Arabs to me, but I'm reminded of them constantly. They make jokes about my religion. I've heard them call Muslims names like "maddas lovers," referring to Saddam's name spelled backwards. It makes Muslims seem even more demon-like.

They confuse Islam with Hinduism. When they find out I'm a Muslim, they ask: "Do you worship cows?"; "Don't you wear red dots on your foreheads?" One boy even asked if Muslims were born with those dots.

From the day I came to the United States as a refugee at the age of 10 in 1983, I don't remember once learning about Islam at school although I've studied both Christianity and some Judaism. My "World Studies" textbooks in the seventh and ninth grades had small sections about Islam, but the teachers never got around to teaching them.

In a recent history class my teacher talked about the way Muslims treat their women. He sounded disapproving. As an example of how repressive Islam was he pointed out that the Saudis don't allow women to drive and asked what the class thought of that. There was a lot of snickering. Some students cracked jokes about how stupid the Saudis and Muslims must be. The teacher gave us no broader information about Islamic culture or the particular interpretation of the Koran followed by the Saudis.

While women can't drive in Saudi Arabia, next door in Kuwait, before the Iraqi invasion, 60 percent of university professors were female. In Iraq, 40 percent of the civil service is made up of women.

I finally stood up and told the class I was a Muslim, that I soon hope to have a driver's license and that the Koran teaches that men and women are equal. Then I asked how Americans can condemn and judge Muslims without knowing anything about the culture or the religion.

Islam is practiced widely, from Nigeria to the Philippines. Each culture interprets Islam in a different way, creating their own rules of dress, prayer and morality. Islam is a religion with one billion adherents worldwide; it is also the fastest growing religion in the U.S.—soon to be the second largest domestically, behind Christianity.

How will my classmates deal with a world that is one-quarter Muslim when they do not learn anything about it in school? Many of their parents already have strong prejudices against it. I find the same slurs and jokes out of school, written on bumper stickers, in editorial cartoons and on the radio—names like "camel jockey."

Muslims often stay to themselves and in that way stick out more than other cultural minorities. If people's husbands and children start dying in the Persian Gulf, they will make an easy scapegoat. Japanese Americans were ostracized in World War II, and sometimes I fear the same thing could happen to American Muslims in a Gulf war.

The bottom line is that we need better education about Islam and the Middle East. Yet even though Islam is getting some attention because of what's happening in the Gulf, most of it is negative. My only hope is that at least in the schools students will start learning that Islam and Saddam Hussein are not identical. Education in the end is the only force that can break through stereotypes.

December 27, 1990

With African Americans making up a disproportionate percentage of the forces preparing to risk their lives in war, many at home are skeptical about the justice of the impending conflict. Ron Walters, chairman of the Howard University Political Science department, argues that the Bush administration is playing race politics in the Gulf.

WHY SHOULD BLACKS FIGHT IN THE GULF?
RON WALTERS
The Washington Post

It appears to fascinate some Americans and annoy others that President Bush's stationing American troops in the Gulf has drawn a decidedly negative response from African Americans. In the past six weeks, blacks' opinion has moved from 43 percent approval of the president's policy in an early national poll to a low of 23 percent in a more recent one. In both, there was a distance of 30 to 40 points difference between the black and white rates of approval.

In assessing the reasons for this difference, the speculation has encountered the normal range of possibilities: blacks feel that Saddam Hussein's aggression was wrong but that Bush's military response is worse, placing them at an unacceptable level of vulnerability and deepening the nature of their disadvantages in society in the process. Then there is the provable fear of high black casualties in the event of war based on the Vietnam experience and given that the Defense Department admits that 28.7 percent of the troops in Saudi Arabia are black.

Blacks, like many other Americans, are suspicious of the motivations for the possible war. If it is to prove that America is still the policeman of the world, then the price is too high. If it is to secure supplies of oil, Africa stands ready to supply oil—including Angola, where Bush is conducting a policy favoring the rebel faction UNITA. If it is to develop a new regime of security in a post-Cold War world, no time could be better than this for experimenting fully with methods of resolving international conflict short of war.

What we know is that billions of petrodollars are now being made as a result of higher oil prices. And we know that the poor, who will fight this war, will not profit from the oil riches or the war itself.

Many feel that blacks and others who think similarly should forgo all of these considerations and approve the president's actions in the name of loyalty to the nation in a crisis. They pose the alternatives of blind loyalty and patriotism. Yet, black patriotism is unassailable: it should be kept in mind that the patriotism of black members of the military has never wavered in times of war. Historically they have felt a demonstration of patriotism was necessary to prove they had legitimate claims to equal treatment within American society once they returned from serving their country. Alas, it has not worked out that way. In fact, it is arguable that, considering the number of high-ranking black officers there, the military is the truest meritocratic system we have, far more so than society as a whole.

Blind loyalty of blacks to the president is prevented by the knowledge that the expenditure of billions of dollars in Saudi Arabia gives the lie to the frequent protestations of the lack of resources available for domestic urban priorities. This duplicity has contributed fundamentally to our own domestic "Gulf" policy, creating the generally different attitudes of blacks and whites toward the current crisis in the Middle East. A stubborn segment of the American public wants to pretend that racial disadvantages do not exist, that social policy must be operated on an individually "objective" basis. As a result, ameliorative policies are held hostage and the racial divide is widening in a country that holds out the promise of multi-racial democracy.

So it is important to understand that the recent actions of President Bush in the field of civil rights take place against the backdrop of a potential war that may require a disproportion-ate sacrifice by many "individual" blacks. But given the state of social policy it is logical to ask where the disproportionate understanding and rewards for their service will be.

There is the agonizing irony that while this philosophical and political debate drones on, black soldiers sit in the sands of Saudi Arabia in splendid equality, mobilized to die for their country, while their president has vetoed a measure—the Civil Rights Act of 1990—that would enhance the possibility for them to have the means to live in dignity. And if they should be lucky enough to return, they would find that he may also have taken away their right to college scholarships and placed them in a dangerous race-neutral pool.

To put it bluntly, the Bush administration is playing race politics in a manner that would continue to deny national resources to blacks, while black lives are disproportionately at stake as a result of his foreign policy. If no one will respect the nature of their sacrifice, then why should blacks especially be motivated to demand that their sons and daughters give it, considering the circumstances?

December 30, 1990

Public opinion in the United States remained divided on the question of war throughout the last six months of 1990. As this last year in a decade-and-a-half of peace draws to a close, *New York Times* columnist Tom Wicker believes that Americans, concerned with the poor state of the economy and the critical social problems in their own country, do not want to go to war in the Persian Gulf.

WAR AND MALAISE
TOM WICKER
The New York Times

Rochester, Vt.

Despite a flood of Christmas sentimentality about "the kids over there"—this time including women—little appetite for war in the Middle East can be found among the American people; quite the opposite.

As the announced deadline of Jan.15 approaches, the problem seems more than the natural reluctance of any nation to send its youth into war. It's more, I believe, than the obvious truth expressed by Senator Pat Leahy of Vermont to President Bush: "Americans support defensive measures to contain the Iraqi Army, but there is no consensus for. . . an offensive war that would cost the lives of thousands of Americans."

The unease is palpable—to some extent because memories of Vietnam remain so corrosive, and because Mr. Bush has not provided convincing reasons for another distant war in which, again, "allies" are likely to become fair-weather friends. No doubt, too, many Americans have heard with anxiety their military leaders' protests that U.S. forces, which will do most of the fighting and dying, are not yet ready for combat.

The end of the cold war, being celebrated only last Christmas, now seems far away and forgotten. The so-called peace dividend is fast disappearing into a military operation costing at least $25 billion a month even before the shooting starts.

Still, even more than all that is at the root of American malaise during a holiday season overshadowed by threats abroad and at home. Americans, it seems to me, are deeply troubled by the sheer incongruity of mounting a huge military operation abroad, the necessary purpose of which remains unclear, while the economy deteriorates at home, our children go begging and shooting, crime spirals upward, the schools educate poorly if at all, millions neither have nor can afford medical care and bridges fall down on the homeless sleeping beneath them.

A sampling of holiday domestic news makes the point:

Dec. 20—The Commerce Department revised its estimate of third-quarter growth in gross national product, from 1.7 percent to an anemic 1.4 percent. The fourth quarter will be worse.

Dec. 21—In 1990, the New York metropolitan area lost about 100,000 private industry jobs, according to a Federal survey. Three more of the nation's largest banks reported millions in bad-loan write-offs or dividend reductions. For 1991, U.S. businesses plan to expand spending by only 0.4 percent, the least in five years.

Dec. 22—The Federal Home Loan Bank Board's senior economist said it would take three to five years for growth to resume in New York City. U.S. health care spending was announced to have reached $304 billion last year; but though the law requires lead-poisoning tests for all the nation's 12 million poor children, only a third actually are being tested.

Dec. 23—In Washington, five children, one only 6 years old, were shot by other youngsters from a passing car; there have been 471 homicides in the city this year. The Federal budget office sought about $1 billion in reductions in aid to mass transit, despite a recent increase in the gasoline tax.

Dec. 24—Experts said the health of Americans in the inner cities had deteriorated to "critical condition," while the rest of us are healthier and living longer. Even the television networks suffered one of their worst years; all lost market share and CBS announced a fourth-quarter loss.

Dec. 25—Retailers reported "the poorest Christmas season in years" as shoppers didn't show up. Signs of the first U.S. price deflation since the 1940's also were reported—bad signs for a government, businesses and people burdened with debt.

Dec. 26—Further signaling recession, a wide spectrum of American manufacturers, caught in a price squeeze, are deferring plans to modernize and expand. Some are laying off employees.

And on and on. It's true that spending for another war might provide stimulus to a sick economy. But that's not only a distasteful way to prime and pump; it's inefficient, in lives and money. Already the Pentagon is having to pay premium prices—sometimes twice standard rates—for shipping space to the Gulf.

Anyway, it's not just economic problems but values that trouble the nation, as Jan. 15 nears. In Britain in 1930, leaders sought "peace in our time" and shrank from a war to defend a people "of whom we know little." Now, in ironic reversal, many Americans sense that their most pressing problems are here at home, largely unattended by leaders in the fatal grip of superpower illusions, who hasten them into ill-considered war.

Chapter 7

JANUARY–FEBRUARY 1991

ASSESSING THE DAMAGES

Chronology

As 1991 begins, the Congress, after a generally lackluster last-minute debate, supports the President, and the nation braces for war in the desert. Both sides portray the impending war as a sort of Armageddon, holding out potential devastation for soldiers and machines.

The U.S. and Iraq finally agree on January 9 as the date for a meeting between Secretary of State Baker and Foreign Minister Tariq Aziz. But prospects for any serious negotiations to stop the war at this stage are remote. President Bush declares that the meeting will not be a bargaining session, and there will be "no negotiations, no compromises, no attempts at face-saving and no rewards for aggression." Some U.S. officials say the meeting has been scheduled to meet criticism of the United States in Europe and criticism at home by Congress. And as expected, the Baker-Aziz meeting, which lasts six hours in Geneva, ends in stalemate. When Baker assures Aziz that if Iraq leaves Kuwait the U.S.-led forces will not attack,

Aziz again ties settlement of the Kuwait issue to the Arab-Israeli conflict, saying that "the Palestinian question is a matter of national security to Iraq." He adds that Iraq will "defend itself in a very bold manner" in a war, and promises to target Israel for attack. By January 10 most Western embassies in Baghdad are closed.

As preparations for war intensify, the FBI begins interviewing Arab-American business and community leaders to collect information on possible terrorism in the U.S. Bush calls Israeli Prime Minister Yitzhak Shamir, asking that Israel continue to stay out of the Gulf conflict.

Just after 7 p.m. in Washington on January 16—seventeen hours after the U.N.'s deadline—White House spokesman Marlin Fitzwater announces that "the liberation of Kuwait has begun," with massive air and missile strikes against Iraq and Iraqi-occupied Kuwait. At 9 p.m. President Bush goes on television to announce that "the allied countries with forces in the Gulf" have "exhausted all reasonable efforts to reach a peaceful resolution, and have no choice but to drive Saddam from Kuwait by force." Among the targets under attack, says Bush, are Saddam's "nuclear bomb potential," as well as his chemical weapons facilities and artillery and tanks. Bush assures the nation that this "will not be another Vietnam . . . Our troops will have the best possible support in the entire world, and will not be asked to fight with one hand tied behind their back."

On January 17 Iraq fires the first Scud missiles into Saudi Arabia and Israel. They do not contain chemical warheads, and Israel, which suffers light damage, does not retaliate.

There are twenty-eight nations with troops, planes, or ships in the allied military coalition. U.S. Army and Marine units make up 70 percent of ground forces. Air forces from the U.S., Britain, France, Saudi Arabia, Kuwait, and Italy participate in attacks during the first two days of hostilities. Allied planes fly over a thousand sorties in the first fourteen hours of the offensive, which has now officially been named "Operation Desert Storm." The U.S. employs an array of high-tech weapons, originally designed for war against the Soviet Union—which has largely organized and armed the Iraqi army.

To thwart an allied amphibious landing in Kuwait, the Iraqis, on January 23, apparently open the spigots on an oil buoy about eight miles off Kuwait, starting an oil spill in the Persian Gulf. These spigots have a capacity to release 100,000 to 200,000 barrels a day. Within a matter of hours, the spill has grown to an area thirty miles long and ten miles wide. Early reports suggest that the Gulf spill will dwarf that caused by the Exxon Valdez.

The bombing raids continue, and the first major ground conflict takes place when the Iraqis launch a ground attack on the Saudi coastal town of Khafji on January 29. Sporadic fighting continues for two days.

On February 1, President Bush visits the families of Gulf soldiers at military bases in North Carolina and Georgia. He describes his morale as "sky high" after these visits. On February 3, the chief of staff of the U.S. Southern Command in Riyadh reports that seven of the eleven Marines who died on in the battle over Khafji were killed by "friendly fire"—a missile from a U.S. aircraft.

At the start of the third week of war, allied commander General Norman Schwarzkopf announces that thirty-one Iraqi chemical, biological, and nuclear munitions sites have been hit, and over half have been "severely damaged or destroyed." Schwarzkopf promises to "continue a relentless attack on this very, very heinous weapon system." Later that week it is reported that the allies have resorted to another kind of unconventional weapon: Fourteen million leaflets, urging Iraqi troops to surrender, have been dropped over Kuwait.

At the end of this third week, the U.S. reports twelve Americans killed in combat and twenty-six noncombat deaths (in addition to the 105 noncombat deaths before the war began). Twenty-two allied planes and thirty-three Iraqi planes have been shot down; an additional 134 Iraqi planes have been flown into Iran, in a move that continues to baffle many U.S. strategists.

In the early weeks—and throughout the war—there is little reliable information on civilian casualties within Iraq. In a press conference on February 5, President Bush says "we are doing everything possible, and with great success, to minimize collateral damage [civilian casualties]," adding that "Saddam is now relocating some military functions, such as command and control headquarters, in civilian areas such as schools." On February 7 U.N. Secretary General Perez de Cuellar says "there appear to be thousands" of Iraqi civilian casualties, but that the Iraqis "don't want to say there are more than a few hundred...they won't allow the Red Cross to certify the situation in Iraq." The same day, however, Western journalists are taken to the southern Iraqi town of Nasiriya, where, they are told, forty-seven people had been killed when a bridge across the Euphrates, filled with cars and pedestrians, was bombed the previous afternoon. Former U.S. Attorney General Ramsey Clark says on February 7, after returning from a trip to the southern Iraqi city of Basra, that he had seen evidence that allied bombs had hit hospitals and houses in that area.

Refugees arriving in Jordan also report that water, power, and sewage systems have been destroyed in Baghdad. While at this point pilots have evidently been aiming only at military targets, the bombs often miss. By the second week in February, allied attacks have apparently expanded to "dual use" targets—public highways and other elements of the infrastructure—causing the bombing and strafing of civilian buses and trucks and other civilian facilities. International relief organizations report lack of food and water. Diseases such as polio, which reappeared after sanctions were imposed, show signs of rising to epidemic proportions, particularly

among the younger population. (Half of the residents of
Iraq are under fifteen years old.)

On February 10, Secretary of Defense Cheney, in
Riyadh to assess the progress of the war, says Iraq's production facilities are "for the most part destroyed; we've
done good work in destroying most of the storage facilities for his chemical and biological capabilities, although
clearly he retains significant chemical weapons."

Cheney and Joint Chiefs of Staff Chairman General
Colin Powell return from their Gulf survey, and the air
war continues. "I'm still amazed at the sparkling lights
of the anti-aircraft fire and missiles and so-forth," says
RAF Squadron Leader Dave Catterson, "and I, stupidly
enough, still find them quite pretty."

On February 12 the Pentagon pledges to increase the
opportunities for journalists to cover frontline military
activities in the Gulf. During the first month of the war,
the Pentagon has exercized virtually complete control
over press coverage: Most news has come from allied
press briefings and from media pools formed by the
Pentagon, and all reports and footage have had to pass
through military censors. Few American reporters remain
in Baghdad.

Bad weather temporarily slows the progress of the
air war, and some chafe at the delay. Congressman Dan
Burton raises the possibility, on February 11, of using
nuclear weapons: "It would be immoral to lose 20,000 or
30,000 young Americans in combat without using weapons we have at our disposal to save their lives." Iowa's
Democratic Senator Tom Harkin responds that Burton
had made "just about the most foolish and dangerous
statement I can think of.... We've got 200,000 Kuwaitis
still in Kuwait. What would they think about having a
bomb dropped on them? Think about the fallout that
would occur on our own troops... [and] all over Iran,
Pakistan, India, with the prevailing winds."

In preparation for a possible ground assault, the U.S.
steps up air attacks beginning February 11—described by

one U.S. official as "a beautiful day for bombing." On February 13, the American stealth bombers destroy a Baghdad air raid shelter which is claimed to house a command and control center for Saddam's military, killing hundreds of women and children who apparently routinely stayed there during the nightly American raids. Iraqi offiicials report that the bodies of 288 civilians, including 91 children, have been recovered from the demolished bunker; many survivors have been badly burned. In Riyadh, Brig. General Richard Neal says, "From the military point of view, nothing went wrong... I am outraged that civilians were put in harms way, and I lay the blame for that on the Iraqi leadership." Lt. General Thomas Kelly, director of operations for the Joint Chiefs of Staff, says at a Pentagon briefing that "we're going to have to examine our consciences very carefully to determine if we can't do something in the future to preclude [further civilian deaths] ... Obviously we didn't know that the civilians were in there or we would not have bombed the thing." Later he promises that "if there is any evidence civilians are present we will look very carefully at the target and probably not strike it." Earlier, Kelly had said that "the U.S. position seems to be that Iraq could move people in and out of the bunker while we're not looking."

White House spokesman Marlin Fitzwater says, on the day of the bunker attack, that Saddam Hussein "does not share our value in the sanctity of human life. Indeed, he time and time again has shown a willingness to sacrifice civilian lives and property that further his war aims." Leslie Cagan, coordinator of the U.S. National Campaign for Peace in the Middle East, says the television footage of the aftermath of the attack gives Americans "their first honest look at the war."

By February 14, the allies have flown over 70,000 bombing sorties, over 2,000 a day, in their offensive against Iraq and occupied Kuwait. Ramsey Clark reports that the head of the Iraqi Red Crescent—the Islamic equivalent of the Red Cross—has told him that over 6,000 Iraqi civilians have died as a result of allied bombings. In the same period, Iraq had fired thirty-two scud missile at Israel and thirty at Saudi Arabia.

On February 15 Saddam Hussein, in a speech broadcast on Baghdad radio, offers to leave Kuwait, and outlines his conditions for withdrawal. Within four hours, President Bush has rejected the offer, calling it a "cruel hoax," and saying that far too many conditions are attached to it. Bush says, "The American people are strongly in support, not only of the troops, but [our] objectives . . . it is my hope that we have kicked once and for all the so-called Vietnam syndrome."

In preparation for the ground war, Pentagon spokesmen talk of "softening up" Iraqi troop positions in the Kuwaiti theater of operations. On February 19 the *Washington Post* reports that Iraqi troops in Kuwait and southern Iraq are "suffering horrendous casualties as U.S. and allied forces pound them with air strikes and artillery barrages." On the same day there are unconfirmed reports that Iraq's deputy prime minister had told Iranian officials that there were 20,000 Iraqis dead and 60,000 wounded during the first twenty-six days of war.

Saddam Hussein seems unmoved by such statistics. "Fight them . . . Oh men of the mother of battles," he tells his soldiers and his people. "Fight them because with their defeat you will be at the last entrance of the victory of victories. The war will end with all that the situation entails of dignity, glory, and triumph for your people, army, and nation. If the opposite takes place, God forbid, there will only be the ignominious abyss to which the enemies are aspiring to push you."

A week of diplomatic activity between the Soviets and the Iraqis begins, ending with the February 21 announcement by the Soviets that Iraq has agreed to a "full and unconditional withdrawal" from Kuwait. The U.S. rejects this plan as well, citing the timetable for withdrawal, among other facets of the plan, as "unacceptable." President Bush gives Iraq until noon on February 23 to begin "an immediate and unconditional withdrawal from Kuwait," or face a ground attack. The Iraqis denounce the U.S.'s "shameful ultimatum," and instead support the peaceful Soviet plan, which would give them three weeks for withdrawal.

The deadline comes and goes. At 10 p.m. on February 23, Bush orders the ground attack to commence, and announces, "The liberation of Kuwait has now entered a final phase." The allied force numbers 700,000 troops, facing an Iraqi army of 545,000. The allies dominate the air with 2,000 planes, and the seas with a flotilla of more than a hundred ships.

More than 200,000 troops move into Kuwait, encountering little resistance and capturing thousands of Iraqi soldiers in the most sweeping armored attack since World War II. Within twenty four hours, a large Marine force is in the outskirts of Kuwait City. The U.S. VII Corps, a heavy tank force with more than 70,000 soldiers, races north across southern Iraq to outflank and envelop the Iraqis. British and French troops, along with the American forces, seek out the Iraqi's elite fighting forces, the Republican Guards.

The invasion stretches across a 300-mile front, from the Persian Gulf to western Iraq. The *Washington Post* reports that "U.S. pilots flying overhead described a kind of huge, mechanical steeplechase, with countless tanks, armored personnel carriers and other vehicles tearing pell-mell northward across the desert." U.S. casualties remain light.

Captain John Sizemore, a bomber pilot, tells the *Washington Post* on February 25, "You could see them in columns. They look like little ants in a row coming from a peanut butter and jelly sandwich somebody left on the ground. Just lots of them down there."

By February 26 Baghdad radio announces that Saddam Hussein has ordered his army to make a fighting withdrawal from Kuwait. The White House dismisses this news as insufficient to end the hostilities. The allied armies continue their rush to encircle the enemy. In another day the allies punch through to the Euphrates River valley, cutting off the route of retreat for the Republican Guards. The allies also bomb and strafe the road from Kuwait to Basra, along which the Iraqis are trying to retreat. Other allied forces pour into Kuwait, which is a smoking ruin.

At 9 p.m. on February 27, with the allies in Kuwait City and Iraqi forces in full retreat, President Bush declares, in a televised speech to the nation, "Kuwait is liberated. Iraq's army is defeated." He orders a ceasefire. The next day, February 28, Baghdad agrees to designate military commanders to discuss military aspects of the ceasefire under the conditions outlined by Bush.

In Washington, the administration lets it be known that it wants to continue sanctions so long as Saddam Hussein remains in power. The emir of Kuwait says there will be three months of martial law in his country.

In the last days of February, the American press is awash in the rhetoric of victory. But Russian journalist Viktor Filatov, writing from Baghdad in *Sovetskaya Rossiya* on February 28, asks, "What further blood do these barbarians of the twentieth century need? I thought the Americans had changed since the brigandage of Vietnam ...But no, they never change. They remain true to themselves."

Assessing the Damages

There are clearly aspects of this war that make it more ominous and dangerous than previous wars; one of them is the environmental havoc it creates.

The U.N. Environment Program points out the Persian Gulf "is regarded as having one of the most fragile and endangered ecosystems" anywhere in the world, and in a speech before the U.N. Second World Climate Conference in November 1990, Jordan's King Hussein has warned that "a war in the Gulf would not only result in devastating human death and injury, tremendous economic loss, and prolonged political confrontation between Orient and Occident, it could also lead to an environmental catastrophe" that would be "swift, severe and devastating."

During the Iran-Iraq war, Iraq blew up several Iranian drilling platforms, causing the Nowruz oil spill, which lasted for nearly eight months and spilled more than half a million barrels of heavy crude into the Gulf—three times as much oil as was spilled by the Exxon Valdez. The Nowruz spill spread all across the Gulf, killing wildlife and disrupting coastal systems for months.

Soon after the Gulf war begins in January 1991, the U.S. military in Saudi Arabia announces that, apparently in an effort to forestall an allied amphibious invasion, Saddam Hussein's forces in Kuwait have pumped oil from land-based storage tanks and heavily laden tankers into the Gulf. Initial reports indicate that the oil released in the Persian Gulf spill amounts to at least 294 million gallons, compared to 11 million gallons for Exxon Valdez and 68 million gallons for Amoco Cadiz, which split open in 1978 off the Brittany coast. (Later, estimates on the amount of oil released into the Gulf will be downgraded to about 60 million gallons—and a third of this will be attributed to several spills caused by allied bombings.)

Slowly drifting down the Gulf, the January spill promises to gum up both the desalinization works in Saudi Arabia and the electricity producing plants along the shore. Although there is some suspicion that American bombing attacks helped to create this spill, General Norman Schwarzkopf captures the world's attention with a Sunday briefing in which he describes the magnitude of the spill and then tells how allied forces, using smart bombs, have blown up a key pipe juncture to stop the oil tanks from leaking into the Gulf. Saddam Hussein is instantly branded an eco-terrorist, and there is speculation about what he might do elsewhere in the world— say, sending teams of saboteurs to set forest fires in late spring in northern California, or to blow up one of the big pipelines that transport natural gas from the Gulf of Mexico to both the East and West Coasts.

As *Newsday* reports, David Ross, a geologist who studied and mapped the area in 1972, warns that oil from the Persian Gulf spill may get bottled up at the Strait of Hormuz, and remain trapped in the Gulf for a long time. The area is unlike Alaska, where Prince William Sound gets a high rate of exchange with the ocean, and is open to rough, stormy waters and powerful tides—all of which provide a steady flow of fresh water and help to dissipate the oil. The Persian Gulf has none of these characteristics. It is bordered on all sides by desert, and it has little inflow of fresh water and rapid evaporation of surface water —adding up, in Ross's words, to a "very stressed environment." Finally, in Alaska, men and equipment were thrown into the cleanup effort. In the Gulf, all energies are concentrated on warfare, with roads, equipment, airfields, and personnel all straining to meet the demands of the coming ground war.

The Persian Gulf has no sea otters or bald eagles, but it does have dugongs, which look like Florida manatees, plus many species of fish, seabirds, sea snakes, shrimp, and dolphins. The Gulf dugongs—which make up the world's second largest population of the species—dwell near Bahrain and Qatar, where the oil is apt to get trapped. The Nowruz spill killed 400 sea turtles in a few months, and marine ecologists who work in the Gulf expect this to be repeated. Oyster beds are also likely to be damaged, and fisheries in the Gulf, while not huge, are important locally; and in the case of shrimp they were just beginning to develop on an international level. It may be decades before this industry recovers from the spill.

As the war began, oil wells in Kuwait were set afire, probably as the result of both allied bombing and deliberate firing by Saddam Hussein's troops. There were fears that the accumulated smoke from oil well fires could have effects similar to those felt in the northwestern United

States during the summer of 1987, when smoke from forest fires blanketed an enormous area, filtering out sunlight and reducing surface temperatures as much as twenty degrees celsius. Dr. John Cox, a British chemical and environmental engineer who worked in Kuwait, predicted that if Iraq were to set the nation's thousand oil wells ablaze, the smoke might waft upwards—disrupting local and regional climatic patterns, creating an equatorial ozone hole, and conceivably disrupting the Asian monsoons. This in turn could lead to crop failures on the subcontinent that would affect more than one billion people. Even Pentagon planners who doubt such dire predictions agree that the fires could have a serious impact on local and regional weather patterns.

Beyond this, air strikes against Saddam Hussein's chemical and biological warfare factories and munitions could cause leakage into the ground water supplies. The chemical complex located near the holy Shiite city of Samarra, forty-five miles northwest of Baghdad on the Tigris River, manufactures a reported 200 tons of mustard gas a month. Large chemical storage areas are located there as well. The chemical complex near Samarra had also produced forty-eight tons of tabun, a nerve gas that disrupts the part of the human nervous system that regulates blood vessels (like the pesticide parathion, only more potent). In addition, Iraq manufactures another more potent nerve gas called sarin, and the poisonous gas phosgene. Tabun and sarin will disperse when released; they are highly toxic, but will not persist in the environment. Mustard gas causes burns and leads to cancer, and is extremely persistent. In Ethiopia patches of active mustard gas, dropped by the Italians before World War II, are still being found. In addition to these gases, Iraq is believed to possess stocks of biological agents, including anthrax and botulism. Their dispersal would have horrible implications. Finally, the allied destruction of Iraq's two small nuclear reactors might have released small amounts of radioactivity and, more significantly, might have led to dispersal of the plutonium that Iraq was amassing for nuclear bombs. And none of this includes the heavy environmental cost of one million troops with their equipment waging battle across the desert.

Many of the environmental effects of the war may take a long time to appear and, unlike the catastrophic results of an oil spill, may occur in perverse and insidious ways. The evolution of the Persian Gulf into an international fishing ground, for example, promises to be retarded if not altogether halted. And although Iraq is dependent on only one product, oil, for its export earnings, the future viability of the country lies in agriculture. Eighty percent of Iraq's water comes from the Tigris and Euphrates rivers. Farming has long been concentrated in the oblong strip of arable land between the two rivers, which converge on the Persian Gulf, and Iraq's population is concentrated there as well. If the rivers become polluted by radioactive materials, chemical agents, and the general destruction of war, Iraq's agricultural activity will be seriously set back. Its population would be susceptible to mass deaths from a variety of causes. All in all, the real casualties of the Persian Gulf war—in human, environmental, and economic terms—will be widespread, long-term, and difficult to calculate.

January 6, 1991

As the new year begins with America on the brink
of war, former President and Commander-in-Chief
Richard Nixon offers some "straight talk" on the reasons for going to war, asserting that "a bad peace is
worse than war."

WHY U.S. POLICY IS RIGHT IN THE GULF

RICHARD NIXON
The New York Times

Woodcliff Lake, N.J.

It is time for some straight talk about why 400,000 young
Americans spent Christmas in the deserts of Saudi Arabia and
why in less than two weeks the U.S. may be once again at war.

We must first be clear about what the conflict is not about.

If we must resort to military force to drive Saddam Hussein
from Kuwait, it will not be a war about democracy. While our
goal is to restore Kuwait's legitimate Government, it is hypocritical to suggest that we hope to bring democracy to Kuwait.
Except for Israel, there are no democracies in the Mideast, and
there will be none in the foreseeable future. The Emir of Kuwait
is among the world's more benevolent dictators, but once he is
back in his palace in Kuwait City, he will still be a dictator.

Nor is intervention justified because Saddam Hussein is a
cruel leader. President Bush has been criticized for equating
him with Hitler. Whether he is that bad is irrelevant. He is
bad enough. His soldiers are murdering, torturing and raping
defenseless Kuwaitis and pillaging their country. He violated
international law by using chemical weapons against Iran and
the Kurds.

But if our policy were to punish cruel leaders, we would
not be allied with Syria's President Hafez al-Assad. He ordered
the massacre of 20,000 innocent people in the city of Hama in
his own country, has supported international terrorism and
presided over an army that has committed brutal atrocities in
Lebanon. Both Syria and Iraq threaten our interests, but today
Iraq poses a profoundly greater threat.

Those who fault President Bush for enlisting President Assad's support should remember Winston Churchill's classic rejoinder to those who criticized him for supporting Stalin after Hitler invaded the Soviet Union during World War II: "If Hitler invaded Hell, I think I would find a kind word to say about the Devil in the House of Commons."

We are in the Persian Gulf for two major reasons.

First, Saddam Hussein has unlimited ambitions to dominate one of the most important strategic areas in the world. When Senator Bob Dole said we were in the Gulf for oil and Secretary of State James Baker said we were there for jobs, they were criticized for justifying our actions on purely selfish grounds. We should not apologize for defending our vital economic interests.

Had we not intervened, an international outlaw would today control more than 40 percent of the world's oil. While, by stringent energy conservation, the U.S. might be able to get along without oil from the Gulf, Western Europe and Japan could not. What happens to the economies of other great industrial nations directly affects the economy of the U.S. We cannot allow Mr. Hussein to blackmail us and our allies into accepting his aggressive goals by giving him a choke hold on our oil lifeline.

Because he has oil, he has the means to acquire the weapons he needs for aggression against his neighbors, eventually including nuclear weapons. If he succeeds in Kuwait, he will attack others, and he will use whatever weapons he has to achieve his goals. If we do not stop him now, we will have to stop him later, when the cost in young American lives will be infinitely greater.

There is an even more important long-term reason for rolling back Iraq's aggression. We cannot be sure, as many believe and hope, that we are entering into a new, post-Cold War era where armed aggression will no longer be an instrument of national policy. But we can be sure that if Saddam Hussein profits from aggression, other potential aggressors in the world will be tempted to wage war against their neighbors.

If we succeed in getting Mr. Hussein out of Kuwait in accordance with the U.N. resolution and in eliminating his capacity to wage war in the future—which must be our goal if he refuses to get out peacefully and forces us to act militarily —we will have the credibility to deter aggression elsewhere without sending American forces. The world will take seriously U.S. warnings against aggression.

Some critics argue that we should continue sanctions for as long as 18 months before resorting to force. They contend that even if sanctions do not work, Mr. Hussein will be so weakened that we will suffer fewer casualties if war does come.

They are wrong on three counts. First, while the Iraqi people suffer the effects of sanctions, President Hussein will direct his resources so that the Iraqi military will not. Second, while the sanctions will weaken Iraq, they will weaken us even more, because of the political difficulty of holding our alliance together abroad and maintaining support for our troop commitment at home. Finally, the most the critics can claim is that it is possible that sanctions might work. It is certain that military force will work. The stakes are too high to risk failure.

Other critics believe diplomacy will eventually convince Saddam Hussein that he should get out of Kuwait. But neither diplomacy nor sanctions has a chance unless he knows that if he does not get out of Kuwait peacefully, the American people and our allies will be united in support of driving him out militarily.

Should Secretary Baker's meeting with the Iraqi Foreign Minister, Tariq Aziz, fail to produce an agreement that complies unconditionally with the U.N. resolution, we must remember that when dealing with an insatiable aggressor a bad peace is worse than war because it will inevitably lead to a bigger war.

If we must go to war, it will not be just a war about oil. It will not be a war about a tyrant's cruelty. It will not be a war about democracy. It will be a war about peace—not just peace in our time, but peace for our children and grandchildren in the years ahead.

If Saddam Hussein gains in any way from his aggression, despite our unprecedented commitment of economic, diplomatic and military power, other aggressors will be encouraged to wage war against their neighbors and peace will be in jeopardy everywhere in the world. That is why our commitment in the Gulf is a highly moral enterprise.

January/February 1991

As time grows short, the Bush administration continues to call the shots in the Persian Gulf. Eric Alterman of the World Policy Institue criticizes what he sees as "Congress's failure" to take control of a situation of such grave importance to the nation.

CONGRESS'S FAILURE
ERIC ALTERMAN
Tikkun

Can anyone imagine being told in say, 1975, that within fifteen years, the United States Congress would be reprising its inglorious role as silent partner in an undeclared presidential war? Amazing as it sounds—and despite some grumbling from the Senate Armed Services Committee—Congress appears *once again* to be forfeiting its constitutionally mandated role as the sole governing body charged with the solemn responsibility of declaring war. And this without even a cold war to silence its critics. It is the Gulf of Tonkin, part II: a sequel shot in the sands of Arabia.

But of course the political epilogue of the Gulf story is that Wayne Morse and Ernest Gruening—the Senate's sole dissenting voices on LBJ's disastrous resolution—were both defeated for re-election. Today, as always, most Congressmen are "more concerned with electoral survival than human survival," as one Democratic aide puts it. Apparently still in the grips of its Reagan-era paralysis, Congress has allowed the war party in President Bush's administration to define the terms of debate. . . .

On the Democratic side of the aisle, reactions have been far more discordant. Initially, most of the voices discernible above the din belonged to House members who clamored for a military solution even more loudly than the president did. Democratic hawks were admirably unequivocal in announcing their enlistment into the Kuwait crusade. As Stephen Solarz (D-N.Y.) put it, America's response to the crisis would "determine the fate and future of the entire world, if we were to permit Saddam Hussein to get away with his brutal aggression." On the other side of the spectrum, a hard-core group of twenty-nine House members and three senators (Bob Kerrey of Nebraska, Mark Hatfield of Oregon, and Ted Kennedy) spoke up in opposition to the heavily U.N.-dependent resolutions Congress passed endorsing Bush's initial deployment to Saudi Arabia. Most Democrats, however, simply tried to stay out of trouble. They ducked Republican calls for a special session of Congress to debate the pros and cons of a declaration of war, and argued feebly that such a debate would either give Bush authority he did not yet have or signal to Hussein that Bush's threats of military retaliation were empty ones. No one wanted to be seen voting in favor of either premature war or unnecessary wimpery.

This situation remained largely unchanged through the 1990 elections. Two days afterward, Bush, virtually without any congressional consultation, announced his decision to deploy another two hundred thousand American troops to Saudi Arabia. This second deployment was mobilized not for deterrence but explicitly for an offensive war to chase Hussein out of Kuwait. The uneasy public reaction to the new moves served as a wake-up call for many Democrats, who suddenly realized that they were about to accept responsibility for what was rapidly becoming a widely mistrusted military adventure. Having failed to object to Bush's all-or-nothing definition of the problem, however, these Democrats were in no position to start questioning the fundamentals of a policy that made definition the basis of a case for war. Instead, they questioned only the particulars of Bush's timing, claiming that the administration was not giving the U.N.-sanctions a chance to cripple the Iraqi economy and force Saddam's capitulation in a relatively peaceful manner. If and when these sanctions were deemed to have failed, however, war, for mainstream Democrats, remained the only viable option.

The key beak to read in this debate belonged to Georgia hawk, and Senate Armed Services Committee Chairman, Sam Nunn. Nunn works a kind of protection racket for liberal Democratic senators: when they are up for re-election, he comes to campaign for them in order to fend off allegations of pacifism and wimpiness from right-wing Republicans. They then mind their own business when Nunn decides how many hundreds of billions will make his friends in the Pentagon happy.

Nunn lay low for the early part of the crisis, but finally called hearings on the subject in late November. There, he

mapped out the boundaries of what would henceforth consti-
tute the safe middle ground (SMIG) for Democrats who
wished to be considered "credible" and "responsible" by the
nation's op-ed pages. In charting the SMIG, Nunn did not, of
course, take issue with the idea of going to war to restore the
Kuwaiti monarchy. "The question is not whether military
action is justified. It is." That was the end of that. . . .

Led by Berkeley firebrand Ron Dellums (D-Calif.), fifty-four
Democratic representatives, along with Senator Tom Harkin
(D-Iowa), petitioned the U.S. Superior Court to prevent
George Bush from going to war without a congressional decla-
ration. Among the signatories were three Jewish members,
Barbara Boxer, Tedd Weiss, and Barney Frank. . . .

[But] after a full four months of reaction time, no one in the
leadership of the Democratic party had yet addressed the fundamental question of whether the "liberation" of Kuwait was
worth going to war over. To say that the United States should
go to war to free Kuwait, without first debating just what
makes this goal worth at least thirty thousand American lives,
is an unconscionable dereliction of the Congress's democratic
responsibilities. Japan and Germany, far more dependent on
Gulf oil than we are, and far more economically competitive,
have taken a good hard look at the stakes and concluded that
determining which antidemocratic tyrant rules Kuwait is not
worth the sacrifice of a single citizen's life, and certainly not
the $2 billion a month it costs to keep American soldiers
sitting there. And yet even to raise the question in Congress
—which is, after all, constitutionally entrusted with responsibility for these decisions—during the first four months of the
crisis, was to be stigmatized as a radical, an appeaser, or
worse.

The obvious solution to the Democrats' dilemma over
whether to declare war would have been for the Democratic
leadership to call a special session of both houses for the
specific purpose of passing a resolution that simply affirmed
this inarguable constitutional prerogative. This could have
prevented Bush from starting a war, Gulf of Tonkin style,
while retaining for Congress the option of forcing Saddam
out of Kuwait if and when it determined this was necessary.
Democratic leaders considered this course at the end of
November, then threw in the towel when Bush announced
Baker's mission to Baghdad.

Cynics such as myself may still be proven wrong. By the time this article appears, Baker may have negotiated the peaceful withdrawal of Saddam Hussein from Kuwait and defused the entire crisis. Needless to say, I would be thrilled with such an outcome. But if, as appears more likely, Bush has merely offered Baker's trip as a symbolic gesture to salve congressional consciences, then the cowardice of the Democratic party in refusing to confront the president, both on constitutional and substantive grounds, will stand as one of the great moral and political failures in its history. The last such failure killed more than fifty-seven thousand Americans and millions more Indochinese.

January 10–12, 1991

Over the course of three days, with the clock ticking toward the deadline, both houses of Congress at last openly debate the American use of force in the Gulf. The discussion is often repetitive and predictable, but the two senators from New York bring the opposing arguments down to common-sense terms.

TRANSCRIPT OF CONGRES-SIONAL DEBATE ON THE USE OF FORCE AGAINST IRAQ
SENATOR DANIEL PATRICK MOYNIHAN AND SENATOR ALFONSE D'AMATO
Washington, D.C.

Senator Moynihan: How did it come about that we are here on the senate floor talking of war, talking of war in a region where the massed forces on either side are larger than any such encounter since the Second World War? A million armed men and women divided by a line in the sand facing the prospect of hideous encounters, all of which arises in the aftermath of the invasion by one small Third World country of another smaller Third World country.

In one of those countries the indigenous population was compounded by about four times by immigrant laborers brought in as servants. Both of them wealthy countries since a Stanford professor in 1938 discovered the Arabian oil dome. Suddenly the wealth appeared—but otherwise these are not very important countries.

Senator Simon was kind enough to mention that I was once Ambassador to India. That part of the world was not unconnected to the Middle East. It had once been governed by the British from New Delhi. Some 7,000 people managed the area.

Iraq as such is an artifact of the Treaty of Sevres which ended the First World War with Turkey and the allies in 1920. The precise borders of Iraq were drawn in a tent in 1925 by a British colonial official.

I was also, if I may just say, once our Ambassador to the United Nations. I remember Kuwait at the United Nations as a particularly poisonous enemy of the United States. One can be an antagonist of the United States in a way that leaves room for further discussions afterwards. But the Kuwaitis were singularly nasty. Their anti-Semitism was at the level of the personally loathsome when Resolution 3379 equating Zionism with racism passed the General Assembly. The Kuwaitis were conspicuously poisonous.

By contrast, the Iraqis were very recently said to be our friends by this, our administration. Last summer the Committee on Foreign Relations held hearings on Iraq. My colleague, Senator D'Amato, pointed out the particularly outrageous behavior of the Iraqi Government with respect to the use of poison gas, the repression of the Kurds, and so forth. Senator Pell, the distinguished chairman of the Committee on Foreign Relations, reported from the committee the Iraqi International Law Compliance Act of 1990. It contained a list of specific violations of international law by Iraq.

Our findings were that the Government of Iraq had systematically detained, tortured and executed thousands of its own citizens. The Government of Iraq had destroyed more than 3,000 villages and towns in the Kurdish regions of Iraq. Iraq had used chemical weapons on an extensive scale against its Kurdish citizens resulting in tens of thousands of deaths.

Amnesty International has documented extensive violations of human rights by the Government of Iraq, including the torture and murder of children as a means of punishing their parents. Iraq has blatantly violated international law in initiating use of chemical weapons in the Iran-Iraq war and against Kurdish citizens. Iraq has failed to ratify the Convention of Biological Weapons. The committee found, therefore, that Iraq had engaged in a consistent pattern of gross violations of internationally recognized human rights and disregard for international law.

We said, that being the case, we will not any longer subsidize sales of agricultural products to Iraq. This matter came to the floor, and we learned from the other side of the aisle, from the distinguished Senator from Indiana, that the State Department "opposes the virtual total economic embargo of Iraq which would result from this amendment."

It is odd. That was July 26—seven days before Iraq invaded Kuwait. This crisis involves Kuwait, a particularly nasty little regime given to poisonous anti-American, anti-Semitic pronouncements, and Iraq who we were subsidizing with

food imports only seven days before the invasion. And when
Senator Pell said here is a country that has been outrageous
—poison, murder, mayhem, violation of human rights, violation of international law—the State Department says, "Do not
touch them, do not bother with them. We are against the
measure."

Well the measure passed. Eventually the State Department
managed to see that it did not become law. But it passed the
Senate.

Here are two countries, neither of them very attractive:
Kuwait openly contemptuous of and hostile to the United
States; Iraq the beneficiary of the United States.

Suddenly, on behalf of Kuwait and in opposition to Iraq we
have seen the largest array of armed forces since the Second
World War. We see the President declaring that he has the
right to send those forces into battle, independently of any
judgment of the Senate.

How could this happen in the first post-cold-war crisis?

I would like to suggest, Mr. President, and I hope this
might help us think about the subject, that the way in which
the President initially proceeded obtained the universal
support of the country and the Senate. Suddenly, however,
there was an institutional lurch back into the manner and
mode of the cold war.

It has been with us so long, we do not know how to act dif-
ferently. We have not acquired the instincts, the institutions,
the institutional memories, to do other than what we have
been doing during the cold war. We know nothing else. That
is what happened on November 8—two days after the election—that suddenly lurched us into a cold war mold.

It happens, Mr. President, that last November, the Committee on Foreign Relations held a series of hearings on the
subject "After the Cold War." We examined changes in the
American Government which have taken place over the long
struggle with totalitarianism which emerged, really, from the
First World War. As Judith Sklar has written, "1914 is, after
all, when it all began."

From 1914 to 1989, there was a 75-year "war" which
inevitably changed attitudes and institutions. In our hearings
we were looking at the attitudes and institutions that had
changed, and the ways in which they did. I chaired the hearings, so I took the opportunity to organize our inquiry around

an extraordinary speech which Woodrow Wilson gave in St. Louis, Missouri, on September 5, 1919. It was on that trip around the country, pleading for public support to influence the Senate to consent to the ratification of the Treaty of Versailles which contained the League of Nations covenant. Wilson was asking for that support. He was twenty days from Pueblo, Colorado where he would collapse. It would be, in effect, the end of his Presidency.

I see the Senator representing St. Louis is on the floor, and I think the senior Senator from Missouri would recognize that Wilson's remarks had about them the quality of prophecy: It was the end of his life. He was trying to tell America what he would leave behind him, what would happen if we did not establish a world order where there was law, where there were procedures, where peace was enforced. And if we did not, what would come instead.

He said, "Very well, then. If we must stand apart and be the hostile rivals of the rest of the world, we must do something else: We must be physically ready for anything to come. We must have a great standing army. We must see to it that every man in America is trained in arms, and we must see to it that there are munitions and guns enough for an army. And that means a mobilized nation; that they are not only laid up in store, but that they are kept up to date; that they are ready to use tomorrow; that we are a nation in arms."

Then he said, "What would a nation in arms be? Well, you know, you have to think of the President of the United States not as the chief counselor of the Nation, elected for a little while, but as the man meant constantly and every day to be Commander in Chief of the Army and Navy of the United States, ready to order it to any part of the world with a threat of war, as a menace to his own people."

Then he said, "And you can't do that under free debate; you can't do that under public counsel. Plans must be kept secret. Knowledge must be accumulated by a system which we have condemned, because we called it a spying system. The more polite call it a system of intelligence."

Then he went on a little further to say, in effect, how this world would shape itself up into one of continuing crises. And so, Mr. President, in that speech in St. Louis, which, as I say, had a prophetic quality which haunts one to this day, Woodrow Wilson said that we would see the emergence of a system of Government in which the President had become Commander in Chief, head of the Armed Forces. That did happen. And nothing is more extraordinary evidence of it having happened than the assertions we have heard in the past month after the lurching from a defensive deterrent position, which we responded to very well, into an offensive position on November 8. This was a decision reached in secret. It suddenly turned what had been a collective security operation with the complete support of the country and the world into an offensive, military crisis situation. . . .

We were following the collective security mode and suddenly lurched out of it. Suddenly, from a situation where the world was defending a small country that had been attacked by a larger neighbor, we switched to a situation where the United States had engaged a major Islamic country in a count-down to Armageddon.

Mr. President, that is a kind of madness where we are living in an earlier world and acting in ways that have no relevance to the situation of the moment. We are not in an international crisis in the sense that events that took place on August 2 necessitate the confrontation of the largest set of armed forces since World War II. Nothing large happened. A nasty little country invaded a littler but just as nasty country. They have their avowed virtues, I do not doubt. There has not been much virtue on display internationally in either case. And the United States shares with the other nations of the world an interest in the resolution of the crisis, principally to establish the fact that the U.N. Charter is an international standard that will be enforced.

The world will not be particularly different after Iraq leaves Kuwait, which it will do. It will not be any better, or it will be better to the extent only that we will have established that the international community will enforce the Charter in the aftermath of the cold war that has become possible.

So, Mr. President, all we are saying on this side of the aisle, and I hope we will hear it from the other side of the aisle, is this: Why can we not continue the President's policy of August, September, and October? That was a policy appropriate to a small disturbance in a distant part of the world where there are interests involved because that part of the world exports oil to Japan and sends oil to Europe. There is an important international interest in maintaining the standards of the Charter. Fine. But not World War III. Is it not clear, Mr. President, that we did not have World War III? It did not happen.

Suddenly our institutions are acting as if to say, "Oh, my God, we missed World War III. Maybe we can have it now here. Not there but here." Mr. President, that borders on the edge of the disturbed. Dr. Strangelove, where are you now that we need you?

This is so unnecessary. With what unanimity in this body the President would be supported if he simply drew back to the defensive positions of the period up to November 8 before his announcement of a secretly planned escalation to an offensive mode.

Mr. President, our armies have been on the Rhine for 45 years. That is the stuff of Roman legions. We are still in Panmunjom. We have a naval force with some land-based facilities in the Gulf since the Second World War. Twelve months will pass, 18 months will pass, life will go on. And we will not have the wrenching constitutional crisis that will come about if the President launches a massive use of our Armed Forces in a distant region of the world without a specific declaration of war by Congress.

I conclude, Mr. President, simply pleading to the President. He will have that constitutional crisis regardless of the outcome of the conflict. The primacy of Congress on this issue under the Constitution will have been denied just at that moment when it would seem possible to return to what was once the normal conduct of foreign affairs by the Presidents and the Congress of the United States.

* * * * *

Senator D'Amato: I say to my friends, we talk about waiting for some sanctions at some mythical time that no one is willing to set forth. We do not say two months, six months, some undetermined time when they will pay their toll, and we have an assessment by Judge Webster, the CIA, by others, that say it is not having an impact. Any darn fool should have known that right from the beginning and it should not have been handled in that manner. We should have said our sanctions are there to deprive him of the fruits of an otherwise great victory.

I begged the administration early on not to take that course of action, not to spell out to the people that sanctions in and of itself would bring victory. They did not. The administration was wrong. And they have come forward today and they admit it because those are the facts. I am not just saying that. I committed that to paper August 24 in an article to the *New York Times*. I said to them, "It is simply naive to believe that an economic embargo will starve Mr. Hussein into capitulating to our demands." It is in the record. It is in the record that we failed to do even a prudent thing, to send a signal to Saddam Hussein, "Do not undertake this aggression."

Now after the aggression is undertaken, after the failure of the administration to stand early and the Congress to do what it should have done, now when the President commits hundreds of thousands of young men and women, what are we going to say to Saddam Hussein? We are going to see if the sanctions will work in the face and in the light of our expert testimony that indicates an evidence and facts that they will not.

So we want to undercut the President, a blow to our President and to future Presidents and to our young men out there? Do it. That is what happens if we pass this resolution. It is incredible.

If Saddam Hussein faces no credible punishment, no credible threat but the continuation of an economic boycott that, yes, is bringing real problems in economic deprivation to his people, but that is not the kind of credible punishment that will move him, he has no incentive to withdraw from Kuwait.

History has pointed that out in the case of Saddam Hussein. But only when he faces overwhelming threat to his well-being and that of his military machine do we have an opportunity to resolve this matter peacefully. So I say if we pass this resolution, we deprive the President of demonstrating that we have the will and the capacity and the ability to inflict the kind of punishment that even Saddam Hussein will not countenance.

January 11, 1991

With only days to go before the January 15 deadline, and on the eve of the historic congressional vote that will authorize the president to wage war, former *New York Times* editorial page editor John B. Oakes expresses his hope that the lessons of history may keep the United States from falling into a "reckless, futile, unnecessary war."

SAYING NO TO A NO-WIN WAR
JOHN B. OAKES
Newsday

One hundred and forty-three years ago, in the midst of the war with Mexico that many Americans thought then and think today was unjustified, a first-term Republican member of the House of Representatives wrote to a friend:

"... Kings have always been involving and impoverishing their people in wars, pretending generally... that the good of the people was the object. This, our [Constitutional] Convention understood to be the most oppressive of all Kingly oppressions; and they resolved to so frame the Constitution that *no one man* should hold the power of bringing this oppression upon us."

One hundred and forty-three years later, the American people have been trapped by George Bush in almost precisely the position that Abraham Lincoln warned against.

For the past five months, we have been under steadily increasing, presidentially induced risk of falling into what Lincoln called "the most oppressive of all Kingly oppressions" —a reckless, futile, unnecessary war.

President Bush, to his credit, successfully orchestrated the most stringent set of economic sanctions the U.N. has ever applied against an aggressor. But sanctions take time to work, and Mr. Bush has not the necessary patience to let that sensible policy mature. Now we are on the edge of a primarily U.S. war for a cause that is primarily a U.N. responsibility.

Now, war or no war, President Bush's policy of brinkmanship has put us in a no-win situation.

If we have a shooting war, it is one we will "win" at the likely cost of thousands of American and non-American lives, the devastation of cities from Baghdad to Tel Aviv, the shattering of remaining American influence in the Arab world and the sustained enmity of most of the third world nations that have suffered from Western colonialism.

Such a war would appear to much of the world as fought not to save Kuwait or punish Saddam Hussein, but to reestablish Western hegemony over the people and resources of their oil-rich Middle East.

The likeliest gainer from such a war could be Hafez Assad, Syria's dictator, Saddam's arch-enemy and our temporary ally. This would be Assad's one chance to destroy Hussein with American help. He would become the undisputed leader of the revolutionary Arab world, once again united in its hostility to Israel and the West.

It is a no-win situation even without a shooting war. If international diplomacy gives Saddam and Bush a face-saving way out of the impasse and no war occurs, Saddam will emerge stronger than ever. He will be left with his jacked-up war machine intact, his prestige enhanced—to the Moslem world, a hero who stood up to imperial America.

If he "capitulates" on the understanding that his basic demands—an adjustment of his border and an international conference on the Palestinian problem—will be carefully considered as soon as he gets out of Kuwait, it certainly won't be President Bush who will be looked upon as the "winner."

Now at last, at two minutes to midnight, the president is reluctantly appealing to Congress to share the onus of waging war for his stated aim of ousting Saddam Hussein from Kuwait. Of all the possibilities in this no-win situation, an American-initiated and American-led war is the worst for the United States.

Congress now has to face up to the critical decision it has been ducking for months. How many of its members have the moral courage and the political wisdom to "just say no"—or, at the very minimum, "not yet"?

January 16, 1991

On January 16, two hours after the first air strikes on Iraq begin, President Bush goes on television to tell the American people why "the world"—and he—"could wait no longer."

PRESIDENT BUSH'S ANNOUNCEMENT OF WAR
Washington, D.C.

9:01 P.M. EST

The President: Just two hours ago, allied air forces began an attack on military targets in Iraq and Kuwait. These attacks continue as I speak. Ground forces are not engaged.

This conflict started August 2nd when the dictator of Iraq invaded a small and helpless neighbor. Kuwait—a member of the Arab League and a member of the United Nations—was crushed; its people brutalized. Five months ago, Saddam Hussein started this cruel war against Kuwait. Tonight, the battle has been joined.

This military action, taken in accord with United Nations resolutions—and with the consent of the United States Congress—follows months of constant and virtually endless diplomatic activity on the part of the United Nations, the United States and many, many other countries. Arab leaders sought what became known as an Arab solution—only to conclude that Saddam Hussein was unwilling to leave Kuwait. Others traveled to Baghdad in a variety of efforts to restore peace and justice. Our Secretary of State, James Baker, held an historic meeting in Geneva—only to be totally rebuffed. This past weekend, in a last ditch effort, the Secretary General of the United Nations went to the Middle East, with peace in his heart—his second such mission. And he came back from Baghdad with no progress at all in getting Saddam Hussein to withdraw from Kuwait.

Now the 28 countries with forces in the Gulf area, have exhausted all reasonable efforts to reach a peaceful resolution, have no choice but to drive Saddam from Kuwait by force. We will not fail.

As I report to you, air attacks are underway against military targets in Iraq. We are determined to knock out Saddam Hussein's nuclear bomb potential. We will also destroy his chemical weapons facilities. Much of Saddam's artillery and tanks will be destroyed. Our operations are designed to best protect the lives of all the coalition forces by targeting Saddam's vast military arsenal. Initial reports from General Schwarzkopf are that our operations are proceeding according to plan.

Our objectives are clear. Saddam Hussein's forces will leave Kuwait. The legitimate government of Kuwait will be restored to its rightful place and Kuwait will once again be free. Iraq will eventually comply with all relevant United Nations resolutions. And then, when peace is restored, it is our hope that Iraq will live as a peaceful and cooperative member of the family of nations, thus, enhancing the security and stability of the Gulf.

Some may ask, why act now? Why not wait? The answer is clear: The world could wait no longer. Sanctions, though having some effect, showed no signs of accomplishing their objective. Sanctions were tried for well over five months, and we and our allies concluded that sanctions alone would not force Saddam from Kuwait.

While the world waited, Saddam Hussein systematically raped, pillaged and plundered a tiny nation, no threat to his own. He subjected the people of Kuwait to unspeakable atrocities—and among those maimed and murdered, innocent children.

While the world waited, Saddam sought to add to the chemical weapons arsenal he now possesses an infinitely more dangerous weapon of mass destruction—a nuclear weapon.

And while the world waited, while the world talked peace and withdrawal, Saddam Hussein dug in and moved massive forces into Kuwait.

While the world waited, while Saddam stalled, more damage was being done to the fragile economies of the Third World, the emerging democracies of Eastern Europe, to the entire world including our own economy.

The United States, together with the United Nations, exhausted every means at our disposal to bring this crisis to a peaceful end. However, Saddam clearly felt that by stalling and threatening and defying the United Nations he could weaken the forces arrayed against him.

While the world waited, Saddam Hussein met every overture of peace with open contempt. While the world prayed for peace, Saddam prepared for war.

I had hoped that when the United States Congress, in historic debate, took its resolute action, Saddam would realize he could not prevail and would move out of Kuwait in accord with the United Nations resolutions. He did not do that. Instead, he remained intransigent, certain that time was on his side....

We have no argument with the people of Iraq—indeed, for the innocents caught in this conflict, I pray for their safety.

Our goal is not the conquest of Iraq—it is the liberation of Kuwait. It is my hope that somehow the Iraqi people can, even now, convince their dictator that he must lay down his arms, leave Kuwait, and let Iraq itself rejoin the family of peace-loving nations.

Thomas Paine wrote many years ago: "These are the times that try men's souls." Those well-known words are so very true today. But even as planes of the multinational forces attack Iraq, I prefer to think of peace, not war. I am convinced not only that we will prevail, but that out of the horror of combat will come the recognition that no nation can stand against a world united. No nation will be permitted to brutally assault its neighbor.

January 25, 1991

Kiren Chaudhry, a professor at the University of California at Berkeley, had lived in Iraq, doing fieldwork on the country's economic reform and privatization program. In an interview with Laura Hagar on January 25 Chaudhry, who has just returned to the United States, provides one of the few first-hand accounts of life in Baghdad as the war began.

BACK FROM BAGHDAD
KIREN CHAUDHRY
The East Bay (California) Express

Laura Hagar: *You were in Iraq ten days before the U.S. attack. What was the mood of the people in Baghdad when you were there?*

Kiren Chaudhry: I think the first and most striking thing was the fear, and along with that, a sense of disbelief—a sense that the Americans couldn't possibly attack Baghdad itself. I think this comes out of the fact that, even though Iraqis have gone through this period of xenophobia and anti-Western, anti-American propaganda for a long time, they still admire a great deal about the United States and they still somehow feel—perhaps because of the repression of their own regime—that the United States has something to offer them in terms of an abstract political alternative, in terms of helping them get out of their current situation. But I don't think they ever imagined or ever wanted the United States to try to do this through war.

Are you saying that a significant portion of the Iraqi population does not support Saddam Hussein? That's something you simply wouldn't get from the mainstream American media, which makes the Iraqi people seem like one vast mob chanting "Saddam, Saddam!"

To give you an idea of how one gleans these things in a police state that's so repressive, where saying something directly to a Westerner could result in not just your death, but the death of your whole family or your whole clan, let me describe two different experiences I had at a very famous and very old Baghdadi restaurant. When I was in Iraq at the end of 1989, I went there several times. The restaurant regularly features singers who, interspersed with other songs, sing eulogies to Saddam which are manufactured by the government on a daily basis. Now, last year when I was there, when these would come on, people would go out of their way to demonstrate how much they were enjoying it. They would clap, get up on the tables sometimes, dance, sing along. This time, after these songs would end, there was no applause at all. While we were in this restaurant, two different fistfights broke out among large groups of people (it's an enormous place).

I came away with the sense that the Iraqis are simply fed up. If you look at what Iraq has gone through in the past decade, you can see why. They had eight years of war with Iran, a war which was very divisive internally because a large proportion of Iraqis are Shiites and many of them actually favored Khomeni and the new system in Iran. About sixty percent of the Iraqi population is Shiite. The other forty percent is Sunni, but within that there's another division, in that approximately fifty percent is Sunni and approximately fifty percent is Sunni-Kurdish—so, politically, these two groups often are at loggerheads because of the ethnic difference.

Besides the war with Iran, Iraq also went through a period of economic liberalization, in which the government tried to promote the private sector and made all kinds of reforms, including the privatization of industry. They dissolved the labor unions. Wages dropped. There was unemployment. There were all the kinds of stresses that we see in Eastern Europe right now, that same kind of economic instability and collapse. All this was going on from October 1988 until the initiation of this new military venture. So Iraqis, I think, are generally fed up. They don't understand why it is that they have to bear the burden of the Arab cause time and time again. They thought that's what was going on with the Iran-Iraq war and now they're doing it again.

What do you mean by the "burden of the Arab cause"?

Well, each one of these conflicts for the Iraqis and the Arabs has been framed in terms of opposing an external non-Arab entity. The Iran-Iraq war, of course, was about opposing the Persians, and particularly the Iranian revolution. And that's why all the Arab countries supported Iraq in this war;

Kuwait and Saudi Arabia loaned Iraq billions of dollars to fight the war against Iran. The current conflict, which started out as a financial disagreement with Kuwait, has now been posed in terms of, first, a conflict between the Arabs and the Israelis, and now a broader conflict between Muslims and non-Muslims, or Arabs and the West. So, in that sense, it's very abstract for most Iraqis. They can't quite understand why basic goals that they have, such as getting a better standard of living, having their children educated abroad, living the kind of life that other people in oil-exporting countries live, have been shelved once again for these abstract, ideological causes.

So how did Iraq get in this position? I mean, these things always seem like they come out of the blue, but, of course, they don't. There's always a history.

A lot of the Middle East's current problems come from the colonial period. After the dissolution of the Ottoman Empire, the borders of Iraq were drawn deliberately to prevent Iraq from having an easy access to the Gulf. So Iraq has, as a country, this persistent problem of not having an outlet to this main waterway. And, of course, once it became a major oil exporter, this became a huge problem for them.

Another thing is that all of these borders were drawn somewhat arbitrarily. When Britain and France carved up this area they did not pay very much attention to the ethnic and religious composition of these countries or to the economic resources that they had. I'm not suggesting that there was a deliberate negative agenda, but there certainly wasn't careful attention given to what these countries were going to look like afterwards. Under the Ottoman Empire, Kuwait was part of a province that was actually administered from Basra, which is a city in Iraq. So that whole historical dimension of the unity between the two countries is actually there. There are a lot of older ties as well: a lot of tribes that you can find in southern Iraq will have kinsmen in Kuwait; there are a lot of trade ties, and so on. I'm not suggesting in any way that, therefore, the historical claim that the Iraqis are making is valid. I'm just saying that Iraq's claims didn't appear out of nowhere. They came right out of the colonial period and affected what happened later.

This isn't the first time that Iraq has tried to press its claim to Kuwait. Under Abdul Kareem Kasim, a populist who came into power immediately after the revolution of '58, the Iraqis did try to take Kuwait after the British moved out of Kuwait in 1961. The British had maintained a base at Aden, which is in the Arabian peninsula in the south. When the British moved out, Abdul Kareem Kasim moved his troops in and captured part of Kuwait. The response at this point from all the Arab states was extremely forceful. Even though the Arab world at the time was tremendously divided—remember, this was the heyday of Nasser, and the Arab world was divided between the monarchies and the republicans and there was a tremendous amount of conflict. Still, Egypt, Jordan, Saudi Arabia, all these countries sent troops to the area, and then the British began to send troops, and Abdul Kareem Kasim then moved the Iraqis back out.

I'm very disturbed by people who attribute this violence to the Arab mentality or to cultural traits of the Arabs. It's not a racial trait, it's the result of political circumstances. Iraq is a deeply divided society. Those divisions are not just economic, but geographical, sectarian, ethnic—Sunni, Shiite, Kurd and non-Kurd, and so on. Combine this with the fact that on each side Iraq is surrounded by hostile powers—Turkey, with its own Kurdish population (there was a story of murder and gore if ever there was one!), and Iran. There's been hostilities and water disputes with Turkey all along. In the southeast, you have Iran, where particularly after the Iranian revolution, there was a real threat to the national integrity of Iraq, because of the strong allegiance of Iraq's Shiite population to post-revolutionary Iran.

And then, of course, you have the persistent problem of the Kurds and the civil war that's persisted in Iraq on and off since its inception. So at some level, a government that could hold these different communities together would almost have to be strong-handed in some ways, unless they wanted to simply allow various parts of the country to section off. As we can see from the Soviet Union, governments are very, very reluctant to let this happen. This process of national integration is extremely painful and brutal and violent, and it always has been. I think to understand this, all Westerners have to do is look at the process of state formation in early modern Europe. France, for instance, was not born as France. It was united from all these different communities that had their own language, their own dialect, and so on. It was a long and bloody process. So at some level you can see what's happening in Iraq in these terms.

*Yes, but France actually did turn into a stable nation-state. It
doesn't look like Iraq is going to make the transition.*

France coalesced after centuries. Iraq's only been at this
thirty years or so. And remember, in Europe you had a core
government that was expanding outwards, conquering territories and then united them administratively. In Iraq, you had
these essentially arbitrarily defined borders given to them by
the British, who then said, "Okay, deal with it!" Suddenly
there was this huge territory that needed to be controlled.
That's very different from the piecemeal way that Europe's
nation-states emerged.

So I think it's unfair to cast this situation in terms of the
Arabs' "violent nature." Most less-developed countries
growing out of a colonial legacy have these sorts of problems
that erupt into violence. As Americans, we simply can't understand the scarcity of resources that exists in the Third World,
the inequalities that exist there. These conditions can push
people into acts of violence that are beyond our understanding. I heard on NPR that since August, 2,600 blacks have died
in South Africa, 300 people in El Salvador, 711 in Lebanon,
40 Israelis, 150 Palestinians, 7,000 Liberians, 7,000 people in
India, 3,000 in Sri Lanka, and 1,500 in Somalia, all in political violence. From the perspective of somebody who studies
developing countries, President Bush's "new world order"
looks much more like the new world disorder to me.

I think your point is well-taken, though, about the image
that Americans have of Arabs. I'm both fascinated and horri-
fied at this. I think that racial hatred against Arabs is the only
remaining socially acceptable racism in the United States
today. And I think it comes from what began as a romantic
notion of what Arabs were, which was grounded in the tradi-
tion of Orientalism, where Arabs were a projection of what we
wanted them to be—Lawrence of Arabia kinds of images—and
then when it turned out that these quaint colonials controlled
the oil, it turned into a real confrontation. Since the OPEC oil
crisis in 1973, through 1979 and the Iranian revolution, right
up to now, it's not a coincidence that our bogeymen have all
been Muslim or Arab. We had the Ayatollah, then we had Gad-
hafi until we bombed Libya, and now we have Saddam Hussein, and who knows who will be next? The way the media
grabs onto these images really alarms me. Have you noticed
this film with Sally Field, *Not Without My Daughter* [about an

American woman and her half-Iranian child trying to escape from post-revolutionary Iran]? The timing of these things is really shocking. It's a schlocky, awful television movie, but the fact that it is released now is significant.

Let's go on to Saddam himself. What do you make of him and the way President Bush and the American media have depicted him as another Hitler or Stalin?

Well, Saddam Hussein is probably one of the more violent modern leaders, just in terms of the recorded and well-known instances of brutality and so on. Not just the Kurdish thing, but personal acts of violence that he himself has committed. But he is not unique in this regard. I haven't heard either the administration or the media mention the fact that Syria's Assad, who's now an ally of the United States, in one attack killed 20,000 unarmed civilians in the town of Hamah in 1982. I don't think there's a comparable instance in Iraq of that many people being killed by their own government.

I think that President Bush has personalized this whole conflict. He's said he has no quarrel with the Iraqi people, but only with Saddam Hussein. And Saddam Hussein does so dominate the political landscape of Iraq that it is, to some extent, he and his regime and not so much the Iraqi people that are confronting the Americans in this conflict. But this sort of characterization of the problem is very dangerous. By focusing so much on Saddam Hussein, you dehumanize the Iraqi people. You run the risk of forgetting that it's the civilians that are going to pay the highest cost for this conflict, and have already paid a tremendous cost for having Saddam Hussein as their leader. When you focus so much on this one personality, you get away from what the horror of war really is, and what it's going to mean. While I was there, citizens were forbidden to leave Baghdad; they weren't being allowed to evacuate the city.

When we started moving massive amounts of troops in and war became a very serious possibility, I asked myself, is there any way we could possibly do this and come out the winner in this situation?

There isn't. There's a frenzy of anti-Western feeling in the whole Third World, particularly in the Muslim world. These sentiments are going to focus on this event. None of the rhetoric about the international coalition and about the fact that this is being done under the United Nations' auspices will

make sense to these people. The Arabs have seen international
laws applied inconsistently for decades. People outside the
United States are incredibly politically sophisticated. They
know the kinds of political and economic deals that the U.S.
cut with each and every country that's been supporting it in
this whole initiative, except maybe Britain and the European
countries. China, for instance. For backing us in the Gulf, the
Chinese have now been forgiven for Tiananmen Square.
They're back in the fold. No more economic sanctions. The
Egyptians have had their entire military debt forgiven by the
United States. The Syrians are getting arms. They got the
green light from the US to move all the way into Lebanon.
This is costing us billions of dollars, not just in terms of the
troops that are deployed, but all the money that we've
committed to different countries. As far as I know, at this
point, the American taxpayer is still responsible for about
seventy percent of these expenses.

*When this all started I thought, if we go through with this, the
Arabs will never, ever forgive us and we will be entangled there in
the worst way for the foreseeable future. That was my fear.*

That's absolutely true. And this argument cuts into the
second part of the answer, which is our oil interests. How are
we going to maintain our oil interests, or even keep a steady
flow of oil coming out of the region, if Israel gets involved and
this becomes a regional war, or if the regimes in Saudi Arabia
and Syria and Egypt topple and become anti-American, or if
you have a condition where it doesn't really matter what the
governments are saying because the people are doing something else (and that is very possible). In Pakistan, for instance,
which has troops in Saudi Arabia ostensibly to protect the
holy places, Muslim fundamentalists have started recruiting
their own private army to fight on the side of Saddam
Hussein. Jordan is technically neutral, but how long can it
remain so if its Palestinians, which make up sixty percent of
the country, go off to fight for Saddam? I wouldn't make any
bets on what the Syrians and Egyptians are really thinking
and feeling at this point.

*I find Saddam Hussein's adoption of the Islamic fundamentalist
line pretty amazing, given that he's supposed to be a godless
socialist.*

Saddam Hussein has *no* religious credentials. The core of
Baathist ideology is secularism. It's not just tangential to

Baathism. It is the very base of it. It's not a coincidence that Baathism arose in Syria, a country just riddled with sectarian differences. It was an ideology that gave a vision of how a state with so much diversity could be set up.

But Saddam Hussein seems to have been very successful at making the connection in the minds of Arabs between his cause and the cause of Islamic fundamentalism. Credentials or no, it seems to have worked.

The response of the Muslim world and Islamic fundamentalists—from Iran to Pakistan to North Africa—is not a reflection of how valid they think his claims to leading the Islamic world are. It's a reflection of a very deep-seated hatred and mistrust of the West. Anybody who comes out confronting the West is going to be a hero in that region and, at some level, we have to ask ourselves why that is.

February 4, 1991

Though the hearings are all but obscured by the daily news of the war, Henry Gonzalez, the Democratic congressman from Texas who is chairman of the House Banking Committee, launched an investigation into U.S.-Iraqi trading patterns that had raised questions over banking practices.

TRANSCRIPT OF HOUSE COMMITTEE HEARINGS ON U.S.-IRAQI TRADE AND BANKING PRACTICES
Washington, D.C.

Congressman Gonzalez: In 1979, during the Carter administration, Iraq was labeled as a nation that had consistently supported international terrorism. At one time or another, Iraq was reportedly providing state sponsored support for the notorious anti-Israeli group the Abu Nidal Organization and other terrorist organizations. Under the export controls operative at that time, a terrorist designation meant Iraq was prohibited from purchasing many United States goods including civilian aircraft or military equipment.

Shortly after this action the Iranian revolution and ensuing hostage crisis rocked United States policy in the region. At the same time, tensions between Iran and Iraq were mounting. In 1980, Iraq invaded Iran, starting a bloody war that would last nearly eight years and claim hundreds of thousand of lives.

The loss of Iran was a severe strategic blow to the United States. The United States feared Iranian hegemony in Middle Eastern affairs and began to tilt toward Iraq as a counterbalance to the rise of Iran. In a controversial decision, the Reagan administration removed Iraq from the terrorist list in 1983, thus easing export controls that had been instituted in 1979. It appears the United States wanted Iran to lose the war so bad that it was willing to reestablish diplomatic relations with Saddam Hussein's terrorist regime after a 17-year interruption even though many believed Iraq was still harboring terrorists.

Iraq was also friendly with Russia, and countering this influence in Iraq probably played a role in this United States decision to tilt toward Iraq. At the time, economic factors played little role.

Removing Iraq from the terrorist list also opened the door for United States Government guaranteed agricultural exports to Iraq which began in 1983. This was convenient, because at about the same time the U.S. agriculture community was experiencing surpluses in many agriculture commodities. The agriculture community supposedly saw Iraq as having long-term food needs that would present significant market opportunities for United States agricultural commodities.

In 1984, the United States officially reestablished diplomatic relations with Iraq even though in that same year Iraq had used poison gas in its war with Iran. Over the remaining years of the 1980s, Iraq continued to be one of the world's worst violators of human rights—a topic I will discuss at some length at a later date. Nevertheless, the administration continued to ignore massive human rights abuses.

As incredulous as it may seem, the United States reacted to all the human rights abuses, including Iraq gassing its own citizens, by expanding United States credit guarantee programs. From 1985 to 1990, the United States authorized over $4 billion in United States guaranteed agricultural exports to Iraq, the peak being $1.1 billion in 1988.

While Iraqi participation in the agriculture export guarantee program was increasing dramatically, Iraq was in default on United States Export-Import Bank credit programs. After settling its differences with Iraq, in 1987, the Export-Import Bank opened up for business with Iraq by providing a $200 million a year line of short-term insurance coverage for United States manufacturing exports to Iraq. These actions were probably taken to appease Saddam and his ambitious economic reconstruction program announced in 1987. The war with Iran ended in 1988, and Iraq was anxious to get the reconstruction program going. BNL would play a major role in the reconstruction effort. . . .

In July 1989, the Federal Reserve Bank of Atlanta was notified by the FBI of a substantial off-book operation at the Atlanta Agency of Banca Nazionale del Lavoro. On August 4, 1989, the Federal Reserve, accompanied in Atlanta by the FBI and the U.S. Attorney in Atlanta, raided the U.S. operations of BNL.

Based on the information gathered from that raid, it was apparent that BNL-Atlanta was conducting massive off-book transactions. The Atlanta office was lending and raising billions that it did not report on its financial statements or its bank regulatory statements.

The off-book lending probably began in February 1987. These transactions, kept on a set of secret books, were purportedly established to conceal the excessive Iraqi loans from BNL's headquarters in Rome.

The off-book transactions were originally used to finance commodity exports to Iraq. The first such transaction occurred in February 1987 with Rafidain Bank of Baghdad, Iraq. . . .

The Iraqis were quite successful in obtaining western technology. During the 1980s, Iraq established ownership or control of a sophisticated network of United States and European front companies whose primary mission was to obtain western military technology and know-how and export it back to Iraq. The Iraqis were very secretive in their dealings and were careful to conceal their true affiliation.

An example of the success of this network is the Taji Complex, a cannon factory outside of Baghdad. This project was long considered a civilian industrial complex, and many western nations provided the technology and know-how to build it. Last year, a German Government investigation concluded Taji was meant for the manufacture of gun barrels. Many European and United States companies provided technology for this plant.

Hopefully, coalition air forces have destroyed the Taji Complex. But the Taji Complex is just one example of the Iraqi strategy. Over the next several months I will acquaint you with other Iraqi military applications made possible by western technology and BNL financing.

A recent example of a company linked to the Iraqi network is the Cleveland, Ohio-based machine tool company, Matrix-Churchill. Iraqis secretly owned Matrix-Churchill and its affiliate in England and used both to obtain computer-controlled lathes and other industrial machinery that went into the Taji Cannon Complex.

Upon gaining control of the Cleveland-based Matrix-Churchill, the Iraqis set up a procurement division within the company. The procurement side of the company received its orders, mostly in Arabic, directly from Baghdad. It was apparently charged with finding other United States companies that would build industrial plants in Iraq. Matrix-Churchill helped find U.S. contractors to build a Fiberglass plant and sophisticated cutting tool plant in Iraq. The cutting plant may have been used to manufacture parts with nuclear applications while the Fiberglass plant was supposedly used to produce missile casings.

Ironically, the U.S. Government and our Western allies often granted export licenses for such plants, thus permitting countries like Iraq access to such sophisticated technology. This was the case with the above plants. The United States Custom Service confiscated Matrix-Churchill in September 1990, calling it an "Iraqi front company."

It is likely that the Iraqi network used dozens of United States and European companies to supply the needed technology and know-how to upgrade Iraqi military capability. It is debatable whether or not these companies knew the ultimate destination of their products. Some probably did, some probably did not. These companies were often lured into supplying Iraq by higher than normal profits and even bribes.

As I stated, earlier, it is hard to believe that the United States intelligence community or that of our allies did not know about the applications of technology being transferred to Iraq. It is also hard to believe BNL escaped the attention of the intelligence community. These organizations monitor overseas telexes and phone conversations. Did they fail to discover the over 3,000 telexes between BNL and Iraqi government agencies, many providing information detailing loans to companies that were building the Taji complex and other military related projects within Iraq?

They also monitor travel between the United States and Iraq. Did they fail to discover the many visits BNL employees made to Iraq and vice versa, and the purpose of such visits?

Given the magnitude of the loans to Iraq, and the projects that some of the loans were going to finance, one would almost be justified in asking the question: If the United States and Western intelligence communities did not know about BNL, did they fail to do their job properly?

February 6, 1991

As the allied nations step up both their air strikes and their censorship of the press, Robert Fisk, writing in the *Independent* of London, is one of a handful of reporters to provide first-hand accounts of the unfolding war. On February 6, he describes how many reporters in the Gulf have become part of the military propaganda apparatus.

FREE TO REPORT WHAT WE'RE TOLD
ROBERT FISK
The Independent (London)

A colonel commanding an American air base in the Gulf last week decided to honour the "pool" reporters who had been attached to his fighter-bomber squadrons since the day the war broke out. He produced for each of them a small American flag which, he said, had been carried in the cockpits of the very first U.S. jets to bomb Baghdad. "You are warriors, too," he told the journalists as he handed them their flags.

The incident said a lot about the new, cosy, damaging relationship between reporters and the military in the Gulf war. So thorough has been the preparation for this war, so dependent have journalists become upon information dispensed by the Western military authorities in Saudi Arabia, so enamoured of their technology, that Press and television reporters have found themselves trapped.

For most journalists in the Gulf—and most of the Western armies—war is an unknown quantity, exciting as well as frightening, historic as well as deadly. The notion that this is a "just" war, a struggle between good and evil (as Messrs. Runcie and Bush would, respectively, have us believe) has presented us with a moral pretext for our presence. If Saddam Hussein is the Hitler of Baghdad—worse than Hitler in President Bush's flawed historical analysis—then it was inevitable that our reporting would acquire an undertone of righteousness, even romanticism.

As RAF fighter-pilots took off from a Gulf airstrip a week ago, a young British reporter told her television audience that "their bravery knows no bounds." When 10 U.S. navy jets took off from the aircraft carrier USS Kennedy at the start of the war—in a campaign that we now know is also causing civilian casualties—a reporter for the *Philadelphia Inquirer* filed a pool dispatch from the ship describing how "Thursday morning was one of the moments suspended in time . . . paving the way for a dawn of hope." Journalists are now talking of Iraq as "the enemy" as if they themselves have gone to war—which, in a sense, they have.

The language is of the early Forties, when Hitler's armies had reached the Pas de Calais and were poised to invade England. Journalists in uniforms and helmets are trying to adopt the *gravitas* of Edward R. Murrow and Richard Dimbleby. We are being prepared for "the biggest tank battle since World War Two" and "the largest amphibious operation since D-Day [or Korea]."

This nonsense is as dangerous as it is misleading. When three of the largest Western armies launch their attack from the Muslim nation containing Islam's two holiest shrines, this is no time to draw parallels with the Second World War. If Ed Murrow were alive today, he would probably be among the reporters in Baghdad describing the effect of allied air raids. Nor is this the "dawn of hope." It may well be the start of renewed decades of hatred between the West and the Arab world. Yet our reporting does not reflect this.

It is not easy for journalists to exercise self-criticism when they are reporting history. And to cast doubt on the world of American or British officers in the Gulf is to invite almost immediate condemnation. Those of us who reported the human suffering caused by Israeli air raids in Beirut in 1982 were told we were anti-Semitic. Any expression of real scepticism about American military claims in the Gulf provokes a parallel accusation. Have we taken Saddam's side? Do we not realise that Iraq invaded Kuwait on 2 August?

There cannot be a reporter in Saudi Arabia who does not realise that Saddam Hussein is a brutal, wicked dictator who rules through terror. There can be no doubt about the savagery of his army in occupied Kuwait. Reporters who wander off to investigate military affairs in Saudi Arabia risk, at worst,

deportation. The last journalist who did that in Iraq, Farzad
Bazoft, was hanged. Long before Saddam invaded Kuwait, we
were reporting on his cruelty—unlike the Saudis during the
Iran-Iraq war, who were bankrolling his dreadful regime
under the illusion that he was the saviour of the Arab world.

Yet, almost three weeks after the start of the war, journalists
have allowed themselves to be duped by the Western
authorities, forced either to participate in pool reporting
under military restrictions or to work independently at the
risk of having their accreditation taken away. In theory the
"pool" means that the reports of journalists travelling with
military units are available to all television networks and
newspapers. In practice, it means that the only reporters
officially allowed to witness events at "the front"—whether
they be with the army, the navy or the air force—have their
reports read and often amended by military censors.

It should be said at once that almost all ordinary soldiers
are invariably friendly and helpful to journalists. It should
also be said that there are journalists in the "pool" who are
valiantly and successfully filing dispatches that describe the
unhappiness as well as the motivation of soldiers at war, the
boredom as well as the excitement, the mistakes as well as the
efficiency. But many of their colleagues can claim no such
record. Most of the journalists with the military now wear
uniforms. They rely upon the soldiers around them for advice
and protection. Naturally (and justifiably) fearful of the
coming land war, they also look to the soldiers around them
for comfort. They are dependent on the troops and their
officers for communications, perhaps for their lives. And there
is thus the profound desire to fit in, to "work the system," a
frequent absence of critical faculties.

This was painfully illustrated last week when Iraqi troops
captured the abandoned Saudi border town of Khafji. Pool
reporters were first kept up to 15 miles from the sighting and
—misled by their U.S. military "minders"—filed stories reporting the recapture of the town. But when *The Independent*
travelled to the scene to investigate, an American NBC
television reporter—a member of the military pool—-
responded as follows: "You asshole; you'll prevent us from
working. You're not allowed here. Get out. Go back to
Dhahran." He then called over an American Marine public

affairs officer, who announced: "You're not allowed to talk to U.S. Marines and they're not allowed to talk to you."

It was a disturbing moment. By traveling to Khafji, *The Independent* discovered that the Iraqis were still fighting in the town long after the Prime Minister had claimed outside No. 10 Downing Street that it had been liberated. For the American reporter, however, the privileges of the pool and the military rules attached to it were more important than the right of a journalist to do his job.

The American and British military have thus been able to set reporters up against reporters, to divide journalists on the grounds that those who try to work outside the pool will destroy the opportunities of those who are working—under military restriction—within it. That is why, when an enterprising reporter from *The Sunday Times* managed to find the Staffordshire Regiment in the desert last week, he was confronted by an angry British major accompanying the British Press pool, who claimed that if he did not leave, "You'll ruin it for the others."

The "others," however, already have problems. When American correspondents on the carrier Saratoga quoted the exact words of air force pilots last week, they found that the captain and other senior officers deleted all swear words and changed some of the quotations before sending on their dispatches after a delay of 12 hours. On the Kennedy, news agency pool reporters recorded how fighter-bomber pilots watched pornographic video tapes to help them relax before their mission. This was struck from their report.

At one American airbase, a vast banner is suspended inside an aircraft hangar. It depicts an American "Superman" holding in his arms a limp, terrified Arab with a hooked nose. The existence of this banner, with its racist overtones, went unreported by the pool journalists of the base. A pool television crew did record U.S. Marine Lieutenant-Colonel Dick White when he described what it was like to see Iraqi troops in Kuwait from his plane. His words are worth repeating: "It was like turning on the kitchen light late at night and the cockroaches started scurrying . . . We finally got them out where we could find them and kill them." These astonishing remarks went unquestioned, although there was certainly one question that was worth putting: what is the new world order worth when an American officer, after only three weeks of war, compares his Arab enemies to insects?

The unquestioning nature of our coverage of this war is one of its most dangerous facets. Many of the American television pool dispatches sound as if they have been produced by the military, which, in a way, they have. For the relationship between reporter and soldier here is becoming almost fatally blurred. Reporters who are working independently of the military have been threatened not just with the withdrawal of their accreditation, but also with deportation from Saudi Arabia—even though they willingly comply with all the security guidelines, which preclude the reporting of military details that could be of use to Iraq.

The system may be convenient for the military, but it is pernicious for the Press. Reporters who worked in Vietnam are now describing official military briefings in Riyadh as even more uninformative than the notorious "five o'clock follies" in Saigon. This is supposed to be a war for freedom, but the Western armies in Saudi Arabia—under the guise of preserving "security"—want to control the flow of information.

There could be no better proof of this than the predicament of the French television crew who filmed the Khafji fighting at great risk to their lives, broke no security guidelines—and then had their tape confiscated because they were not members of the pool. In reality, the French were merely doing their job. If reporters were trusted to travel independently to the front, as they have done in so many other wars, obeying local military commanders, betraying no secrets, but taking responsibility for their own lives, the whole charade of pools and restrictions could be abandoned.

As it is, we probably do not yet appreciate how sad and humiliating is our acceptance of the present system. How are we going to justify what amounts to sycophancy if the forthcoming land battle turns into a bloodbath for the West? What excuses will we find for those uncritical reports? Generals will always blame the Press for their failures, however much we bow to their rules. But when the bodies start coming home—when the West really begins to suffer—the public, whose support for this conflict is partly shaped by what it reads and sees on television, may not forgive us for our weakness in so humbly accepting those little flags handed out by the colonel.

February 25, 1991

As casualties mount in the ground war that has been launched despite the Soviet-initiated peace proposals, columnist Sheryl McCarthy declares, "I've known for a while that the United States' decision to go to war with Iraq had nothing to do with our claims to want to liberate Kuwait."

TRUTH OF THE GULF WAR ON THE STREETS
SHERYL MCCARTHY
Newsday

The cab driver was missing some of his teeth, so his speech was rather mushy.

"Any news on the war?" he asked me.

I told him I hadn't heard anything new. He shook his head and uttered a sarcastic laugh.

"We're over there for the oil," he said. "He [by which I assumed he meant President George Bush] got an offer to make peace, but he turned it down. We're just over there for the oil...What kind of world is this we're living in?"

Understanding often comes slowly and late in the game. But when one seeks clarity, one ultimately finds it, though the process may unfold as slowly as watching a plant grow. So it was heartening amidst the epidemic of boosterism about this war to meet this cab driver who has begun to see the truth.

I've known for a while that the United States' decision to go to war with Iraq had nothing to do with our claims to want to liberate Kuwait from the illegal grip of Saddam Hussein. Something more venal, corrupt and self-serving was clearly at work. But to know something and to have actual proof of it are two different things. Over the weekend President Bush gave me ample proof of what I suspected.

Last week the Bush administration was broadsided by Soviet President Mikhail Gorbachev's peace agreement with Iraq. The leader of what used to be "the evil empire" had actually come up with a reasonable plan to get Hussein out of

Kuwait. And Hussein, beaten down by the deadly barrage from the allies, had actually agreed to the terms.

What could be more reasonable, if our true goal was restoring the integrity of Kuwait, than to accept this plan and end the carnage? But the Bush administration began to squirm. Not to accept the plan would seem to be at cross purposes with its stated mission in Iraq. But to accept the plan would have undermined its real goal. So the administration hedged, then came up with its own plan which it demanded that Iraq implement within 48 hours. When Iraq didn't snap to our demands, we rushed in with ground troops in what may prove to be a bloody and unnecessary ground war.

Joshua Epstein, a defense analyst with the Brookings Institution, best summed up the real Bush strategy. The U.S. plan, he said, wasn't all that different in substance from the Soviet plan. "When you come right down to it, it is now evident that all along the Bush administration and its military allies wanted to destroy Hussein and annihilate his military power so that it can never be a threat. So we were not prepared to negotiate and we set a deadline to avoid the political pressure of a debate."

With John Wayne type bravado, yesterday's headlines reported how the allied forces, in one of the greatest ground battles since World War II, had moved in to liberate Kuwait from the grip of Saddam Hussein. The fact is we didn't accept the Soviet peace plan because we didn't care squat about Kuwait's integrity. Nor did we care about bringing the war to a speedy end. We rolled our troops into Iraq because our goal from the beginning was to topple Hussein, who had gotten too uppity and too uncontrollable for the western powers who feel it is their manifest destiny to control that region of the world.

The rhetoric of U.S. officials further tipped their hand. One official said the Soviet peace plan should be rejected because it would not "punish" Hussein enough, and Stormin' Norman Schwarzkopf mused about how, once the allies have destroyed Hussein's Republican Guard, " his chances of staying in power are pretty low." Now, I ask you, if Hussein was willing to pull out of Kuwait, which is what we said we wanted, then who are we to talk about "punishing" him? And who are we to engineer the toppling of his government, which, from all indications, is supported by the Iraqi people?

The U.S. actions in Iraq are reminiscent of our actions in Vietnam, where we helped to destroy that country by using it as a pawn in the now-dead Cold War. Even now our government continues to foment turmoil and misery in Cambodia by trying to help overthrow the Vietnamese-installed government there.

Much has been made of our military prowess in the Persian Gulf, and of how Hussein, who has been so rudely beaten, didn't have the military might he had boasted of. We vilify him as a desperate man and an environmental criminal for taking steps like burning Kuwaiti oil fields. But the fact is that to achieve our political goals, the U.S. and its powerful allies are bombing the hell out of a country a fraction of the size of our own and killing hundreds of its people. Given the overwhelming odds against him, Hussein's actions merely seem like those of a wily general who is taking what steps he can against overwhelming superior forces.

Finally, given the chance to end the war and get Iraq to withdraw from Kuwait, we rejected it. That, more than anything else, revealed the total lack of any moral imperative in this war. The presence of political imperatives became even more blatant.

Coming to an understanding of all this is a painful process, but to see the world with clarity is redeeming and is worth the struggle. Like the cab driver, I can only shake my head over the moral bankruptcy of my country, and repeat his words:

"What kind of world is this we're living in." Indeed, and what kind of country?

February 27, 1991

Shortly before President Bush orders a ceasefire in the Gulf war, the allied commander, General Norman Schwarzkopf, provides the following account of the campaign.

HOW THE WAR WAS WON
GENERAL NORMAN SCHWARZKOPF
Riyadh, Saudi Arabia

As you know, very early on we took out the Iraqi air force. We knew that he had very, very limited reconnaissance means. And therefore we took out his air force, for all intents and purposes we took out his ability to see what we were doing down here in Saudi Arabia.

Once we had taken out his eyes, we did what could best be described as a "Hail Mary" play in football. I think you recall when the quarterback is desperate for a touchdown at the very end what he does is, he steps up behind the center and all of a sudden every single one of his receivers goes way out to one flank, and they all run down the field as fast as they possibly can and into the end-zone, and he lobs the ball. In essence, that's what we did.

When we knew that he couldn't see us any more, we did a massive movement of troops all the way out to the extreme west, because at that time we knew that he was still fixed in this area [Kuwait] with the vast majority of his forces, and once the air campaign started he would be incapable of moving out to counter this move, even if he knew we made it.

There were some additions to Iraqi troops out in this [northern] area. But they did not have the capability nor the time to put in the barrier that had been described by Saddam Hussein as an absolutely impenetrable tank barrier that no-one would ever get through, I believe those were his words...

Not only did we move troops out there, but we literally moved thousands and thousands of tons of fuel, of ammunition, of spare parts, of water, and of food out here into this area, because we wanted to have enough supplies on hand so that if we launched this and got into a "slugfest" battle, which

we very easily could have gotten into, we'd have enough supplies to last for 60 days...

But by Feb. 23, what you have found is this situation: the
front lines had been attritted down to a point where all of
these [Iraqi] units were at 50 per cent or below. The second
level—and these were really tough fighters that we were
worried about—were attritted to some place between 50 and
75 percent, although we still had the Republican Guard, and
parts of the Republican Guard were very strong. We continued to hit the bridges all across this area, to make absolutely
sure that no more reinforcements came into battle.

This then was the morning of Feb. 24. Our plan initially
had been to do exactly what the Iraqis thought we were going
to do, and that's take them on head-on into their most heavily
defended area.

Also, at the same time, we launched amphibious feints and
naval gunfire, so that they continued to think that we were
going to be attacking along the coast, and therefore fixed their
forces in this position. They wouldn't know what was going
on. I believe we succeeded in that very well.

At four in the morning, the Marines—the 1st Marine
Division and the 2nd Marine Division—launched attacks
through the barrier system. They were accompanied by the
2nd—the Tiger Brigade, U.S. Army Tiger Brigade of the 2nd
Armoured Division.

At the same time, two Saudi task forces also launched a
penetrator through the barrier. But while they were doing
that, the 6th French Armoured Division, accompanied by a
brigade of the 82nd Airborne, also launched an overland
attack to their objective—Salman airfield.

We were held up a little bit by the weather, but by eight in
the morning, the 101st Airborne launched an air assault deep
in the enemy territory to establish a forward operating
base...

What we found was as soon as we breached these obstacles
and started bringing pressure, we started getting a large number of surrenders.

We were worried about the weather. The weather, it turned
out, was going to get pretty bad the next day and we were
worried about launching this air assault, and we also started
to have a huge number of atrocities—of really the most
unspeakable types—committed in downtown Kuwait City,

to include reports that the desalination plant had been destroyed. And when we heard that, we were quite concerned about what might be going on.

Based upon that, and the situation as it was developing, we made the decision that, rather than wait till the following morning to launch the remainder of these forces, we would go ahead and launch those forces [VII Corps.] that afternoon.

This was the situation you saw the afternoon of the 24th. The Marines continued to make great progress going through the breach in this area—and we were moving rapidly north.The task force on the east coast was also moving rapidly to the north and making very, very good progress.We launched another Egyptian-Arab force, and another Saudi force, again to make the enemy continue to think that we were doing exactly what he wanted us to do, and that was to make a headlong assault into a very, very tough barrier system. At the same time, we continued to attack with the French. We also launched an attack on the part of of the entire VII Corps.

The First Infantry Division went through, breached an obstacle and minefield barrier, established quite a large breach through which we passed the 1st British Armoured Division.

At the same time—and because of our deception plan and the way it worked, we didn't even have to worry about a barrier—the 3rd Armoured Division just went right around the enemy and were behind him in no time at all. And the 1st Armoured Cavalry.

The 24th Mechanised Division also launched out in the far west. Once the 101st had their forward operating base established here, they went ahead and launched into the Tigris and Euphrates valleys.

There are a lot of people who are still saying that the object of the U.S. was to capture Iraq and cause the downfall of the entire country of Iraq. Ladies and gentlemen, we were 150 miles away from Baghdad and there was nobody between us and Baghdad. If it had been our intention to take Iraq, if it had been our intention to destroy the country, if it had been our intention to overrun the country, we could have done it unopposed, for all intents and purposes. But that was not our intention. Our intention was purely to eject the Iraqis out of Kuwait and destroy the military power that had come in.

Epilogue

THE UNQUIET PEACE

The war in the Gulf ended with the United States victorious and President Bush enjoying unparalleled popularity. At home, Bush's new-found appeal dispelled any impression there might once have been of weakness, and gave the Republican minority in Congress a substantial boost in its drive to pass more conservative domestic programs, redirecting the country further away from the already distant New Deal and towards free enterprise. Abroad, the United States had shown itself to be the surviving superpower, and more than capable of policing the new world order. In the Middle East, the victory promised to provide the Bush administration with the authority it needed to remain in control of oil resources and to tackle the heretofore seemingly intransigent problems of Israel and the Palestinians.

Civil Violence

If the United States appeared, for the moment, triumphant and united, Iraq seemed sunk in ruin and chaos. Within days of the ceasefire at the end of February, the Shiites in southern Iraq revolted, reportedly with the support of Iran, and there was unrest and sporadic fighting in Basra and other cities across the southern part of the country. Dispirited and broken remnants of the retreating Iraqi regular army sometimes joined in.

"The ground war that might have taken place in Kuwait is now being fought in Iraq, not between Baghdad and its coalition adversaries but between the government and its internal enemies," wrote Chris Hedges, the *New York Times* reporter who was captured and then traveled with the Iraqi military around Basra before being freed in Baghdad.

The rebellion inside Iraq against Saddam Hussein spread into the North, with Syria encouraging Kurds and other Iraqi opposition groups to fight against the government. Leaders of the Iraqi Kurdistan Front said Irbil, a city of 900,000, along with Sulaimaniya, the provincial capital, had fallen under their control. There, too, units of the Iraqi army were said to have surrendered or joined in the rebellion.

At an early March meeting in Damascus, Syria's President Assad, Saddam Hussein's arch rival in the Baath party, staked out a new postwar role for his country. Together with Egypt, it would provide security for Kuwait, Saudi Arabia, and the other defenseless Gulf sheikhdoms. Syria and Egypt have more than 50,000 troops in the area, which could provide the core of a regional defense network. The two countries had been enemies until January 1990. (Syria broke with Cairo over its 1979 peace treaty with Israel.) Both remain deeply in debt, and their new role would bring increased foreign subsidies in the form of military aid. "So this will come as pennies from heaven," said Cairo University professor Ali Hillal Desouki. Iran was excluded from the new regional security plan.

For a while, there was serious talk that Iraq might break up—becoming another Lebanon or, more likely, splitting in two like North and South Korea, with the Sunni and Shiite populations divided by a new border. But by the end of the first week in March, Saddam Hussein seemed to have regained control of Basra, which refugees called a "dead zone"—its streets full of beaten soldiers and littered with bodies. In Baghdad residents clustered at the bus depots for bits of news coming from returning soldiers. The mood was sullen and angry.

Saddam expelled all foreign journalists and began the process of putting down the insurgencies. He recalled Republican Guards to defend the capital, where there was rioting in the Shiite areas. U.S. intelligence intercepted commands from Baghdad to troops in the South to use poison gas, and the State Department warned Saddam it would bomb his troops if that was allowed to happen. While President Bush, in his address to a joint session of Congress, said Saddam must be held accountable for his actions, Saddam remained in power.

The Human Cost

Information on civilian casualties during the Gulf war was unreliable. Foreign reporters who stayed in Baghdad during most of the bombing believe they were relatively light; under 10,000 dead. If this figure is correct, it is surprising given the escalating rate of civilian deaths in recent warfare.

Allied losses were light—139 soldiers were killed in action. (In fact, the numbers of noncombat deaths in the Gulf surpassed the number of combat deaths. Together, they totalled 324 as of March 17). Tens of thousands of Iraqi soldiers were killed; some estimates ran as high as 100,000. More than 100,000 Iraqis were taken prisoner. Asked for his impression of Saddam Hussein as a military leader, allied commander General Norman Schwarzkopf replied, "Ha! As far as Saddam Hussein being a great military strategist, he is neither a strategist, nor is he schooled in the operational art, nor is he a tactician, nor is he a general, nor is he a soldier. Other than that, he's a great military man."

Iraqi chemical and biological warfare, which might have caused countless additional casualties, never materialized, and there was never any real question of Saddam's ability to use nuclear weapons.

But the conflict saw germ warfare of another sort, and environmental warfare of horrendous proportions. The long-range effects of destroying the infrastructure of Iraq—roads, electric power, water, sewer systems, and bridges—are difficult to calculate. Certainly, the ruin of this infrastructure places the population at grave risk from an epidemic of disease—not the botulism or anthrax that Saddam was believed to be ready to employ, but typhoid, cholera, and polio. With half of the people of this nation of eighteen million under fifteen years old, and from one-third to two-thirds of that number five years of age or less, children are likely to be the hardest hit by the epidemics.

Dollars and Cents

Of Kuwait's 1,080 oil wellheads, the Iraqis rendered more than 800 inoperable, including 535 that were fractured and set afire with explosives as part of their scorched earth retreat. Fire-fighting teams soon landed to begin the job of getting them under control. The work was expected to go faster than originally believed, but the experts said it could take them years. Hydrogen sulfide pouring out of the flaming wells blew eastward, dumping acid rain on Iranian and even Indian agricultural lands. Smoke plumes from the fires could be seen for 400 miles.

Oil well fires in Kuwait threatened to reduce the nation's reserves of 92 billion barrels by 10 to 15 percent, and, if not checked, could burn for a hundred years. Experts predicted that even if efforts began immediately some of the fires would take up to five years to extinguish at a cost of as much as $3 million per well.

A postwar Kuwaiti survey found the Iraqis had destroyed up to half of the country's petroleum-gathering centers, sabotaged pumping stations along the pipeline network, destroyed all the surface oil storage facilities, and damaged or destroyed spare parts for the oil industry. Sabotage of Kuwait's refineries was sporadic and of little serious consequence.

In the United States, too, the damage wrought by the war was more profound and wide-ranging than the surface jubilation indicated. With the nation in economic recession, the costs of war threatened to further harm the economy. At the war's beginning, the Defense Budget Project, an independent Washington, D.C. group, estimated that the intensive air war might cost in the neighborhood of $500 million a day. Add to that an intense ground war, and the cost would jump to $1 billion a day, assuming the U.S. replaces its equipment. The Congressional Budget Office initially projected the war would run $17 to $35 billion if the equipment is not replaced, and as much as $86 billion if it is.

The cost of maintaining peace in the chaotic Middle East is unknown, but if past experience in similar situations is a guide, it might add up to a considerable amount of money. A study by James Love of the Center for the Study of Responsive Law in Washington points out that in the recent past, foreign nations have deployed one soldier per 48 to 194 occupied citizens. The report projected that in Iraq, which has a population of 17.6 million, the U.S. would have to keep a force of anywhere between 91,000 and 367,000 men as a garrison. A 100,000-man army would run $4.6 billion a year. Add to that humanitarian, economic, and reconstruction aid and the total becomes between $15 and $30 billion over the next five years. And if a regional "peacekeeping" force is needed to bolster this garrison, that would increase the cost even more.

As it turns out, some of these early cost estimates were far too high. Based on Defense Department estimates, the total cost of the buildup, air, and land operations for

Desert Shield/Storm are likely to be less than $47.5 billion. If the coalition members and supporting countries meet their commitment of $53.5 billion towards the U.S. effort, foreign contributions will end up paying for the entire operation. As for keeping the peace, the U.S. anticipates maintaining a naval presence in the area along with periodic land maneuvers. That will surely be far less expensive than garrisoning an army in the region indefinitely. But there remains the constant possibility of a dramatic increase, for strategic reasons, in the number of U.S. forces.

Reconstruction

It had been widely assumed that the rich sheikhdoms of the Gulf would pay for the war as well as reconstruction. But as the war went on, some doubt arose as to whether this would be possible. For one thing, the Gulf sheikhdoms would be spending anywhere from $50 billion to $100 billion for Western contractors to rebuild Kuwait. And then there would be the cost of restoring the economic infrastructure of Iraq, which would probably run upwards of $50 billion. (As President Bush made clear, the vast majority of those funds must come from the region. He said "not a dime" for Iraqi reconstruction would come from the U.S.)

These figures may be daunting even to the shiekhs and emirs of the Gulf states. Our perceptions of the Gulf are still colored by the imagery of the 1970s, when the sheikdoms were hugely rich. In the ten years ending in 1982, the Saudis chalked up a $170 billion surplus from high oil prices. But after that, the desert kingdom ran a deficit averaging about $15 billion a year, finally toting up a debt of about $80 billion by last year. When you subtract the cost of Desert Shield/Storm ($13.5 billion in early 1991), expected contributions to Egypt and Syria, and the cost of cleaning up the oil slick (which some estimates say could cost as much as $5 billion), the Saudis won't have much left over to help rebuild the region.

The situation could get worse. At the end of February, oil was running at about twenty dollars a barrel, a long-time low. And five dollars of that was a war premium (the markets figured maybe the Iraqis would get lucky with a Scud and take out a big oil processing station). But now that the war is over, the price of oil will drop. If oil goes to fifteen dollars a barrel, then the price of Saudi crude drops to around twelve or thirteen dollars a barrel. At that price, production declines. The Saudis will end up with an oil income that is closely balanced against their imports, and little or no surplus to spend.

What does this bode for rebuilding the region? The regional development bank that was discussed in February in Cairo might have gone some way toward narrowing the great gaps between the handful of small, thinly populated, petrorich Arab states and their populous but poor neighbors. But with so much money going to Western contractors to rebuild Kuwait, there won't be much left to go into the development bank—planned to be capitalized at $15 billion—let alone to rebuild the civilian infrastructure of Iraq. And shortly after the idea of the bank was made known, the U.S. Treasury Department sought, apparently with success, to kill the idea altogether for fear the U.S. would get dragged into funding its operations.

No one will want to loan money to a country controlled by Saddam. The Saudis and Kuwaitis may control Iraq's oil output, and they can be expected to demand reparations in terms of a certain pumping percentage. The Saudis have spent billions in improvements to increase production. Having spent this money, they will not now want to reduce their share of production. But at the same time, in their straitened condition, the Saudis won't want to see overall production increased if it would bring a further decline in oil prices and worsen their already precarious financial situation. Taken together, these factors point to a new fragility in the economics of the Gulf.

"Liberated" Kuwait

Kuwait's postwar position is precarious. All its liquid assets are likely to be consumed in the rebuilding, so to avoid spending all its money, the small nation has made plans to borrow as much as $20 billion. The oil fires are likely to delay the return to oil production for a year or more. Over the short term, Kuwait may become an oil importing nation. The longer it takes to produce oil, the stronger will be the political opposition.

A 200-page planning document prepared for the Pentagon by the U.S. Army's 352nd Civil Affairs Command in Riyadh (and obtained by Pacific News Service in late February) provided a detailed look at how the U.S. expects to reconstruct Kuwaiti society, from health care to public safety. While the document set forth plans for medical care for Kuwaiti citizens, it made clear that only rudimentary care will be made available for the more than half a million guest workers and their families. Many of these guest workers have spent most of their lives in Kuwait, and many of them are children. The Pentagon acknowledged, "Kuwait will only pay for evacuation and extramural treatment of their own citizens." (Kuwaiti citizens number about 200,000 of the 800,000 total population.)

A tough security section seemed aimed at Palestinians and other "expatriates" who accounted for more than 60 percent of the prewar Kuwaiti population. At several points the document equated "stay-behind Palestinians" with the Iraqis, and said terrorist action was expected from both groups.

The Pentagon planning document looked forward to a period of martial law and an American presence for up to five years. It called for tough press control, and a reorganized banking system under control of the royal family, excluding Palestinians: "This is a very sensitive political decision," the document said, "because the prominent merchant families are linked through the interlocking ownership of these institutions. The Palestinians virtually controlled the banking system."

The document also stated that "war crimes will be prosecuted in Kuwaiti tribunals, conducted by personnel from the Kuwaiti public safety and security agencies, with assistance from allied personnel." And the plan envisioned what could turn out to be a lengthy American presence in Kuwait. "Throughout all phases of the recovery period, and into the reconstruction phase, additional support will be provided to the established security force."

While the Pentagon planning papers are no more than plans, events in the early days of liberation tended to bear them out. The Kuwaiti resistance, including gangs of armed teenagers, rounded up, beat, and executed those they considered to be collaborators, including numerous Palestinians. Reporters described one case in which an American Special Forces soldier stood by while the resistance beat a young Palestinian boy. Two British reporters intervened to save the Palestinian boy. One of them, Robert Fisk, later wrote in *The Independent* of London, "When I asked the American officer why he allowed the Kuwaitis to beat civilians, he replied, 'You having a nice day? We don't want your sort around here with your dirty rumors. You have a big mouth. This is martial law, boy. Fuck off.'" On March 8 Middle East Watch, an international human rights group, reported that some 6,000 Palestinians accused by the Kuwaitis of collaborating with Iraq were being held in Kuwait without charges on the authority of a local militia acting in conjunction with U.S. forces.

If these indications are representative of what is happening inside Kuwait, the American military has become the enforcer of a class war in the Gulf, serving the interests of a tribal hierarchy out to discipline a servant class. This will add fuel to the anger of impoverished nations of the Third World—Pakistan, India, Yemen, Sudan, Egypt, etc.—providing explicit reasons for them to hate the new world order.

Iraq's Future

At war's end, no member of the international community was anxious for Iraq to be split apart. Iran let it be known it would not allow a change in Iraq's geographical make-up even though it clearly longed to replace the Baathist Sunni Moslems with an Islamic Republic, and called for Saddam to resign. It seemed unlikely that Turkey would permit an independence movement among the Iraqi Kurds, which might lead its own large Kurdish population into rebellion. Syria wanted to maintain a united front against Israel, which the Balkanization of Iraq would not help. The very thought of an Islamic Republic in Iraq was unthinkable to the Saudis—even Saddam was preferable to that.

Still, the potential outlines of a divided Iraq must be considered. *The Economist* provided a guide of what such a partition might look like: A southern Islamic republic would have a population of eight million, an oil reserve of 60 billion barrels (one third of Saudi Arabia's), two large ports opening to the Gulf, heavy industry and agricultural potential. A Kurdish republic in the mountainous north would have 20 to 30 billion barrels of oil (as much as Libya) and a population of up to four million. There is industry in the North, but Kurdistan would be land-locked. A Sunni Moslem state in central Iraq would have 15 billion barrels of oil (equivalent to reserves in Nigeria or Norway). It too would be landlocked, and mostly desert, with a population of three million, industry, and farm potential. It would claim Baghdad, but half the capital's four million people are Shias, and a quarter of the rest Kurds or Christians, creating the potential of a violently divided city like Beirut.

King Hussein of Jordan, who had supported Saddam Hussein with ammunitions, which were found by attacking American forces in the frontline defenses, also faces a precarious future. In his own way, King Hussein is as clever a survivor of Middle East politics as Saddam, and it remains to be seen whether he will reinstate himself with the United States and become a negotiator of a peace between Israel and the Palestinians.

The Legacy Stateside

The U.S. won the war. "As commander in chief, I can report to you: Our armed forces fought with honor and valor," Bush told a joint session of Congress on March 6. "As president, I can report to the nation: Aggression is defeated. The war is over."

But underlying issues remain. Among these, oil is foremost, and the United States remains schizoid on the subject. Big industry wants foreign oil at the lowest possible price, especially during a recession: Cheap oil makes it possible to make up for inefficiency in industrial production. At the same time, the Southwestern independent oil and gas prospectors want higher international prices, so as to shore up their own income. With Bush even now preparing for the 1992 campaign, these domestic concerns are—just as they were in 1986, when he made his trip to the Gulf to convince the Saudis and other Gulf producers to raise prices—no academic matter.

To some degree this decision about the price of oil will be made within the Congress, as it grapples with the various bills that attempt to set out a national energy policy. Victorious in war, Bush must still win acceptance for a conservative domestic program in what the press calls "Operation Domestic Storm." He will continue to seek a new energy policy, based not on efficiency or renewable energy, but on nuclear power, synthetic fuels made from coal and corn, and an expanded oil drilling program in the far north of Alaska and along the coasts. But while the environmental lobby in Washington is against the legislation, it lacks the means of organizing support for a different approach.

Amidst the celebration of victory, two committees in Congress began investigations of U.S. involvement with Saddam Hussein before the war, which brought about revelations reminiscent of the Iran-Contra scandal.

Details of an extensive network of agricultural and industrial relationships have already been exposed. The committe's investigation suggests that before the U.S. warred against Saddam, it may have helped to build up his regime, even to the point of assisting him in achieving the ability to manufacture unconventional weapons, including poison gas.

In another congressional investigation, records obtained by a subcommittee of the House of Representatives in early March revealed that the day before Iraq invaded Kuwait, the Bush administration approved $695,000 worth of advance data transmission equipment to the Iraqi government. The records show that between 1985 and 1990, the Reagan and Bush administrations approved 771 sales of technology to Iraq, including advanced devices for reading satellite gear and graphics terminals to help design rockets.

The *Wall Street Journal* reported on March 10 that Oscar Wyatt, chairman of Coastal Corp., a big importer of Iraqi crude before the war, had been trying to sell Saddam a half interest in Coastal's $800 million American oil refining and marketing network. Coastal is one of the largest U.S. refineries, and sells gas in twenty-three states.

There were other ramifications of the war, among them the effect of censorship during hostilities on the press. In April 1990, Saddam had complained to Senator Bob Dole and his party about his unfair treatment by the press, and Wyoming Senator Alan Simpson responded that the American press was a "pampered" lot, and encouraged Saddam to let reporters come and see Iraq for themselves. When Peter Arnett did so, staying through the war to report from Baghdad, Simpson assailed him as a "sympathizer." In her meeting with Saddam just before the war, Ambassador April Glaspie had also pointed out to the Iraqi leader that "if the American president had control of the media, his job would be much better." The war gave Bush an excuse to exercise such control. He and Saddam were in total agreement on the subject of censorship, and the press, for the most part, trailed along like proper spaniels.

The war also saw the reinvigoration of the military, and the United States' victory should give the volunteer army a push ahead—making it easier to recruit, and perhaps widening the purview of the military and making it more of a focus in American life. For many, military service is the only financial road to college or a technical education, and it will undoubtedly continue to be so. With industry, the universities, and civilian government in decline, the United States may well become a nation where the best and the brightest enter the military.

New World Order

The angry and sullen people in Baghdad and Basra are the survivors of World War III—or, more aptly put, the first of the Third World wars. The collapse of the Soviet Union has meant the end of the Northern Hemisphere's longest running civil war—the ongoing power struggles between the various Western industrialized powers—which began in 1914. The war with Iraq is the first of many on a North-South rather than an East-West axis. These will be high-tech versions of nineteenth-century colonial wars. Not content with wresting resources and labor from the Third World—taking rubber from Southeast Asia, say, or slaves from Africa—these wars are designed to impose an economic relationship that more fully exploits all the resources of a conquered nation. Iraq will not be merely an oil field to be pumped dry, but also a market for American goods and services and, ultimately, a cultural satellite.

"What is the new world order?" asked one Baghdad woman in the week after the fighting stopped, her voice rising in rage. "Is it based only on killing and money? Bush insisted on this war, and now he has what he wanted. We are nothing."

U.N. Security Council Resolutions on the Persian Gulf Crisis

Aug. 2, 1990

Resolution 660: Condemned the invasion of Kuwait. Demanded Iraq's unconditional, immediate withdrawal and called on both countries to begin negotiations. (Adopted 14-0; Yemen did not participate.)

Aug. 6

Resolution 661: Imposed a trade and financial embargo on Iraq and occupied Kuwait. Established a special sanctions committee to implement the resolution. Called on U.N. members to protect the assets of Kuwait around the world. (Adopted 13-0; Cuba and Yemen abstained.)

Aug. 9

Resolution 662: Declared Iraq's annexation of Kuwait null and void. (Adopted by unanimous vote.)

Aug. 18

Resolution 664: Demanded the immediate release of foreigners from Iraq and Kuwait and the right of diplomats to visit their nationals. Insisted that Iraq rescind its order closing diplomatic and consular missions in Kuwait. (Adopted by unanimous vote.)

Aug. 25

Resolution 665: Called on U.N. members with ships in the region to enforce sanctions by inspecting and verifying cargoes and destinations. (Adopted 13-0; Cuba and Yemen abstained.)

Sept. 13

Resolution 666: Reaffirmed that Iraq was responsible for the safety and well-being of foreign nationals. Specified guidelines for the delivery of food and medical supplies. (Adopted 13-2; Cuba and Yemen opposed.)

Sept. 16

Resolution 667: Condemned Iraqi aggression against diplomats and diplomatic compounds in Kuwait. Demanded immediate release of foreign nationals. (Adopted by unanimous vote.)

Sept. 24

Resolution 669: Emphasized that only the special sanctions committee had the power to permit food, medicine or other humanitarian aid shipments to Iraq or occupied Kuwait. (Adopted by unanimous vote.)

Sept. 25

Resolution 670: Expanded the economic embargo to include air traffic in or out of Iraq and Kuwait, except for humanitarian aid authorized by the special sanctions committee. Called on U.N. member nations to detain Iraqi ships that could be used to break the naval embargo. (Adopted 14-1; Cuba opposed.)

Oct. 29

Resolution 674: Demanded that Iraq stop mistreating Kuwaiti and other foreign nationals. Reminded Iraq that it is liable for damages to foreigners of their property resulting from the invasion and occupation of Kuwait. (Adopted 13-0; Cuba and Yemen abstained.)

Nov. 28

Resolution 677: Condemned Iraq's attempts to change Kuwait's demographic composition. Also condemned Iraq's destruction of Kuwaiti civil records. (Adopted by unanimous vote.)

Nov. 29

Resolution 678: Demanded Iraq's unconditional withdrawal from Kuwait by Jan. 15. Authorized U.N. members "to use all necessary means" to bring about Iraqi withdrawal after that date. (Adopted 12-2; China abstained; Yemen and Cuba opposed.)

Acknowledgements

Alterman, Eric, "Congress's Failure," from Tikkun Magazine, Copyright ©1991. Reprinted from Tikkun Magazine, a bi-monthly Jewish Critique of Politics, Culture and Society published at 5100 Leona Street, Oakland, CA 94619.

Arkin, William, "U.S. Hangs Nukes Over Iraq," Copyright ©1990 by the Author. Reprinted by permission.

Buchanan, Patrick J., "Declare War, or Come Home," Copyright ©1990 by Tribune Media Syndicate. Reprinted by permission.

Carpenter, Ted Galen, "Bush Jumped the Gun in the Gulf," from The New York Times, 8/18/90. Copyright ©1990, The New York Times. Distributed by Special Features/Syndication Sales.

Chaudry, Kiren, "Back from Baghdad," from an interview which appeared in the East Bay Express, 1/25/91. Copyright ©1991 by Laura Hagar. Reprinted by permission.

Chomsky, Noam, "America's Isolation in the Gulf," Copyright ©1990 by Noam Chomsky. Reprinted by permission of the Author.

Cockburn, Alexander, "The Last Temptation of George Bush," Copyright ©1990 by the Author. Reprinted by permission.

The Economist, "The Old Arab Order Passes," from The Economist, 9/1/90. Copyright ©1990, The Economist Newspaper Limited. Reprinted by permission.

Ehrenreich, Barbara, "The Warrior Culture," from Time Magazine, 10/15/90. Copyright ©1990 by Time Magazine.

Fisk, Robert, "Free to Report What We're Told," from The Independent of London, 2/6/91. Copyright ©1991 by permission of The Independent of London. Reprinted by permission.

Flavin, Christopher, "Cold War Ends, Oil War Begins," Copyright ©1990 by the Author. Reprinted by permission.

Greider, William, "Learning Wrong Lessons from the Mideast Crisis," from Rolling Stone Magazine, October 4, 1990. Copyright © 1990 by Straight Arrow Publishers, Inc. All rights reserved. Reprinted by permission.

Hunter, Shireen T., "Iraq is Not the Lesser of Two Evils," Copyright ©1990 by the Author. Reprinted by permission.

Hussein Ibn Talal, King of Jordan, "It's Not Too Late to Prevent a War," from The Washington Post, 9/23/90. Copyright ©1990 The Washington Post.

Kinsley, Michael, "Winners in the Oil Crisis," from The Washington Post, 11/01/90. Copyright ©1990 The Washington Post.

Kissinger, Henry, "The Game Has Just Begun," Copyright ©1990 by the Author. Reprinted by permission.

Kupperman, Robert H., "President Bush's Options on Iraq," Copyright ©1990 by the Author. Reprinted by permission.

Lewis, Anthony, "Paying for Reagan's Contemptuous Folly," from The New York Times, 10/24/90. Copyright ©1990 by The New York Times Company. Reprinted by permission.

McCarthy, Sheryl, "Truth of the Gulf War on the Streets," from Newsday, 2/25/91. Copyright ©1991 by Newsday. Reprinted by permission.

Molnar, Alex, "If My Marine Son Is Killed..." from The New York Times, 8/23/90. Copyright ©1990, The New York Times. Distributed by Special Features/Syndication Sales.

Nawa, Fariba, "A 'Camel Jockey' in an American Classroom," Copyright ©1990 by Pacific News Service. Reprinted by permission.

Nixon, Richard, "Why U.S. Policy is Right In The Gulf," from The New York Times, 1/6/91. Copyright ©1991, The New York Times. Distributed by Special Features/Syndication Sales.

Oakes, John B., "Saying No to a No-Win War," Copyright ©1991 by the Author. Reprinted by permission.

Safire, William, "A Dangerous Thing," from The New York Times, 3/19/90. Copyright ©1990 by The New York Times Company.

Said, Edward, "Shattering Effects of Saddam's Invasion," 9/5/90. Copyright ©1990 by the Author. Reprinted by permission.

Schlesinger, Arthur, "Iraq, War and the Constitution" from The Wall Street Journal, 11/12/90. Reprinted with permission of The Wall Street Journal. Copyright © 1990 Dow Jones and Company, Inc. All rights reserved.

Scott, Peter Dale, "U.S. Hungry for Kuwaiti Petrodollars—Not Just Oil," Copyright ©1990 by Pacific News Service. Reprinted by permission.

Viorst, Milton, "War and Consequences," from The Washington Post, 11/13/90. Copyright ©1990 The Washington Post.

Webb, James, ". . . And the Horrors of a Desert War" from The New York Times 9/23/90. Copyright ©1990, The New York Times. Distributed by Special Features/Syndication Sales.

Wicker, Tom, "War and Malaise," from The New York Times, 12/30/90. Copyright ©1990 by The New York Times Company.

List of U.N. Security Council Resolutions courtesy of The Washington Post.